Fassaden
Façades

Dirk U. Hindrichs · Winfried Heusler (Eds.)

Fassaden – Gebäudehüllen für das 21. Jahrhundert
Façades – Building envelopes for the 21st Century

Birkhäuser – Publishers for Architecture
Birkhäuser – Verlag für Architektur
Basel · Boston · Berlin

Inhalt
Contents

Büro- und Verwaltungsbauten   **28**
Office buildings

Mit der Architektur im Dialog
In dialogue with architecture

Liebe Leserinnen und Leser,

die Fassade, lexikalisch auch „Gesicht", ist gleichbedeutend mit Begrenzung und innerer Ansicht, sowie Kulisse von Straßen- und Stadträumen. Die Fassade als Gebäudehülle steht aber auch für intelligente Systeme, die mit einem breiten Spektrum an Technologie und Werkstoffen perfekt geplant und umgesetzt werden können. Dabei sind effizientes Energiemanagement, Steuerung des Innenraumklimas sowie der Schutz vor Außeneinflüssen wie Lärm, Hitze, Kälte oder Sonneneinstrahlung Grundanforderungen an ein modernes Gebäude, an die Gebäudehülle schlechthin.

Schücos Ziel ist es, mit all seinen Partnern, Architekten, Fachplanern, Ausführenden, Investoren und Nutzern gemeinsam die gestellten Anforderungen mit einem Höchstmaß an technischer Qualität, Design und Produktion zu erfüllen, dabei immer auf der Suche nach der besseren Lösung.

Schüco setzt auf intelligente Produkte und Systeme, die in puncto Technik, Architektur, Wärmedämmung und Energieeinsparung kreative Lösungen

Dear Reader,

Semantically, the façade is synonymous with "a boundary and inner face, and a backdrop of streets and urban spaces". But the façade as a building envelope also stands for intelligent systems, which can be planned and executed perfectly with a broad range of technology and materials. Here, efficient energy management, interior climatic control and protection from outside influences such as noise, heat, cold or the sun's rays are the fundamental requirements of a modern building, and of the building envelope per se.

In conjunction with all its associates – architects, developers, contractors, investors and users – Schüco's aim is to fulfil all requirements to the highest standards of technical quality, design and production, whilst constantly searching for a better solution.

Schüco is committed to intelligent products and systems that produce creative solutions in terms of technical operation, architecture, thermal insulation and energy efficiency. This innovative strength is also what sustainability demands

„Architektur tritt in den Mittelpunkt des gesellschaftlichen
Lebens und erzeugt Nachhaltigkeit der Zeitepoche."
„Architecture strikes right at the heart of all our lives
and defines an era for generations to come."

hervorbringen. Diese Innovationskraft steht auch dafür, was heute als Nachhaltigkeit vorausgesetzt und von jeder Planung erwartet wird.
Ganz in diesem Sinne ist dieses Buch entstanden; nämlich besondere Lösungen und Ideen von Fassadenkonzepten aufzuzeigen, die städtebaulich, architektonisch, technisch, konstruktiv und funktional außergewöhnlich sind.

Dafür stehen internationale Architekturbeispiele und innovative Planungen namhafter und renommierter Architekten, die Gebäude-typologisch geordnet einen umfassenden Überblick über die technischen Möglichkeiten moderner Gebäudehüllen aufzeigen.

Das vorliegende Buch gibt den hohen Anspruch des Unternehmens an Architektur wieder. Es gibt Ausdruck darüber, dass Schüco zusammen mit den Marktpartnern Außergewöhnliches erreicht sowie Architektur in großer Vielfalt und hohem qualitativen Anspruch realisiert.

Dirk U. Hindrichs
Geschäftsführender und persönlich haftender Gesellschafter der Schüco International KG

and what is expected of every design.

This is the driving force behind the creation of this book: to demonstrate special solutions and ideas for façade designs that are unusual architecturally, technically, structurally, functionally and in terms of town planning.

There are examples of international architecture and innovative designs by renowned architects, with the buildings divided into categories, offering a comprehensive overview of the technical possibilities for modern building envelopes.

This book reflects the company's high regard for architecture. It gives expression to the fact that Schüco, together with its market partners, is achieving something extraordinary, and helping to bring to life a rich variety of architecture of the highest quality.

Dirk U. Hindrichs
President and CEO,
Schüco International KG

Gebäudehüllen für das 21. Jahrhundert

Dr.-Ing. Winfried Heusler
Chief Technical Officer (CTO)
Schüco International KG

Winfried Heusler arbeitete nach einem Studium des allgemeinen Maschinenbaus bei einem großen Metallbauer in Süddeutschland als Leiter Forschung und Entwicklung sowie Leiter des Bereiches Aluminiumfassaden. Zahlreiche Grundlagenentwicklungen, Großprojekte und Veröffentlichungen. Seit 1998 Chief Technical Officer (CTO) bei der Firma Schüco International KG, Bielefeld.

Grundlagen und Tendenzen

1. Einführung

Bis zu Beginn des 20. Jahrhunderts waren Gebäude und Bauweisen einerseits durch die jeweiligen Gesellschafts-, Wohn- und Arbeitsformen, andererseits durch die lokal verfügbaren Materialien und Konstruktions- sowie Fertigungsmethoden charakterisiert. Im 20. Jahrhundert nahmen die Globalisierung und die Geschwindigkeit, mit der neue Technologien entdeckt und (nicht zuletzt auf Grund des verbesserten Informationswesens) in der Breite angewandt wurden – insbesondere in anderen Branchen als im Bauwesen – kontinuierlich zu. Lokale Traditionen traten zunehmend in den Hintergrund. Am Eintritt ins 21. Jahrhundert geht es den Entscheidern beim Bauen längst nicht mehr nur noch darum, einen Raumbedarf mit möglichst geringen Investitionskosten zu decken, sondern vielmehr um die ganzheitliche Maximierung von Chancen und Minimierung von Risiken. So stellen heute nicht nur im Bauwesen die wesentlichen Erfolgsfaktoren langfristige Kundenzufriedenheit und Wirtschaftlichkeit dar! Basis hierfür sind Gebäude, die einerseits dem Bauherrn, andererseits den letztendlichen Nutzern nicht (wie viel zu oft üblich) Probleme bereiten, sondern bei ihnen Zufriedenheit bewirken:

- Gebäude aus gesundheits- und umweltverträglichen Materialien, mit geringem Energiebedarf und minimierten Emissionen.
- Gebäude mit anwendungsgerechten Funktionalitäten sowie nutzungsgerechtem Raum- und Bedienkomfort.
- Gebäude mit hoher Flexibilität bei veränderter Nutzung, mit einer langen Lebensdauer und mit geringen Wartungs-, Instandhaltungs-, Umbau- und Entsorgungskosten.

Wenn Gebäudehüllen dem Anspruch „anwendungsgerecht im 21. Jahrhundert" tatsächlich genügen sollen, müssen bereits in einem frühen Stadium der Gebäudeplanung die objektspezifischen Anforderungen identifiziert, die gebäudehüllenrelevanten Randbedingungen geklärt sowie die Gebäudehülle, der Gebäudekörper, die Gebäudetechnik und der Innenausbau im Laufe eines (mehrstufigen) Planungsprozesses unter Kenntnis bzw. Nutzung der verfügbaren und geeigneten (technischen) Möglichkeiten – in Form einer architektonisch-technischen Lösung – aufeinander abgestimmt werden.

2. Erfahrungen aus der Baupraxis

Nachdem in den 80er- und 90er-Jahren eine Reihe von Gebäuden mit innovativen Gebäudehüllen gleichsam als Prototypen geplant und ausgeführt wurden, die zwischenzeitlich genutzt werden, liegen aus der Praxis Erkenntnisse vor, die bei künftigen Produktentwicklungen und Gebäudeplanungen Berücksichtigung finden sollten.

So sind viele der heute angebotenen innovativen Produkte nicht so ausgereift, dass eine wirtschaftliche Vor- und Werkstattfertigung sowie Baustellenmontage und Inbetriebnahme möglich ist. Darüber hinaus lassen diese sich unter den auf einer Baustelle üblichen Bedingungen häufig nicht fachgerecht mit anderen Komponenten des Gebäudes problemlos zu sinnvollen Gesamtsystemen vernetzen. Zudem werden die relevanten Normen und Vorschriften der Fassaden-, Elektro- sowie Heizungs-, Lüftungs- und Klimatechnik – soweit für diesen speziellen Einsatzfall überhaupt vorhanden – nicht immer beachtet.

Die Analyse ausgeführter Gebäude legt aber auch Schwächen in der Planungs- und Ausführungsphase offen. So werden mit dem Bauherren häufig dessen individuelle Anforderungen nicht ausreichend detailliert diskutiert bzw. frühzeitig zweifelsfrei geklärt. Auch sind vielen Planern die relevanten äußeren und inneren Randbedingungen des Gebäudes nicht ausreichend genau bekannt sowie die tatsächlichen Möglichkeiten innovativer Produkte nicht vertraut. Schließlich werden – insbesondere aus finanziellen Gründen – nur selten die ursprünglichen

Overview and trends

1. Introduction

Until the beginning of the 20th century, buildings and the building process were shaped as much by our social systems, living arrangements and modes of working, as by locally available materials and construction methods. During the 20th century, with globalisation progressing apace, new technologies were being developed and applied with ever greater speed, particularly in industries outside the construction sector. Local traditions increasingly took a back seat. At the start of the 21st century, decision-makers in the construction industry have long had to consider more than just meeting space requirements with as low an investment as possible; now they must also endeavour to maximise opportunities and minimise risks. Today, therefore, as in other industries, the key to success lies in long-term customer satisfaction and economic efficiency. Instead of causing problems for the client or user (which is all too often the case), buildings must provide satisfaction:

- Buildings constructed using materials that are not harmful to the environment or human health, with low energy requirements and minimised emissions
- Buildings that provide the necessary functionality and levels of comfort
- Buildings that can easily be adapted to changed usage requirements, have a long useful life and offer low maintenance, conversion and waste management costs

If building envelopes are to be truly "functional in the 21st century", it is important to identify project-specific requirements and boundary conditions relevant to the building envelope early on in the planning phase. In addition, the building envelope, structure, technology and interior must be considered together in a (multi-phase) planning process that draws on all the techno-logical options available, to create a solution that combines the best of architecture and technology.

2. Practical experience

Following the planning and construction of buildings with innovative building envelopes as "prototypes" in the 1980s and 1990s, which have since come into general use, many practical findings have emerged that should be considered in future product developments and building planning activities.

Many of the innovative products available today are not yet mature enough for the processes of prefabrication, workshop fabrication, on-site assembly and commissioning to be cost-effective. Furthermore, it is often difficult under normal conditions to integrate them with other building components to create a professional and effective overall system. Furthermore, the relevant standards and regulations for façade technology, electrics, heating, ventilation and air conditioning – if at all available for such a special case – are not always observed.

The analysis of completed building projects also reveals weaknesses in the planning and realisation phases. For example, the client's specific requirements are often not discussed thoroughly enough or clarified unequivocally at an early stage. Many planners are not familiar enough with the relevant external and internal building conditions, or the true possibilities of innovative products. Indeed, only seldom do the project planners and companies responsible for completing the project properly implement the original objectives – usually for financial reasons.

Another finding was that, in practice, users or control units did not operate the components of the building envelope and building technology in the manner that was assumed during planning. For example, the use of natural light to

After completing his studies in Mechanical Engineering, Winfried Heusler worked for a large aluminium fabricator in southern Germany as Head of Research and Development and Head of the Aluminium Façades Division. Numerous fundamental developments, large projects and publications. Chief Technical Officer (CTO) at Schüco International KG, Bielefeld since 1998.

Building envelopes for the 21st century

Dr.-Ing. Winfried Heusler
Chief Technical Officer (CTO)
Schüco International KG

Zielvorgaben von den Objektplanern und ausführenden
Firmen konsequent umgesetzt.

Darüber hinaus werden die Komponenten der Gebäudehülle und
der Gebäudetechnik von den
Nutzern oder der Regelung in
der Praxis nicht so, wie es in der
Planung angenommen wurde,
situationsgerecht und ereignis-
abhängig betätigt. Die verbes-
serte Raumausleuchtung durch
Tageslicht kann eben nur dann
zu einer Energieeinsparung
führen, wenn die künstliche
Beleuchtung tatsächlich ausge-
schaltet bzw. zurückgedimmt

und gestalterischen Spiel-
raumes – deutlich reduzieren,
wenn künftig so weit wie möglich auf Grundlage aufgaben-
spezifischer Standards
(„Systemtechnik"), nur so weit
nötig mit projektspezifischen
Standards („Plattformstrategie")
und so selten wie möglich ohne
Standard geplant und gebaut
wird.

Beim Prinzip der „Systemtechnik" werden bauliche Elemente
für unterschiedliche aufga-
benspezifische Anforderungen
in Baureihen- und Baukasten-
systemen mit Wiederhol- oder
Gleichteilen standardisiert und
die Korrelationen zwischen den
Elementen (Abmessungen und
geometrische Schnittstellen) har-
monisiert, d.h. vereinheitlicht
bzw. aufeinander abgestimmt.
Je umfangreicher sowie besser
durchdacht der Baukasten ist
und je geschickter die Planer
und Konstrukteure diesen in der
Anpassungsplanung sowie
Variantenkonstruktion anwen-
den, desto individueller und
rationeller lassen sich projekt-
spezifische technische und
gestalterische Anforderungen
durch unterschiedliche Kombi-
nationen der Baukastenelemente
realisieren. Dann bringt die
bewährte Basistechnik Sicherheit sowie ökonomische Vorteile
und verkürzt in der Objektan-
wendung die Entwicklungszeiten
bei großer Gestaltungsfreiheit
für den Architekten.

Im Entwicklungsprozess werden
die einzelnen Systemkomponen-
ten der Gebäudehülle und die
Schnittstellen zwischen diesen
Komponenten sowie zwischen
der Fassade und den angrenzen-
den Gewerken (Rohbau und
Innenausbau) in wirtschaftlicher,
ökologischer, funktioneller, ferti-
gungs- und montagetechnischer
sowie in gestalterischer Hinsicht
optimiert. Zum einen wird die
Projektkomplexität durch die
geringere Anzahl unterschiedli-
cher Konstruktionstypen und
Teile grundsätzlich reduziert.
Zum anderen haben wirtschaft-
lich und industriell (vor)gefertig-
te Komponenten und/oder
Module als Serienprodukt eine
geringere Komplexität und einen
höheren Reifegrad als Sonder-

McLaren
Technology Centre,
Woking, Great Britain

Flexibilität der Gestaltung
- Form
- Farbe
- Transparenz

Flexibilität der Nutzung
- veränderte Raumaufteilung
- veränderte innere Kühllasten
- veränderte Komfortanforderungen

Flexibilität der Funktionen
- bei variablen Außeneinflüssen
- bei variablen Inneneinflüssen
- bei variablen Nutzerbedürfnissen

wird. Weitere Schwierigkeiten
ergaben sich in Fällen, bei denen
sich einzelne Komponenten in
der Praxis als nicht langfristig
funktionstüchtig, wartungsfrei
oder zumindest wartungsfreund-
lich erweisen, insbesondere
wenn im Schadensfall die kurz-
fristige Versorgung mit kompa-
tiblen Ersatzteilen nicht sichergestellt ist. Es ist jedoch auch
anzumerken, dass die nötigen
Reinigungs- und Wartungs-
arbeiten nicht in jedem Fall
tatsächlich durchgeführt wurden
und dass bei späterer Umnutzung einzelner Räume Umrüst-
arbeiten nicht genauso fachgerecht wie bei der Erstausrüstung
erfolgten. Als problematisch
erweist sich bei gewerkeüber-
greifenden Konzepten in der
Nutzungsphase gelegentlich
auch die Klärung der Verant-
wortlichkeiten bei Themen wie
Gewährleistung und Mängeln.

3. Grundlagen und Tendenzen bei Komponenten der Gebäudehülle

Ein erheblicher Teil der in der
Baupraxis identifizierten
Probleme lässt sich – unter
Beibehaltung des technischen

First East
International Bank,
Sofia, Bulgaria

improve lighting conditions will only save energy if the artificial lights are actually switched off or dimmed. Other difficulties were caused by individual components failing to remain in working order, maintenance-free or even maintenance-friendly in the long term, especially when damaged components could not be quickly replaced with compatible parts. However, we should also note that the required cleaning and maintenance work was not always carried out in every case and, when the usage of individual rooms was later changed, the conversion work was not carried out to the original high standards. In building projects that integrate all trades, it has sometimes proven difficult to establish who is responsible for warranties and defects during the usage phase.

3. Overview and trends for building envelope components

It is possible to greatly reduce the number of problems identified in practice while still observing technical and design limitations. To do this, planning and construction must in future be based as far as possible on task-specific standards (system technology), project-specific standards (platform strategy) should only be applied where necessary, and using no standards at all is an approach that must be avoided.

The "system technology" principle involves standardising building components for different task-specific requirements in construction series and modular systems with identical parts, and harmonising the link between the components (dimensions and geometric interfaces). The more extensive and well thought-out the module and the more intelligently the planners and designers use it in adapting the design to fit the plan and in variant construction, the greater the chance of combining the modular components to meet project-specific technical and design requirements in an

anfertigungen. Der Aufwand für Planung, Fertigung und Montage sinkt, während die Qualität steigt. Vorteile, die aus dem hohen Wiederholfaktor und den einfachen, sicheren System- lösungen resultieren, bestehen auch in den geringeren Anfor- derungen an die konstruktive und handwerkliche Qualifikation der Mitarbeiter von Fassaden- baufirmen. Auch die grundlegen- de dokumentations- bzw. soft- waretechnische Aufbereitung der Produkte zahlt sich später in zahlreichen Objektanwendungen aus. So kann der Fassadenbauer auf zeitsparende Software und Datenbanken mit einem umfang- reichen, aufeinander abgestimm- ten Sortiment zugreifen.

Bei technisch komplexen und architektonisch besonders anspruchsvollen Gebäuden, deren technische und gestalteri- sche Anforderungen sich mit dem Baukasten nicht mehr abdecken lassen sowie bei großen Objekten, bei denen sich auf Grund eines hohen Wieder- holeffektes für den spezifischen Einzelfall wirtschaftlichere Lösungen als mit dem Bau- kasten finden lassen, werden auch objektspezifische Sonder- konstruktionen auf Systembasis entwickelt ("Plattformstrategie"). Wenn dann die funktionsrelevan- ten Komponenten aus dem System übernommen werden, bleiben auch hier die wesent- lichen Vorteile des Systems erhalten.

4. Grundlagen und Tendenzen bei der Konzeption und Planung von Gebäudehüllen

Bauherren und Nutzer von Gebäuden werden mit ihrer Gebäudehülle nur dann wirklich zufrieden sein, wenn zum einen die objektspezifischen Anfor- derungen und Randbedingungen sauber geklärt sowie die relevan- ten technischen Möglichkeiten den Planern bekannt und von diesen bezüglich ihrer Anwend- barkeit gründlich bewertet sind und wenn zum anderen die da- raus abgeleiteten Zielvorgaben von den Objektplanern und aus- führenden Firmen konsequent umgesetzt werden. Dabei ist zwingend die Tatsache zu beach- ten, dass zu Beginn des Pla-

nungsprozesses viele Faktoren ohne nennenswerte Mehrkosten verändert werden können, während die Änderungskosten mit zunehmender Planungstiefe steigen. Teuer wird es, wenn Änderungen während der Bauzeit auftreten. So ist in jeder Planungsphase zu hinterfragen, wie das spätere Gesamtergebnis genau jetzt besonders stark beeinflusst werden kann, was zu einem späteren Zeitpunkt nicht mehr optimal beeinflusst werden kann und was deshalb genau jetzt entschieden werden muss. Deshalb wird bei einem zeit- gemäßen Planungsprozess zwi- schen einer vorgelagerten Konzeptionsphase und der daran anschließenden eigentlichen Planungsphase unterschieden. Letztere sollte aus den oben genannten Gründen zumindest bei innovativen Gebäudekon- zepten in mehrere Teilschritte untergliedert werden, die in sich abgeschlossene optimierende Iterationsprozesse darstellen.

4.1 Klärung der Anforderungen und Randbedingungen

Vor der Konzeption und Planung der Gebäudehülle steht sinn- vollerweise die Klärung der Aufgabenstellung. Es geht dabei zunächst um die frühzeitige Definition der Zielvorgaben einschließlich des Budgets für Investitions-, Betriebs- und Unterhaltskosten durch den Bau- herrn. Die Möglichkeiten inno- vativer Gebäudehüllen können umso besser ausgeschöpft werden, je früher das Thema Gebäudehülle im Planungs- prozess wirklich ernsthaft be- trachtet wird. Je später dies der Fall ist, umso mehr Randbedin- gungen sind bereits festgelegt und umso geringer sind die Spielräume einer kreativen Gebäudeplanung. Mindestens genauso schwierig wird es jedoch, wenn im Laufe des Planungsprozesses zu viele Randbedingungen zu lange offen gehalten werden sollen.

Je nach Gebäudenutzung (z.B. Schwimmbad, klimatisiertes Bürogebäude...) und Gebäude- typ (z.B. Hochhaus) herrschen unterschiedliche Randbedingun- gen (z.B. Raumlufttemperatur und -feuchte sowie Windge-

efficient and individual way. The proven underlying technology is thus secure and cost-effective and, when applied in projects, reduces development times while maintaining plenty of design scope for the architect.

In the development process, the individual system components of the building envelope are optimised from the point of view of the environment, functionality, fabrication, assembly and design, as are the interfaces between components and between the façade and the adjacent carcass and interior. Because there are then fewer different construction types and parts, the project is less complex. In addition, components and modules that are commercially and industrially (pre)fabricated as standard products are less complex and more "mature" than custom designed products. Thus the cost of planning, fabrication and assembly is lowered, while quality increases. The benefits resulting from the high repetition factor and the simple, reliable system solutions also mean lower training requirements for the employees of façade construction companies – whether engineers or skilled manual workers. In addition, the documentation and software prepared for the products can be reused many times over in future projects. For example, façade builders can access time-saving software and databases containing an extensive range of compatible products.

For buildings with technically complex and sophisticated architectural requirements that cannot be met by the modular system, special project-specific constructions are developed on a system basis (platform strategy). This also applies to large projects involving a high degree of repetition, for which the modular system is not necessarily the most economical. If the components relevant to the function are then used from the system, the key benefits of the system are retained.

4. Overview and trends in the design and planning of building envelopes

Clients and users of buildings are only truly satisfied with their building envelope when the project-specific requirements and conditions have been properly clarified, the planners are aware of the relevant technical possibilities and have thoroughly evaluated their effectiveness, and the project planners and companies performing the work have properly implemented the defined objectives. It is, however, important to remember that it is cheaper to make alterations at the beginning of the planning process, and that the costs increase as the planning activities progress. Making changes at the construction stage comes at a high price. At each stage of planning, therefore, it is important to identify what part of the plans will strongly affect the end result, what cannot easily be altered later, and what therefore must be decided straightaway. That's why a modern planning process will distinguish between the concept phase and a subsequent (actual) desing phase. For the aforementioned reasons, the latter must be divided – at least for innovative building concepts – into several sub-phases, each of which is a self-contained iterative process.

4.1 Clarifying requirements and conditions

It makes sense to clarify the precise task prior to designing and planning the building envelope. First, the client must define the objectives at an early stage, including the budget for investment, operating and maintenance costs. The earlier in the planning process the subject of the building envelope is properly examined, the more successfully the possibilities of innovative building envelopes can be exploited. The later this is left, the more constraints have been laid down, which in turn limits the scope for creative building design. However, it is just as difficult, if not more so, if too many constraints are left

Jumeirah Beach Hotel, Dubai, U.A.E.

Schutzfunktionen
- Luft- und Schlagregendichtigkeit
- Wärme-, Feuchte- und Schallschutz
- Sonnen- und Blendschutz

Sicherheitsfunktionen
- Brand- und Rauchschutz (mit RWA)
- Blitzschutz
- Einbruch- u. Durchschusshemmung
- Radardämpfung

Nutzfunktionen
- Tageslichtnutzung
- Solarenergienutzung
- natürliche Lüftung

schwindigkeiten) vor, die zwangsläufig unterschiedliche Anforderungen an eine Gebäudehülle stellen. Die bezüglich der Gebäudenutzung relevanten Einflussgrößen sind im Wesentlichen die Betriebszeiten, die inneren Wärmelasten (während und außerhalb der Betriebszeiten) und die Anforderungen an den Raumkomfort sowie das Nutzerverhalten. Die Entscheidung für ein bestimmtes Fassadenkonzept hängt insofern auch davon ab, ob es sich um ein Büro- oder Verwaltungsgebäude, um eine Unternehmenszentrale, um ein Hotel, um ein Shopping Center, ein Kino, ein Freizeit- oder Tagungscenter, um ein Gebäude für Kultur, Lehre, Forschung oder Bildung, um ein Museum oder Ausstellungsgebäude, ein Theater, ein Krankenhaus, ein Fertigungscenter bzw. eine Fabrik oder um einen Flughafen bzw. einen Bahnhof handelt. Einfluss haben auch das Flächen-, Raum- und Funktionsprogramm sowie die Grundform und Höhe des Gebäudes. Berücksichtigt der momentane Planungsstand Einzel-, Gruppen- bzw. Großräume (Büro, Besprechung, Aufenthalt, Verkauf...) oder soll eine flexible Raumeinteilung möglich sein? Gibt es eine Eingangshalle, ein (mehrgeschossiges) Atrium oder Passagen zwischen Gebäudebereichen? Wo sind Treppenhäuser und sonstige Verkehrsflächen, insbesondere mit Fluchtwegfunktion vorgesehen? Genauso entscheidend ist aber auch die Frage, wo gebaut werden soll? Bezüglich der am Gebäudestandort (z.B. innerstädtisch in Mitteleuropa) vorherrschenden Außenbedingungen spielen hinsichtlich der Gebäudehülle die zeitlichen Verläufe der Außenlufttemperatur und der Solarstrahlung eine maßgebliche Rolle. Starken Einfluss haben darüber hinaus die zeitlichen Verläufe der Windgeschwindigkeit und Windrichtung. Der Gebäudestandort bestimmt aber auch die Belastung der Gebäudehülle durch Lärm und Feuchte im Auslegungsfall sowie deren zeitlichen Verlauf im laufenden Betrieb. Die Freiheitsgrade der Gebäude-

hüllenplanung hängen auch davon ab, ob es sich um einen Neubau, einen Umbau oder eine Renovierung handelt.

Je nachdem aus welchem Blickwinkel die Gebäudehülle mehr oder weniger optimiert wird, haben die nachfolgend aufgelisteten Kriterien im Planungsprozess unterschiedlich hohe Priorität: Aus Sicht des Gesetzgebers geht es insbesondere um das Thema Sicherheit, aus Sicht des Bauherrn bzw. Investors überwiegen zunächst die Aspekte Wirtschaftlichkeit, Kosten- und Terminsicherheit. Je längerfristig Bauherrn und Investoren denken, desto stärker treten die Anforderungen des späteren Betreibers bzw. Mieters (Betriebskosten, Image, Flexibilität...) und der letztendlichen Gebäudenutzer (Komfort, Sicherheit...) in den Vordergrund der Planung. Da sich unsere Gesellschafts-, Wohn- und Arbeitsformen sowie die individuellen Ansprüche der einzelnen Menschen tendenziell immer schneller ändern, gewinnt zwangsläufig auch die Flexibilität unserer Gebäude mehr und mehr an Bedeutung. Dies gilt umso mehr, wenn man berücksichtigt, dass für die langfristige Wirtschaftlichkeit eines Gebäudes auch ein kurzer Nutzungsausfall und niedrige Kosten bei Bauunterhaltsmaßnahmen, bei späterem Umbau (z.B. wegen geänderter Anforderungen bei Nutzerwechsel) sowie bei Renovierung (z.B. spätere Nachrüstung bezüglich neuer, energiesparender oder komfortsteigernder Maßnahmen) entscheidend sind. Kostengünstige Gebäude zeichnen sich dadurch aus, dass sie zunächst nur insoweit ausgerüstet werden, wie dies dem tatsächlichen, momentanen Bedarf entspricht und bei veränderten Anforderungen möglichst schnell, mit geringem Aufwand und möglichst ohne Unterbrechung bzw. Betriebsstörung in der Gebäudenutzung nachgerüstet werden können. Architekten, Projektsteuerer und Fachplaner berücksichtigen zudem den bei ihnen selbst entstehenden Planungsaufwand, während die ausführenden Firmen (Generalunter-

undefined for too long during the planning process.

The purpose (e.g. swimming pool, air-conditioned office) and type (e.g. high-rise) of a building will affect the constraints (e.g. room air temperature and humidity, wind speeds), which in turn affect the requirements of the building envelope. The main influencing factors relevant to building usage are operating hours, internal thermal loading (during and outside of operating hours), room comfort requirements and user behaviour. In this respect, the decision in favour of a particular façade design also depends on whether the building is an administrative building, company headquarters, hotel, shopping centre, cinema, leisure or conference centre, cultural or educational building, museum or exhibition building, theatre, hospital, production facility, airport or railway station and so forth. The decision will also be affected by use of space and function, as well as the basic shape and height of the building. Do the current plans include individual rooms or open-plan rooms (office, meeting room, reception room, sales area) or should the room arrangement be flexible? Is there a foyer, a (multi-storey) atrium, or passages between zones of the building? Where will the staircases and corridors be located, particularly those that function as escape routes? But just as crucial is the matter of where the building is to be constructed. The local external conditions that have the greatest impact on the building envelope are the prevalent external air temperatures and solar radiation levels. Wind speed and direction also play a key role. The location of the building also determines the noise and humidity levels. The degree of freedom available in building envelope planning is also affected by whether the project is a new building, a conversion or a renovation.

The level of priority given to the various planning criteria as listed below will depend on whose point of view is being considered. For example, the legislator will place the emphasis on safety, while the client or investor will primarily be interested in cost efficiency, meeting deadlines, and staying on budget. Clients and investors who think in the long term are more likely to focus their planning on the needs of the future operator or tenant (operating costs, image, flexibility and so on) and the eventual user of the building (comfort, security). Since our social systems, tastes, and the way we live and work seem to change with increasing speed, the flexibility of buildings is bound to become more significant. This is particularly true if we consider that for a building to be cost-effective in the long term, vacancy periods must be short and the costs of building maintenance, conversion (e.g. if a new user has different requirements) and renovation (e.g. addition of new energy-saving or improved comfort features) are low. Cost-effective buildings are those that need only be equipped to meet current

Protective features
- Air and weathertightness
- Thermal, condensation and sound insulation
- Solar shading and anti-glare protection

Security features
- Fire and smoke protection (with smoke extraction unit)
- Lightning protection
- Burglar and bullet resistance
- Radar absorption

Beneficial features
- Utilisation of natural light
- Utilisation of solar energy
- Natural ventilation

Sphinx, Jungfraujoch, Switzerland

nehmer und Fachfirmen) auch ihre Kosten und ihre Auslastung im Auge behalten. Alle im Bauwesen professionell Tätigen versuchen darüber hinaus – egal wie innovativ und selbstlos sie zunächst wirken – ihre jeweiligen Risiken zu minimieren.

Am Ende dieser Phase liegt ein detailliertes, verbindliches Lastenheft vor. Dieses schafft Klarheit für alle Beteiligten. Es vermeidet nicht nur Missverständnisse, sondern es reduziert auch die Risiken und Kosten.

4.2 Konzeption der Gebäudehülle

In der Konzeptionsphase geht es darum, innerhalb des Planungsteams mehrere grundsätzliche Lösungsansätze zu erarbeiten, mit denen die im Lastenheft definierten objektspezifischen Randbedingungen und Anforderungen unter Nutzung der heutigen konstruktiven und funktionalen Möglichkeiten sowie unter Berücksichtigung gestalterischer Gesichtspunkte so erfüllt werden können, dass – je nach Blickwinkel – die optimale Lösung erzielt wird. Welche Nutzwerte stehen welchen Kosten und Risiken in der Planungs-, Herstellungs-, Montage- und Inbetriebnahmephase sowie bei der späteren Wartung und Instandhaltung des Gebäudes (auch über den Gewährleistungszeitraum hinaus), bis hin zu Umbau- und Renovierungsmaßnahmen, gegenüber?

Dabei versteht sich von selbst, dass die heutigen Möglichkeiten nur dann ausgeschöpft werden können, wenn gewerkübergreifend gedacht wird. Es geht also nicht um eine Optimierung einzelner Gesichtspunkte oder Komponenten, sondern um eine Gesamt-Kosten-Nutzen-Optimierung von Gebäudekörper, Gebäudehülle, Innenwänden, Böden, Decken, Speichermassen, Anlagen der Technischen Gebäudeausrüstung und Gebäudeleittechnik. Beim Gebäudekörper sind als Einflussgrößen einerseits die Geometrie des Baukörpers mit Vor- und Rücksprüngen, die Frage nach leichter oder schwerer Bauweise

(nutzbare Speichermassen) und nach offenen Strömungswegen innerhalb des Gebäudes relevant. Noch wichtiger sind hier aber die Größe und Aufteilung transparenter und nichttransparenter Rohbauteile in der Gebäudehülle (z.B. maximal möglicher Fensterflächenanteil) sowie die Orientierung (Himmelsrichtung) und Neigung transparenter und nichttransparenter Rohbauteile. Auswirkungen auf den Energieverbrauch und den Raumkomfort resultieren auch aus konzeptionellen und konstruktiven Kriterien des Gebäudeinneren und seiner Ausstattung. Entscheidend sind hier die Breite, Höhe und Tiefe des Innenraumes, die Ausbildung der Raumumschließungsflächen (z.B. Masse, Reflexionsgrad und Struktur), die Zugänglichkeit der Speichermassen sowie die Anzahl, Größe, Formgebung und Öffnungsart sowie der Strömungswiderstand von Öffnungen (z.B. Innentüren) in den Raumumschließungsflächen. Optimale Ergebnisse lassen sich meist durch die Kombination eines klima- und nutzungsgerechten Gebäudekörpers und einer klima- und nutzungsgerechten Gebäudehülle sowie durch die entsprechende Gebäude- und Regelungstechnik, mit gebäude- und nutzungsspezifisch optimierten Steuerungs- und Regelungsstrategien, erzielen.

4.3 Planung der Gebäudehülle

Die eigentliche Planung teilt sich bei komplexen Bauvorhaben in die Varianten- und Integrationsplanung sowie in die Baugruppen- und Detailplanung auf. Dabei werden, aufbauend auf den Ansätzen der Konzeptionsphase, objektspezifische Lösungsansätze bezüglich Wirtschaftlichkeit (Investitions-, Betriebs- und Bauunterhaltungskosten), gestalterischer Gesichtspunkte, Energiebedarf (Heizen, Kühlen, Lüften, Beleuchten...), Ökologie, Raumkomfort (thermisch, visuell, akustisch...), Nutzungskomfort (Bedienung, Gebrauchstauglichkeit), Wartungsaufwand und -freundlichkeit sowie Flexibilität bei Umnutzung und Nachrüstung Schritt für Schritt detail-

requirements, and then as those requirements change, can be altered quickly, easily and causing as little disruption as possible. Architects, project managers and specialist planners will also consider the planning overhead involved, while companies carrying out the work (general contractor and specialist trades) will keep an eye on their own costs and workload. And all construction professionals will endeavour to minimise their own risks, even if at the start they are bursting with ideas and demonstrating the best of intentions.

This phase concludes with a detailed and binding set of design specifications. This ensures clarity for everyone involved, not only to avoid misunderstandings but also to reduce risks and costs.

4.2 The preliminary concept phase

In the preliminary concept phase, the planning team considers several possible solutions that meet the project-specific conditions and requirements defined in the specifications, that exploit the latest construction and functional possibilities and that include different design viewpoints. The idea is to work out the best solution from each point of view. How do the benefits measure up against the costs and risks in the planning, manufacturing, assembly and commissioning phase, during building maintenance (including after the warranty period) and during conversion and renovation?

It goes without saying that current options can only be exploited when the work of all trades are taken into consideration. The point is not to focus on improving individual components, but to optimise the overall cost-effectiveness of the building structure, building envelope, interior walls, floors, ceilings, storage mass, technical fixtures and fittings, and building management technology.
The factors significant to the building structure are its

geometry (including projections and recesses), the issue of light-weight or heavy construction (usable storage masses) and open air flow within the building. Even more important here are the size and distribution of transparent and non-transparent carcass components in the building envelope (e.g. maximum possible window area) as well as the angle and orientation (direction) of these components. The design and construction criteria of the building interior and equipment also affect energy consumption and room comfort. Important factors here are the height, width and depth of the interior spaces, the construction of the surfaces enclosing the rooms (e.g. mass, degree of reflection and structure), accessibility of storage masses and the quantity, size, shape, opening type and flow resistance of openings (e.g. internal doors) in the surfaces enclosing the room. The best results are usually achieved by ensuring that both building structure and building envelope are designed to suit the climate and purpose of the building, using the appropriate building and control technology, and choosing control strategies that fit the purpose of the building.

4.3 Designing the building envelope

In complex building projects, the actual design activities can be divided into four phases: design option phase, integration design phase, module design phase and component design phase. At this stage, the project-based solutions are subjected to a detailed, step-by-step analysis with respect to the following factors: cost-efficiency (investment, operating and maintenance costs), design considerations, energy requirements (heating, cooling, ventilating, lighting etc.), environmental impact, room comfort (thermal, visual, acoustic etc.), ease of use/operation, cost and ease of maintenance, as well as the flexibility to change use and upgrade facilities. For façade planners and builders, the

lierter betrachtet und bewertet. Aus Sicht des Fassadenplaners und -bauers geht es in den einzelnen Phasen auch um fertigungs- und montagetechnische Gesichtspunkte.

In der Variantenplanung werden von den Planungsbeteiligten alternative Planungskonzepte konkretisiert und bewertet sowie dem Bauherrn als Lösungsvorschläge vorgestellt. Dabei stellen sich den Planern folgende Fragen: Welche grundsätzlichen Dezentralisierungsgrade (TGA und Sicherheit) und Modularisierungsgrade (Gebäudehülle) sind als Teil des Lösungsvorschlages vorstellbar? Welchen Manipulations- und Automationsgrad könnten Gebäudehülle und Gebäudetechnik aufweisen? Welche passiven, aktiven, adaptiven oder integralen Komponenten eignen sich für die spezifische Aufgabenstellung? Welche Schutz-, Sicherheits- und Nutzfunktionen sollen durch die Gebäudehülle bzw. durch die Gebäudetechnik, den Gebäudekörper oder den Innenausbau, bzw. durch deren zielgerichtetes Zusammenspiel realisiert werden? Es geht dabei um die Funktionen Lüften, Heizen, Kühlen, Beleuchten und Stromversorgung (zumindest für Hilfsenergie) sowie um die Wärme-, Kälte- und Stromerzeugung („konventionell und alternativ" [PV, Wind…]..). Welche Betriebsweisen bieten sich bei dem Gebäudetyp, den betrachteten Gebäudekonzepten und bei der beabsichtigten Gebäudenutzung an?

Bei komplexeren Bauvorhaben werden zur Absicherung in dieser Planungsphase häufig mehr oder weniger umfangreiche planungsunterstützende Untersuchungen durchgeführt. Beispielsweise kann die später in einem konkreten Gebäude zu erwartende natürliche Be- und Entlüftung simuliert sowie analysiert werden. Hierzu ist zunächst das aerodynamische Verhalten des Baukörpers und seiner Umgebung und dann das strömungstechnische und thermodynamische Verhalten innerhalb der Gebäudehülle und im Gebäudeinneren zu ermitteln.

Zu diesem Zweck können Fachplaner beispielsweise in Zusammenarbeit mit Forschungs- bzw. Hochschulinstituten und Herstellern Computersimulationen (in denen „die Physik" abgebildet wird) sowie Windkanalversuche (maßstäblich verkleinerte Gebäudemodelle), für genauere Vorhersagen sogar Freilandversuche (originalgroße Musterfassaden oder Gebäudeausschnitte) durchführen. Das gilt sinngemäß auch für Überlegungen zum wärme- und lichttechnischen Verhalten von Bauteilen und Gebäuden. Entscheidend für die Zuverlässigkeit der dabei erzielten Ergebnisse sind beim heutigen Stand in erster Linie nicht mehr die Verfügbarkeit der relevanten physikalischen Gleichungen und der notwendigen Berechnungsalgorithmen (diese Themen sind zwischenzeitlich weitgehend „Stand der Technik"), sondern schlichtweg die Verfügbarkeit realistischer Eingabedaten bzw. Muster und Versuchsaufbauten.

Während der Integrationsplanung wird das ausgewählte Konzept durchgearbeitet und unter Mitwirkung der Fachingenieure und Behörden sowie beratender Unternehmer und Produkthersteller eine integrierte Lösung erarbeitet. Zur Erzielung optimaler Ergebnisse sind komplette Systeme, deren Teile in Wechselwirkung zueinander stehen, zu betrachten. Die Beschränkung auf Einzelteile oder Teilsysteme ist nur dann zulässig, wenn diese ohne maßgeblichen Einfluss auf andere Gebäudebestandteile sind. Gefragt ist deshalb nicht eine Einzeloptimierung spezieller Bauteile oder Kriterien, sondern eine gewerkeübergreifende, ganzheitliche Betrachtung des ganzen Gebäudes, mit allen Schnittstellen zwischen geometrisch oder funktionell verknüpften Baugruppen. Die Systemintegration (Außenwand, Speichermassen, Gebäudetechnik und Gebäudeleittechnik) sowie die Frage nach dezentraler Gebäudetechnik in der Gebäudehülle spielt hier künftig eine größere Rolle als heute. Die Vorteile innovativer Gebäudekonzepte können aber nur dann

individual phases also deal with fabrication and assembly.

In the design option phase, the planning team defines and evaluates alternative design concepts and presents them to the client. In this process, the planners consider the following questions: What degree of decentralisation (technical building equipment and security) and modularisation (building envelope) is possible as part of the proposed solution? What degree of manipulation and automation could the building envelope and building technology offer? What passive, active, adaptive and integral components would be appropriate for this specific set of requirements? What protective, security and beneficial functions should be offered by the building envelope, building technology, building structure or interior, or by a combination of these elements? These include ventilation, heating, cooling, lighting, electricity (emergency supply, at least) as well as the generation of heat, cold and electricity (by conventional and alternative means, e.g. photovoltaic, wind). What modes of operation are suitable for the type of building, the building designs under consideration and the purpose of the building?

In more complex building projects, additional studies – some more extensive than others – are often conducted in support of this planning phase to ensure certainty. Such studies include simulating and analysing the level of natural ventilation anticipated in a particular building. First it is necessary to determine the aerodynamic behaviour of the building structure and its surroundings, followed by the fluid mechanics and thermodynamic behaviour within the building envelope and inside the building. To do this, specialist planners can team up with organisations such as research institutes/universities and manufacturers to conduct computer simulations (which model the "physics") and wind tunnel tests (scale models of

the building) or, for more accurate results, outdoor tests on original size specimen façades or building sections. This also applies to considerations on the behaviour of heat and light with respect to building components and buildings. The key to the reliability of the results obtained is now no longer the availability of the relevant physical equations and calculation algorithms (which have now more or less become the norm), but simply the availability of realistic input data and samples and test structures.

During the integration design phase, the chosen concept is studied and, with the help of specialist engineers, the relevant authorities, consultant contractors and product manufacturers, an integrated solution is produced. To achieve the best possible results, it is important to consider complete systems whose components interact with each other. Concentration on individual parts or parts of systems is only admissible, if they do not have a significant impact on other building components. Thus the purpose is not to optimise individual building components or criteria, but to consider the building as a whole, including all the trades involved and all interfaces between geometrically or functionally connected modules. The issues of system integration (exterior wall, storage masses, building technology and building management technology) and decentralised building technology in the building envelope will play a more important role in future than they do at present. But the benefits of innovative building concepts can only be exploited if the components of the technical fixtures and fittings as well as the building envelope are easy to control and are linked to an intelligent control system. Building management technology allows building envelope and building technology devices and systems to be connected to one another using conventional electrical cabling, via a building BUS

ausgeschöpft werden, wenn nicht nur die Gebäudehülle, sondern auch die Komponenten der Technischen Gebäudeausrüstung über eine gute Regelfähigkeit sowie über eine intelligente Regelungseinrichtung verfügen. Dann bietet die Gebäudeleittechnik die Möglichkeit, Geräte und Systeme der Gebäudehülle und der Gebäudetechnik, über konventionelle Elektroverkabelung oder über einen Gebäude-BUS (z.B. EIB oder LON) bzw. über das PC-Netzwerk (z.B. Ethernet), miteinander zu verbinden und zwischen ihnen eine Kommunikation herzustellen. Die Technische Gebäudeausrüstung kommt nur in Extremsituationen zum Einsatz, wenn die Möglichkeiten der Gebäudehülle erschöpft sind.

Erst wenn die Ergebnisse der Integrationsplanung mit den Zielvorgaben übereinstimmen und die Anforderungskriterien geklärt sind, kann die Baugruppenplanung gestartet werden. Jetzt geht es um die Optimierung und planerische Umsetzung der Schnittstellen innerhalb der Baugruppen. Dabei geht es aus fassadentechnischer Sicht um die Fragen Lochfassade, Vorhangfassade oder Skelettausfachung, Pfosten-Riegel-Fassaden oder Elementfassade sowie um Details wie die Ausbildung der Fassadenbefestigungen und Wandanschlüsse. In zunehmendem Maße sind auch spezielle Gesichtspunkte wie „interaktive" Außenwandkonstruktionen (Funktionalität, Reaktionsfähigkeit und Flexibilität) und Steuerungstechnik für die Außenwand (Gebäudeautomation und Prozessoptimierung) zu berücksichtigen. Die Entscheidung fällt unter den Kriterien Reduzierung von Investitions- und Betriebskosten, Komplexität und Risiken sowie Erhöhung der Flexibilität und Funktionalität. Die Baugruppenplanung endet mit der Festlegung funktioneller Anforderungen an die Baugruppen und definierter Schnittstellen zwischen den Baugruppen, die in der Ausschreibung Niederschlag finden.

Nach erfolgter Vergabe erarbeiten Architekten, Fachingenieure, Unternehmer und Produkthersteller in der Detailplanung gemeinsam die ausführungsreife Planung, welche die Werkplanung und die mit dem Architekten abgestimmte Ablaufplanung für die Ausführung beinhaltet. Jetzt geht es um die Optimierung und planerische Umsetzung der in der Baugruppenplanung getroffenen Festlegungen.

4.4 Projektorganisation für die Konzeption und Planung anwendungsgerechter Gebäudehüllen

Da ein Einzelner die oben beschriebenen, weitreichenden Verknüpfungen im Umfeld anwendungsgerechter Gebäudehüllen einerseits gewerkeübergreifend und ganzheitlich, andererseits im Detail, nicht mehr überblicken kann, bietet sich als Alternative eine jeweils objektspezifisch angepasste Projektorganisation mit koordinierter Teamarbeit und strategischen Netzwerken an. Dabei geht es um Spezialisierung und Arbeitsteilung, sowohl bei Unternehmen als auch bei einzelnen Menschen. Integral denkende Generalisten – die in einer „Makro-Welt" leben und alle derzeit bzw. mittelfristig zur Verfügung stehenden Möglichkeiten und die entscheidenden Risiken kennen – visionieren, konzipieren, organisieren, koordinieren oder managen. Diesen gegenüber stehen die hoch effizienten Spezialisten, die in ihrer „Mikro-Welt" leben und dort alle Details perfekt beherrschen. Sie forschen, entwickeln, beraten, konstruieren, fertigen oder montieren. Jeder hat seine eigenen Stärken bzw. Kernkompetenzen, wobei Leistungs- und Kompetenzspitzen des einen die Defizitbereiche des anderen ausgleichen. So werden je nach Bauvorhaben von Fall zu Fall neben Architekten und Bauingenieuren auch Tragwerksplaner, Elektroplaner, Lichttechniker, Heizungsingenieure, Klimatechniker, Bauphysiker und Bauklimatiker sowie Fassadenplaner, Controller und weitere Experten für Spezialthemen – auch von ausführenden Unternehmen – in das Projektteam aufgenommen.

(e.g. EIB or LON), or via a PC network (e.g. Ethernet), enabling communication to be established between them. Technical fixtures and fittings are only used in exceptional circumstances, when the options within the building envelope have been exhausted.

It is only when the results of integration planning come into line with the objectives, and the requirements criteria have been clarified that the module design phase can begin. This stage involves optimising and implementing the planned interfaces within the modules. As far as the façade is concerned, this means considering options such as punched openings, curtain walls or skeleton infill panels, mullion and transom façades or unitised façades and details such as the configuration of façade fixing brackets and wall attachments. Increasingly, attention must be paid to special aspects such as "interactive" exterior wall constructions (functionality, responsiveness and flexibility) and control technology for the exterior wall (building automation and process optimisation). The decision should be based on minimising investment and operating costs, complexity and risks, and maximising flexibility and functionality. By the end of module design, the team will have defined the functional requirements for the modules as well as the interfaces between the modules – information that is then reflected in the tender specifications.

Once the contract has been awarded, the architects, specialist engineers, contractors and product manufacturers team up during the component design phase to examine the completed plans, which contain the works plans and the building schedule as agreed with the architect. This stage involves optimising and translating the functional requirements and design of interfaces defined during the module design phase.

4.4 Project organisation for the design and planning of functional building envelopes

Since no single person can possibly keep track of the extensive network of activities involved in a functional building envelope, retaining an overview of all trade operations yet still understanding the details, one option is to organise the project on the basis of coordinated teamwork and strategic networks. This involves specialisation and division of labour, for both companies and individuals. The "generalists", who live in a "macro world", have an integrated view of the project and are familiar with all current and medium-term possibilities as well as the main risks, are responsible for shaping the vision, designing, organising, coordinating and managing. In contrast, the specialists live in a "micro world" and have perfect knowledge of all its details. They research, develop, advise, design, fabricate and assemble. Everyone contributes specific strengths and core competencies, with the major strengths of one person compensating for the weaknesses of another. For example, depending on the building project, the project team can include (alongside the architects and construction engineers) load-bearing structure planners, electrics planners, light engineers, heating engineers, air conditioning engineers, building physicists, building climate control specialists, façade planners, supervisors and other experts (including those of the companies contracted to do the work).

Gerhard Matzig

**Eine Verteidigung der Ober-
fläche gegen die Oberfläch-
lichkeit ihrer Kritiker**

Friedrich Nietzsche hat es
gesagt. Roland Barthes hat es
auch gesagt. Platon hat es ebenfalls gesagt. Was? Dass es
nichts Tieferes als die Oberfläche gibt. Nur leider hat sich das
Lob der Philosophen nie so recht
gegen den allgemeinen Sprach-
gebrauch durchsetzen können:
Wer von Fassaden und Oberflächen, gar von Kulissen und
anderen vermeintlichen „bloßen
Äußerlichkeiten" spricht, der tut
dies zumeist in einem negativ
kritischen Sinn.

Man müsste in diesem Zusam-
menhang nicht einmal die
Historie bemühen und vom russischen Fürsten Grigorij
Alexandrowitsch Patjomkin,
genannt Potemkin, erzählen;
dessen legendäre „Potemkin-
sche Dörfer", zum Schein und
als Blendwerk aufgebaute Dorf-
Attrappen, sollten einst der
Großen Katharina blühende
Krim-Landschaften vorgaukeln.
Nein, man muss nur mal fünf
Minuten in eine beliebige Unterhaltung hineinhören – dann fällt
er gewiss: der Satz, wonach der
oder die, dieses oder jenes
„doch nur Fassade" sei.
Gemeint ist: Bluff, Täuschung,
Betrug. Gemeint ist: ein hüb-
sches Gesicht und nichts dahinter. Was der ursprünglich vom
lateinischen Wort „facies" abgeleiteten Fassade sogar vollkom-
men gerecht wird. Facies heißt
Gesicht.

Gerhard Matzig, geb.
1963, hat Architektur
und politische Wissen-
schaften studiert; er ist
stv. Leiter des Feuille-
tons der Süddeutschen
Zeitung.
Gerhard Matzig, b.1963,
studied architecture
and political science;
he is deputy features
editor of the
Süddeutsche Zeitung.

Facies heißt aber auch: äußere
Erscheinung. Woraus sich
schließlich ein fester Begriff der
Baukunst herausgebildet hat.
Unter Fassade versteht man
die vorzugsweise äußere Erscheinung, also die Schauseite
eines Bauwerks.

Man kennt die Kirchenfassade
und die Schlossfassade. Man
spricht von Steinfassaden, Holz-
fassaden oder Glasfassaden.
Man unterscheidet zwischen
ein- und zweischaligen Fassaden. Man weiß von Blendfassa-
den, gegliederten Fassaden oder
sogar von eigenständigen Fassa-
denvorbauten. Man diskutiert
den Fassadenschmuck oder
eben deren Negation: die so
genannte schmucklose Fassade.

Wir haben es also mit einem
regelrechten Fachwort zu tun.
Allerdings mit einem, das wie
kein anderer Terminus technicus
der Architektur im Zwielicht seines öffentlichen Gebrauchs
steht. Weshalb der „Fassadenkletterer" auch kein besonders
alpin wirkender Architekt ist –
sondern ein kletternder Einbre-
cher. Das Wort Fassade ist also
erhellend und zugleich dunkel,
es ist schlicht und zugleich gla-
mourös. Es ist, mit einem Wort,
interessant.

Kein Wunder, dass es die Künste
beschäftigt. Kein Wunder auch,
dass der Fassade eben dort, wo
es schon naturgemäß um Kulissen geht, eine besondere
Bedeutung zukommt: in der
Filmkunst. Wobei es die Fassade
in der jüngst vorgestellten
„Matrix"-Trilogie der regieführen-
den Brüder Andy und Larry
Wachowski zu einer Hauptrolle
der finstersten Art gebracht hat.
In allen drei Matrix-Episoden
steht sie für das Böse schlechthin. Denn die – in ferner Zukunft
– von einer dominanten Com-
puterintelligenz generierten, in
Wahrheit natürlich immateriellen
Fassaden wirken als suggestive
Wahnbilder, mit deren Hilfe die
Menschen in einem rauschähnli-
chen Zustand der Abhängigkeit
gehalten werden. Abhängig von
Bites und Bytes. Abhängig von
der Matrix als Ort der perfekten
Architektur-Illusion. Die Fassade:
ein anderes Wort für Perfidie.

Womöglich hätten die Matrix-
Filme sogar Adolf Loos gefallen.
Dem Wiener Baumeister und
Ahnherren der modernen Architektur (1870–1933) verdanken
wir einen berühmt gewordenen
Fassadenstreit. In dessen Verlauf
bekämpfte der Architekt die tra-
dierte, höchst ornamentreiche
Fassadenbaukunst seiner Zeit –
Keanu Reeves, der Matrix-
Hauptdarsteller, hätte von diesem Kampf alles über das
Thema „gerechter Zorn" lernen
können. Es geht um das legendäre „Haus am Michaelerplatz"
in Wien. Im ersten Jahrzehnt des
zwanzigsten Jahrhunderts sollte
Adolf Loos für die Firma
Goldman & Salatsch ein Wohn-
und Geschäftshaus errichten.
Und zwar als Bekenntnis zur for-
malen Reinheit der funktionalen
Moderne. Dummerweise stand
und steht die Hofburg genau
gegenüber. Und so kam es – wie
es kommen musste. Der Entwurf, ein gebautes, naturgemäß
schmuckloses Manifest im Sinne
der Loos-Schrift „Ornament und
Verbrechen" musste einem mit
architektonischem Pomp und
vielerlei Zierrat verwöhnten Publikum missfallen. Der Wiener
Gemeinderat befand: „Scheusal
von einem Haus". Loos wurde
mit Steinen beworfen. Am
Michaelerplatz kam es zu
tumultartigen, hollywoodreifen
Szenen. Spätestens jetzt war
klar, dass sich vor allem darüber
im öffentlichen Raum streiten
lässt: über den Geschmack.
Beziehungsweise: über die Fassade. Was in der Rezeption zeit-
genössischer Architektur beina-
he aufs Gleiche hinausläuft.

Über die gesellschaftliche
Diskussion der Architektur gibt
es einschlägige Untersuchungen: Das allgemeine Publikum
interessiert sich demnach –
sofern es nicht um das eigene
Häuschen im Grünen geht – nur
mäßig für Fragen der Konstruktion und Haustechnik. Die Stil-
Frage, ob also womöglich ein
Fall von „dynamistischer" oder
„dekonstruktivistischer" Baukunst vorliege – oder ob das
jeweilige Haus nicht doch viel
mehr dem „Biomorphismus"
zuzurechnen sei: Das überlässt
man gerne den Theoretikern.
Und die Diskussion der

Gerhard Matzig

Defending the outer surface against the superficiality of its critics

Friedrich Nietzsche said it; Roland Barthes too, even Plato said it: there is nothing beneath the surface. Unfortunately, the praise of the philosophers has never quite triumphed over everyday language. When one talks about façades and outer surfaces, or even backdrops and other supposedly 'mere external appearances', it is usually meant negatively.

To illustrate this point, one need look no further than the story of the Russian prince Grigori Aleksandrovich Potyomkin – known as "Potemkin", who reputedly gave the order for sham villages to be built for Catherine the Great's tour of the Crimea. Indeed, one only has to eavesdrop on any conversation for five minutes to hear this or that described as "just a façade". What's meant is a false or deceptive appearance, suggesting there is little behind an attractive face. Which, in truth, is completely in keeping with the original Latin word facies (meaning 'face'), from which "façade" is derived.

But facies also means 'external appearance', and it is this that architecture has ultimately taken as a fixed term. The façade is understood as the principal external appearance, i.e. the side of a building on display. Everyone is familiar with the façade of a church or castle, and we talk about stone, timber and glass façades; a distinction is made between single and double skin façades; there are faceted façades and forward-standing, free-supporting façades; and the embellishment of a façade or lack thereof (plain façade) is also discussed.

So what we're dealing with here is a specialist term. But it's a term like no other technical architectural term, one which is overshadowed by its public usage. Which is why the German word "Fassadenkletterer" (literally "façade climber") has nothing to do with Alpine architecture – it actually means "cat burglar". The word façade is at once illuminating and dark, simple yet glamorous; in a word, intriguing.

Is it any wonder then that it infiltrates the arts? No surprise either that the façade has a particular importance in a world already filled with backdrops, namely, in film-making. Brothers Andy and Larry Wachowski, who directed the Matrix trilogy, have given the façade a lead role of the most sinister kind: in all three Matrix films, the façade represents evil. In the distant future, the computer-generated (in reality immaterial) façades work as suggestive illusions, which help to keep the people in a state of dependency, like an intoxication. Dependent on bits and bytes; dependent on the matrix as the site of the perfect architectural illusion. Façade is another word for perfidy.

Adolf Loos would doubtless have enjoyed the Matrix films too. We have this master builder and progenitor of modern architecture (1870–1933) to thank for a famous argument about façades. He fought against the time-honoured, highly ornamental façade designs of the age – in fact, Keanu Reeves (the lead character in the Matrix) would have been able to learn everything about "righteous anger" from this fight. It all centred around the famous "Haus am Michaelerplatz" in Vienna. At the beginning of the 20th Century, Adolf Loos was commissioned to build a residential and commercial property for Goldman & Salatsch. It was intended as a declaration of formal purity of functional modernity. Foolishly, however, the Hofburgs were and still remain quite set against it. Eventually something had to give, as indeed it must. The design – a natural, plain manifesto, with the Loos signature "Ornament and Crime" – must have seemed alien to a public more accustomed to

Photonics Centre, Berlin-Adlershof, Germany sauerbruch hutton architekten, Berlin

architectural pomp and ornate decoration. The Vienna district council called it "a monster of a house". Loos was stoned. On Michaelerplatz, there were tumultuous scenes more akin to a Hollywood movie. Now, at last, it was clear that such things could be debated in the public domain – matters of taste, that is to say, the issue of façades. Which in the world of modern architecture amounts to the same thing.

There have been relevant studies made on the social discussion of architecture. However, unless it concerns their own house and garden, the general public is not overly interested in questions of construction and domestic services. The question of style – 'dynamic' or 'deconstructive' architecture, whether it's more a matter of attributing 'biomorphism' to the house… that's something we'd rather leave to the theorists. And the discussion of functionality? This should ideally be carried out by the occupants. But, what really gets the passer-by, the casual observer, the city user, or – to use Adolf Loos' words – the public witness of architecture, going is the shape and form of the façade. They may not argue with any real knowledge, but they do so with verve; and that is what counts.

The outside of a house is always the showcase for public viewing of architecture. But anyone who believes that the public perception of architecture and how it is discussed publicly does

Funktionalität? Die soll gefälligst von den Bewohnern geführt werden. Was den Passanten, den Flaneur, den Stadtbenutzer – oder nach einem Wort von Adolf Loos: den öffentlichen Architektur-Zeugen – dagegen wirklich umtreibt, das ist die Fassadengestaltung. Darüber wird nicht immer mit Kenntnis gestritten – aber immer mit Verve. Und darauf kommt es an.

Die Schauseite eines Hauses ist auch immer der Schauplatz der öffentlichen Architekturbetrachtung. Wer aber glaubt, dass es darauf – auf die öffentlich wahrnehmbare Architektur wie auf die öffentlich geführte Diskussion darüber – wegen Laienbeteiligung nicht so sehr ankomme, der hat noch immer nicht begriffen, dass die Architektur als „Öffentlichste aller Künste" (Lebbeus Woods) auch deshalb gefährdet ist, weil die Öffentlichkeit davon zu wenig berührt wird. Die Folge: Architektur und Baukultur wird – abseits der bekannten Flughäfen, Museen oder anderer Bau-Sensationen, abseits auch der ubiquitären Star-Architektur, viel zu wenig nachgefragt.

Mitten in diese vielfach analysierte und dokumentierte „Krise der Baukultur" wird allerdings vermeldet, dass die „Kunst der Fassade" einen wahren Boom erlebe. „Mit all den heutigen Möglichkeiten – gestalterisch wie konstruktiv – ist das Thema Fassade" [1], so spannend wie selten zuvor.

Neue Materialien und Konzepte werden allerorts erprobt, Grenzen werden ausgelotet, überlieferte Sehgewohnheiten in Frage gestellt. Und es entwickelt sich sogar die „neue Lust an Ornament und Dekor in der Fassadengestaltung" [2]. Tatsächlich scheint jene Hauptforderung der Moderne, wonach das Äußere eines Bauwerks nur getreulich dienend und bescheiden vom Inneren erzählen dürfe, kaum mehr gültig zu sein. Insofern kann man womöglich auch hoffen, dass die tiefsinnige Kunst der Oberfläche zukünftig von allzu oberflächlicher Kritik verschont bleibt.

Beispielsweise werden Architekten, die sich in besonderer Weise um die Effekte der Fassadengestaltung bemühen, nicht selten gerade deshalb von der Kritik mit Häme überzogen. Jean Nouvel wird dann schon mal als „Marquis de Fassade" bezeichnet. Und Daniel Libeskind wird als „Verpackungskünstler" abgeurteilt. Dabei könnte schon längst klar sein: Natürlich kommt es auch auf die Verpackung an. Natürlich kommt es auch auf die Inszenierung an. Natürlich kommt es auch auf den Anschein an in einer Zeit, die mit spielerischer Leichtigkeit das Sein und den Schein zur Deckung zu bringen vermag. Kulturpessimismus ist also eher unangebracht im Angesicht der neu entdeckten Fassadenhaftigkeit. Im Gegenteil: Der baukulturellen Vitalität können die neuen Form-, Farb- und Materialexperi-

mente nur gut tun. Selbst wenn die Architektur zunehmend auch als Lifestyle-Faktor, Image-Träger und Corporate-Identity-Garant fungiert: Das muss kein Schaden sein.

Wer sich zum Beispiel die spektakuläre Glas-Feier beim Laban Centre in London betrachtet (Architekten: Jacques Herzog, Pierre de Meuron, Basel), das raffinierte Spiel von Transparenz und Transluzenz, die Balance von Einsichten, Aussichten und Ansichten, der ahnt, dass dem Material Glas in Zukunft eine völlig neue Sinnlichkeit zugetraut werden kann. Dafür steht auch die geschwungene, in die Umgebung fließende Fassade des neuen McLaren Technology Centre in Woking/England (Architekten: Foster and Partners, London, in diesem Buch Seite 180). Und wer sich die straffe Rankgitter-Inszenierung eines simplen Autobahn-Kontrollstandes in der Nähe von Wien betrachtet (Architekt: Adolf Krischanitz, Wien), der ahnt, dass der reichhaltige Material-Fundus der Architektur gerade erst geöffnet wurde. Und wer sich das neue Contemporary Arts Center in Cincinnati/USA betrachtet (Architektin: Zaha Hadid, London), der ahnt, dass selbst der Baustoff Beton immer noch einmal uraufgeführt werden kann. Beton, Stahl, Aluminium, Glas, dazu auch Holz und Papier, ja Erde und Wasser und Luft: Der Kunst der Fassade scheinen keine Grenzen gesetzt. Es gibt Hüllen aus Tarnnetzen und Häute aus Plastikbahnen, es gibt Schichten aus Gras und Kleider aus Kunststoffkugeln: Die Zukunft könnte durchaus den Couturiers unter den Architekten gehören: den Modeschöpfern und ihrer Lust an der Sinnlichkeit der Oberfläche. Denn es gibt, sofern die Architektur insgesamt stimmig ist, nun einmal nichts Tieferes als die Oberfläche.
Let`s face it.

McLaren
Technology Centre,
Woking, Great Britain
Foster and Partners,
London

1) Editorial der Fachzeitschrift „Detail",
   Deutschland (Heft 7/8 2003)
2) „Frankfurter Allgemeine Sonntagszeitung",
   Deutschland (26. Oktober 2003)

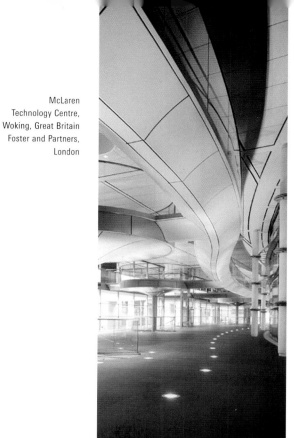

McLaren
Technology Centre,
Woking, Great Britain
Foster and Partners,
London

not matter, has not understood that architecture, as "the most public of all the arts" (Lebbeus Woods), is actually endangered, because the public is not sufficiently moved by it. As a result, apart from the well-known airports, museums and other high profile projects, there is simply not enough call for architecture and building culture.

Within this much analysed and widely documented "crisis in building culture", the news is that the "art of the façade" is actually experiencing a real boom. "With all the design and construction options available today, the topic of façades has rarely been more exciting. New materials and ideas are being tried out everywhere, boundaries are being tested, and traditional perceptions are being questioned." [1]. There is also a "new desire for ornament and decoration in façade design" [2]. In fact, the principal demand of the modern age – that the exterior of a building should only be allowed to tell truthfully and modestly of the interior – seems hardly to apply any more. To that extent, one can only hope that the profound art of the outer surface will in future be spared from any superficial criticism. For example, architects who are particularly concerned about the effects of façade design are often heavily criticised for that very reason. Jean Nouvel has already been dubbed the "Marquis de Façade", whereas Daniel Libeskind has been denigrated as a "packaging artist". But all of this should have been clear long ago. Of course, the packaging is significant; of course, stage management is key; of course, appearance is also important at a time when essence and appearance might coincide with playful lightness. Such cultural pessimism is therefore misplaced in the face of the new 'façadism'. In fact, the latest experiments with shape, colour and material can only be good for the vitality of building culture. Even if architecture functions increasingly as a lifestyle indicator, an image booster and a guarantee of corporate identity – this does not necessarily do any harm.

For example, anyone looking at the spectacular celebration of glass at the Laban Centre in London (architects: Jacques Herzog, Pierre de Meuron, Basle), the exquisite play between transparency and translucence, the balance of looking in, looking out and looking upon, would assume that in future glass as a material will be capable of an entirely new sensuality. The curved façade of "Paragon", the new McLaren Technology Centre in Woking, England (architects: Foster and Partners, London, page 180 of this book), with its flowing lines is another case in point. And anyone looking at the rigid trellis development of a simple motorway toll booth near Vienna (architect: Adolf Krischanitz, Vienna) would believe that the rich fund of architectural materials had only just been opened. Again, anyone studying the new Contemporary Arts Center in Cincinnati/USA (architect: Zaha Hadid, London) would guess that even concrete was staging a comeback as a building material. Concrete, steel, aluminium, glass, as well as timber and paper, even earth, water and air: the art of the façade appears to know no bounds. There are coverings made of camouflage netting and skins made of plastic sheeting; there are layers made from grass and clothing made from plastic balls. The future could well belong to the couturiers amongst the architects: to the trend setters and their indulgence in the sensuality of the outer surface. For there is nothing deeper, as long as the overall architecture is coherent, than the surface – let's face it!

1) Editorial in the technical magazine "Detail",
Germany (Vol. 7/8 2003)
2) "Frankfurter Allgemeine Sonntagszeitung",
Germany (26th October 2003)

Büro- und Verwaltungsbauten
sind Orte der Büroarbeit und
werden von unterschiedlichsten
Raumkonzeptionen bestimmt.
Hightech, Lowtech, all das sind
Anforderungen, die intelligente
und innovative technische
Lösungen erfordern, für die
Gebäudehülle ebenso wie für
den gesamten technischen
Innenausbau.

Office buildings are places
where administrative work is
carried out and are defined by a
host of different designs for the
use of space. Hi-tech and low-
tech; both are requirements
that demand intelligent and
innovative technical solutions for
the building envelope and all the
technical facets of the interior.

Büro- und Verwaltungsbauten

Office buildings

Vienna, Austria

Städtebauliche Situation

Die „UNO-City", ein 1972–78 auf der Insel zwischen linkem Donau-Ufer und einer alten Donau-Schleife für die UNO errichteter Hochhauskomplex, wurde in den 90er-Jahren zum Kristallisationspunkt für den neuen Stadtteil „Donau-City" mit seinen Dienstleistungs- und Wohnhochhäusern.

Diese Hochhaus-Agglomeration markiert zugleich die vom Stadtzentrum ca. 3 km entfernte Donau und das Übergreifen der städtischen Bebauung auf das linke Donau-Ufer. Daraus entwickelte sich dann die städtebauliche Leitidee, den eigentlichen Donau-Raum auch flussaufwärts bis etwa zur nördlichen Stadtgrenze durch weitere Hochhäuser zu markieren. So Ende der 90er-Jahre mit Gustav Peichls „Millennium-Tower" und jüngst mit dem „Florido-Tower" des Architekturbüros Müller-Hartburg.

Der Florido-Tower bildet den point de vue für den nördlichen Ausläufer der Wiener „Gürtelstraße" und zugleich das neue Wahrzeichen des Bezirks Floridsdorf, einer eher etwas farblosen Vorstadt auf dem linken Donau-Ufer.

Urban development

"UNO City" is a high-rise complex built for the organisation in 1972-78 on the island between the left bank and an old loop of the Danube. In the 90s it became the focal point of the new "Danube City" district, with its mixture of residential and service buildings.

This agglomeration of skyscrapers marks the onset of urbanisation on the left bank of the river about 3 km from the city centre. The theme has been developed upstream towards the northern outskirts with further multistorey buildings, such as Gustav Peichl's "Millennium Tower" built in the late 90s and, most recently, the "Florido Tower" by the architectural practice of Müller-Hartburg.

This tower dominates the northern periphery of Vienna's ring road, while forming the new symbol of the district of Floridsdorf, one of the formerly rather colourless left-bank suburbs.

Ansicht von Südwesten bei Nacht
View from the southwest at night

Bauherr
Client
Bayernfonds Immobilien GmbH & Co., Florido-Tower AG c/o UBM Realitätenentwicklung AG, Vienna

Entwurfsplanung und künstlerische Oberleitung
Conceptual Design and Aesthetics
Müller-Hartburg ZT GmbH Architekten + Generalplaner, Vienna
Architekt Dipl.-Ing. Andreas Müller-Hartburg

Ausführungsplanung
Working Design
Projektierungsbüro für Industrie-, Hoch- und Tiefbauten GmbH & Co. KG, Vienna

Bauleitung
Construction Management
Porr Projekt und Hochbau AG, Vienna

Bauphysikalische Projektbearbeitung
Thermal and Acoustic Design
Dipl.-Ing. Dr. Harald Koch Zivilingenieur für technische Physik, Wiener Neudorf

Fassadenplanung
Façade Design
Consultplan, Technisches Büro für Maschinenbau GmbH, Stoob

Ausführung der Fassaden
Façade Construction
Arbeitsgemeinschaft Alu-Glas-Fassade Florido-Tower, bestehend aus: Fa. Alu-Sommer GmbH, Stoob
Fa. Matec, Neutal

Die Aufgabenstellung des Bauherrn

Bauplatz war eine 8.000 m² große Gewerbebrache – unmittelbar an der Hauptstraße zum Wiener Stadtzentrum – zwischen dem „Auepark" an der Donau und dem Kern von Floridsdorf mit seiner heterogenen 2- bis 5-geschossigen Wohnbebauung. Auf diesem Platz sollten ein Büro-Hochhaus mit möglichst flexibler Aufteilung und Mittelhochbauten mit Büros und Läden errichtet werden. Der ganze Komplex sollte im Hinblick auf die Betriebskosten natürlich belüftet und nur das Hochhaus mit einer unterstützenden künstlichen Be- und Entlüftung versehen werden.

Das Entwurfskonzept des Architekten

Der Architekt löste diese Aufgabe, indem er einen 30 Geschosse hohen Büroturm mit elliptischem Grundriss entwarf, der durch eine 3-seitig umlaufende 5- bzw. 4-geschossige Blockrandbebauung an die umgebende Bebauung angebunden wurde. Der begrünte Innenhof des Blocks öffnet sich durch die vollverglas-

Luftbild von Süden
Aerial photograph from the south

te 2-geschossige Eingangshalle auf einen vorgelagerten repräsentativen Vorplatz, der – wie die Längsachse des Turmes – nach SW auf das Stadtzentrum von Wien ausgerichtet ist.

Die Hüllflächen des Turmes weisen an dessen „Längsseiten" mit ihren geschlossenen Brüstungen eine horizontale Tendenz auf, während die zurückspringenden „Schmalseiten" mit ihrer geschosshohen Verglasung dagegen eine ausgeprägte Vertikal-Tendenz haben, die bei abendlicher Beleuchtung noch unterstrichen wird.

Der Rücksprung auf der SW-Seite wird im oberen Drittel durch eine vorspringende 6-geschossige Spange „zusammengehalten", deren Körper durch dunkler reflektierende Fenster- und Brüstungsverglasungen noch betont wird.

Die Büroflächen von 700 m²/ Geschoss können durch Trennwände in Ebene der Längsachse in 2 Mietflächen von je 350 m² oder über demontierbare Deckenfelder in Mietflächen von 1.350 + 350 m² auf 2 Geschossen unterteilt werden. Sie sind je nach Bedarf für Einzel-, Gruppen- und Großraumbüros verwendbar.

Im 2-geschossigen Bauteil am Innenhof ist eine große Cafeteria mit ihren Funktionsräumen angeordnet. Der Gesamtkomplex hat 3 Untergeschosse inklusive einer Tiefgarage mit 600 PKW-Stellplätzen.

Client's Brief

The 8,000 m² brownfield site was right on the main artery into the centre of Vienna, between the "Auepark" on the Danube and the heart of Floridsdorf with its heterogeneous 2 to 5-storey residential buildings. It had to accommodate an office tower with an extremely flexible layout, and medium-rise commercial buildings with offices and shops. To minimise overheads the natural ventilation of the entire complex was only to be artificially boosted in the skyscraper.

Overall Architectural Concept

The architect's interpretation of this brief was an elliptical 30-storey tower with a 4/5-storey transition block around 3 sides to harmonise with the existing built environment. The block's atrium garden opens out through the fully glazed 2-storey entrance hall into an imposing forecourt, which – like the longitudinal axis of the tower – is aligned south-west towards the centre of Vienna.

Continuous spandrels emphasise the horizontal lines of the longer elevations of the tower envelope, while floor-to-ceiling glazing emphasises the vertical lines of the set-back shorter elevations. The contrast becomes even more striking when the lights come on. The top third of the south-west recess is "held together" by a projecting 6-storey mass accentuated by darker reflective window and spandrel glazing.

The 700 m² of office space per storey can be partitioned on the longitudinal axis into two 350 m² full-height rental units, or removable floor panels used to

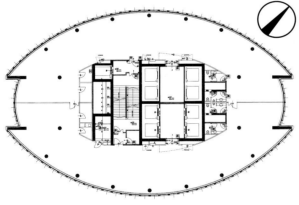

Das Konzept der Turmfassade

Die Forderung des Bauherrn nach natürlicher Fensterlüftung führte zwangsläufig zu dem System der „Glas-Doppelfassade", d.h. einem System mit innerer klimatrennender Fensterkonstruktion, einer äußeren nicht klimatrennenden Festverglasung und einem dazwischen liegenden Raum, der mit der Außenluft in Verbindung steht. Die Vorteile dieses Systems:

* natürliche, von Niederschlägen und Windanfall (d.h. von Luftanströmung und Luftdruckdifferenzen = Böen) unabhängige, individuelle Fensterlüftung;
* optimaler „äußerer" (d.h. unmittelbar hinter der äußeren Festverglasung liegender) beweglicher Sonnenschutz, i.d.R. in Form der an sich windanfälligen Horizontal-Lamellenstoren;
* zusätzliche Schalldämmung gegen Außenlärm durch die äußere Festverglasung.

In der Regel erhält eine derartige Glas-Doppelfassade einen für Wartungs- und Reinigungszwecke begehbaren Luftraum. Diese Konstruktion ist allerdings relativ teuer (Faktor ca. 2,2 im Vergleich zu 1-schaligen Fassadenkonstruktionen) und vergrößert das Gebäudevolumen um die Tiefe dieses begehbaren Luftraumes.

provide 1,350 and 350 m² of floor space on two levels. This accommodation is suitable for single through to open-plan offices.

The large 2-storey atrium cafeteria offers various function rooms. The entire complex has 3 basement levels, including a 600-space underground car park.

Tower Façade Concept

The client's requirement for natural window ventilation necessitated the adoption of a "structurally glazed twin-wall façade", ie a system with fixed inside glazing isolating indoor air conditions, non-isolating fixed outside glazing and an intermediate space connected to the outside air. The advantages of this system are as follows:

* Natural ventilation through individual windows that is unaffected by rain and wind (ie by air flow and pressure differentials causing gusts);
* Optimum "external" (ie immediately behind the fixed outside glazing) movable solar shading system, generally in the form of blinds that cannot otherwise withstand the wind;
* Additional insulation against external noise provided by the fixed outside glazing.

The air space of this type of twin façade is generally accessible for maintenance and cleaning. However, this design is relatively expensive (about 2.2 times as much as its single-skin equivalent) and its air space increases the volume of the building.

Untere Ecke des Alu-
Aufsatzprofils 02
The bottom corner
of the aluminium
section 02

Detailansicht von
Südosten mit „Spange"
Detail-view from the
southeast with "clasp"

Die Konstruktion der Turmfassade

Für den Florido-Tower wurde das kostengünstigere Prinzip des „Kastenfensters" weiter entwickelt, das schon bei dem IZD-Tower in der Donau-City angewendet wurde, und bei dem die Tiefe des Luftraumes nur ca. 10 cm beträgt. Die Wartung der Lamellenstoren und die Reinigung der Innenseiten der äußeren Festverglasung kann infolgedessen vom Raum her erfolgen. Diese Konstruktion ist daher wesentlich preiswerter (Faktor ca. 1,4 im Vergleich zu 1-schaligen Fassadenkonstruktionen).

Der Luftraum steht durch einen umlaufenden Aufsatzrahmen – in dem auch die äußere Festverglasung gehalten wird – durch untere und seitliche Lüftungsöffnungen 40 x 20 mm mit der Außenluft in Verbindung, während die Oberseite durch die Abdeckung der Lamellenstoren geschlossen ist. Die Führung der Zu- und Abluft erfolgt über die 30 mm breiten Schattennuten der Elementstöße, also von unten nach seitlich oben.

Der Kastenfenster-Teil bildet zusammen mit der hinterlüfteten Glasverkleidung und Wärmedämmschicht der Betonbrüstung des darüber liegenden Geschosses ein 1.200 x 3.350 mm großes Element, das bei der Montage in die Ankerplatten an der Deckenvorderkante eingehängt wird. Die horizontalen Elementstöße liegen also jeweils in Höhe OK Betonbrüstung. Die vertikalen Elementstöße, die zugleich Anschlussmöglichkeiten für innere Trennwände bieten müssen, werden nach der Montage der Fassadenelemente durch fenster- bzw. brüstungshohe Glaslisenen in Aluminium-Rahmen abgedeckt.

Die bauphysikalischen Daten für die Konstruktion

Der k- und g-Wert wurde an 2 Muster-Fensterelementen gemessen mit
- $k = 1,5$ W/m^2 K,
- $g = 0,15$ (bei Lamellen in 45°-Stellung)

Der Rw-Wert wurde an einem analogen Referenzobjekt mit ca. 39,5 Rw ermittelt.

Design of Tower Façade

The more cost-effective principle of the "box window" (with air space of only about 10 cm) already used on the IZD Tower in Danube City was further refined for the Florido Tower. As a result the blinds can be maintained and the inside of the fixed outside glazing cleaned from the space. This design is therefore much cheaper (by a factor of about 1.4) compared with a single-skin façade.

A frame holds the fixed outside glazing and connects the air space to the outside air via 40 x 20 mm bottom and side openings, while the top is sealed by the cover of the blinds. The supply and exhaust air are therefore ducted though the 30 mm wide channels of the unit's shadow joints, ie sideways and upwards from the bottom.

The box window unit together with the rear-ventilated glass cladding and thermal insulation of the concrete spandrel of the next storey form a 1,200 x 3,350 mm unit, which is mounted on the outside edge of the slab with anchor plates. The units' horizontal joints are therefore flush with the top of the spandrel. The vertical joints, which also have to allow connection of internal partitions, are window and spandrel height glass covers in aluminium frames.

Glazing Design Parameters

The solar and thermal values measured for two specimen window units were:
- $k = 1.5$ W/m^2 K,
- $g = 0.15$ (with blinds in 45° position)

The Rw value measured on a similar successful project was approximately 39.5 dB.

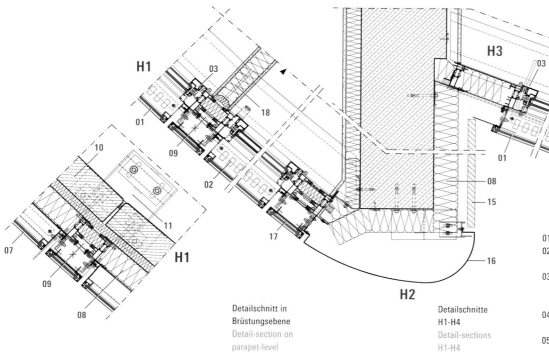

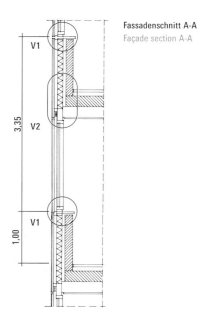

H1

H2

H3   **H4**

Detailschnitt in
Brüstungsebene
Detail-section on
parapet-level

Detailschnitte
H1-H4
Detail-sections
H1-H4

01 Einfach-Festverglasung 8 mm Weißglas ESG
02 Alu-Aufsatzprofil mit 3-seitiger umlaufender
   Lochung 40 x 20 mm
03 thermisch getrennte Fenster-/Brüstungs-
   Elemente aus der Serie Schüco Royal S 70B in
   Sonderkonstruktion, mit Drehkippflügeln
04 Isolierverglasung Wärmeschutzglas
   k = 1.1, außen 6 mm ESG, innen 4 mm Float
05 Isolierverglasung wie 04, jedoch innen VSG zur
   Absturzsicherung
06 Elt-Lamellenstoren b = 25 mm mit Seilführung,
   Kopfleiste mit Alu-Blech abgedeckt
07 hinterlüftete Brüstungsverglasung 8 mm ESG,
   rückseitig RAL 7035 emailliert
08 Min-Faserplatte 100 mm, rückseitig verzinktes
   Stahlblech 3 mm
09 horizontaler bzw. vertikaler Elementstoß
10 Beton-Fertigteilbrüstung mit eingelegter
   Wärmedämmung
11 Verankerungselement Stahl verzinkt
12 Fixpunkt für Reinigungsgondel
13 Hohlraumboden
14 abgehängte Alu-Schallschluckdecke
15 hinterlüftete Bekleidung aus glasierten Keramik-
   Elementen
16 hinterlüftete Bekleidung aus Alu-Blech 3 mm
17 Verglasung der Lisenen-Elemente 6 mm ESG,
   sonst wie 07
18 Anschlussmöglichkeit für Trennwände d =
   10–15 cm

01 Single fixed glazing
   (8 mm toughened opal safety glass)
02 Aluminium section with perforation.
   40 x 20 mm on 3 sides
03 Thermally broken window/spandrel units
   from the Schüco Royal S 70B series, special
   construction with turn/tilt vents
04 Double glazing, k = 1.1, 6 mm toughened
   safety glass outside, 4 mm float inside
05 Double glazing as 04, but with laminated safety
   glass to prevent accidents
06 25 mm wide, cord operated electric blinds.
   Sheet aluminium top cover
07 Rear ventilated spandrel units using 8 mm
   toughened safety glass, back enamelled
   (colour RAL 7035)
08 100 mm microfibre board, 3 mm sheet steel
   galvanised on back
09 Horizontal and vertical unit joints
10 Precast concrete spandrel incorporating
   thermal insulation
11 Galvanised steel anchor
12 Fixing point for cleaning gondola
13 Raised floor
14 Suspended acoustic ceiling made of aluminium
15 Rear ventilated cladding consisting of glazed
   ceramic panels
16 Rear ventilated 3 mm sheet aluminium cladding
17 Cover units with 6 mm toughened safety glass,
   otherwise as 07
18 Partition connection, d = 10–15 cm

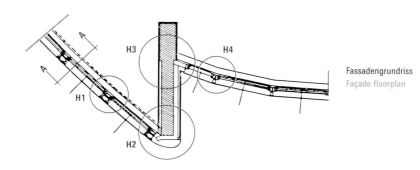

Fassadengrundriss
Façade floorplan

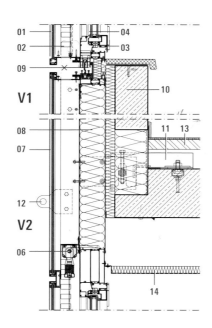

V1

V2

Fassadenschnitt A-A
Façade section A-A

Detailschnitte V1 + V2
Detail-sections V1 + V2

Poznán, Poland

Planung
Design
CDF Architekci,
Biuro Projektowe, Poznán

Mitwirkende Sachverständige
Consultants
Arch. Karol Fiedor

Fantasievolle expressionistische Architektur, ein Spiel mit Formen, Anspielungen und vielen verschiedenen Materialien. Geschlossenen Flächen stehen transparente oder transluzente Bauteile gegenüber.
Die zwei Hauptkörper werden auf drei unterschiedlichen Ebenen durch Brücken miteinander verbunden. So entsteht trotz eigenwilliger Erscheinungsbilder der einzelnen Solitäre ein harmonisches Gesamtensemble.
Die interessanten Dachabschlüsse, einer mit riesiger Andreaskreuz-Aussteifung, verleihen den Gebäuden ihren starken Ausdruck.

Imaginative and expressionist, the architecture is a blend of forms, references and a medley of materials. Windowless areas are contrasted with transparent and translucent components. Bridges connect the two main structures at three different levels to achieve a dovetailing effect.
The most striking and imposing feature is the roof attachments with their massive bracing section.

Objekt-Skizze
aus der Entwurfsphase
Preliminary sketch
from the design phase

Außenansichten
PGK II Centrum
Outside views
PGK II Centrum

„Die Architektur bildet den Raum für den Menschen. Der Mensch bildet den Raum für die Seele. Die Seele bildet den Raum für das All."
"Architecture creates space for people. People create space for the soul. The soul creates space for the universe."

CDF Architekci – Marcin Cholaszczyński, Maciej Dominik, Karol Fiedor

Berlin, Germany

Planung
Design
RHWL ARCHITECTS
Renton - Howard - Wood - Levin
Partnership, London

Außenansichten
Neubau
Axel Springer Verlag
Outside views
New building
Axel Springer Verlag

Frankfurt/Oder, Germany

Planung
Design
Planteam West, Cologne

Mitwirkende Sachverständige
Consultants
Albrecht Memmert + Partner
GbR, Neuss

Eine große Rotunde bildet den markanten Eckpunkt des in ländlicher Umgebung liegenden weitläufigen Gebäudekomplexes. Die differenzierte Rasterfassade, Säulen und die Gebäudeteile überspannenden Brücken verleihen der Anlage eine Leichtigkeit, die durch die voll verglasten, kopfseits aufgebrachten Fluchttreppenhäuser noch unterstützt wird.
Für die Lichtdächer wurde das System SK 60 eingesetzt, für die Profilfassade FW 50, die Fensterelemente sind in dem System Royal S 65 gestaltet.

**Außenansichten
LVA Brandenburg**
Outside views
LVA Brandenburg

A large rotunda forms a striking corner point of a large building complex in a countryside environment. The distinctive modular façade, the columns and bridges between sections of the building give the structure a light and airy appearance, which is sustained by the fully glazed emergency stairways at the front.
The SK 60 system was used for the sky lights, FW 50 for the profile façade, and the window units were made using the Royal S 65 system.

Duisburg, Germany

Planung
Design
Foster and Partners, London,
Great Britain

Fassadenberatung
Eternal skin
Emmer Pfenninger Partner AG,
Münchenstein, Switzerland

Das Gebäude ist Teil des
Electronic Park Duisburg, der
nach Fertigstellung 30.000 m²
flexible Nutzflächen umfassen
wird. Für die Fassaden wurde
das System FW 50 eingesetzt,
mit 190 Lüftungsflügeln aus
Royal S 65. Die Atrien sind mit
Lichtdachsystem SK 60 überdacht.

The building is part of the
Electronic Park Duisburg, which
when completed will provide
a floor area of 30,000 m² for
flexible use. System FW 50
was chosen for the façades
with 190 vents intalled in
System Royal S 65. The atria
are roofed with SK 60 skyline
construction.

Außen- und
Innenansichten
Micro Electronic
Centrum
Outside and
inside views
Micro Electronic Centre

Copenhagen, Denmark

Planung
Design
3xNielsen A/S, Århus

Das Haus der Architekten liegt
zwischen alten Lagergebäuden
am Hafen. Es nimmt die Höhe
der umgebenden Bebauung auf,
zeigt aber eine Fassadengestaltung ganz neuer Art. Das gesamte Gebäude ist in einer
Aluminium-Glas-Konstruktion
allseitig eingehüllt. In den
Fensterbereichen sind in die
Konstruktion fast unsichtbare
Klappfenster-Elemente eingear-
beitet. Für die gläsernen Hüllflächen – Fassade und Dach –
wurde eine Sonderausführung
des Systems FW 50 eingesetzt.

Architects' House is situated
between old warehouses in
the harbour. In height, it
matches the surrounding
buildings, however, it features
a completely new type of façade
design The building is clad on all
sides with an aluminium glass
construction. For the glazed
outer skin – façade and roof – a
special construction of System
FW 50 was used.

Außen- und
Innenansichten
Arkitekternes Hus
Outside and
inside views
Arkitekternes Hus

Hamburg, Germany

Planung
Design
BRT Architekten
Bothe Richter Teherani,
Hamburg

Mitwirkende Sachverständige
Consultants
PBI, Wertingen
DS-Plan, Stuttgart

Vom Wasser betrachtet wirkt das Gebäude wie eine Interpretation eines in sich ruhenden rechteckigen Speichergebäudes. Nimmt man nun jedoch die anderen Ansichten wahr, scheint sich der Bau einem Schiff gleich in Bewegung zu setzen. Betont wird dieses durch die Anordnung und mit dem Spiel der Fassade, besonders im durchlaufenden Mittelteil. Die Doppelkonstruktion der Fassade zeigt die Auseinandersetzung der Architekten mit moderner Energietechnik und verleiht gleichzeitig Tiefe.

Viewed from the water, the building has the appearance of an unassuming rectangular warehouse. Seen from different angles, however, it looks more like a ship about to set sail. An impression emphasised by the forms and patterns used in the façade, particularly through the continuous middle section. Whilst lending depth to the façade, the twin wall construction also showcases the architect's use of modern energy technology.

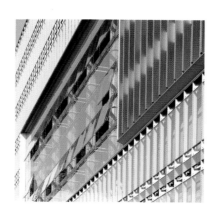

Detailansichten
Deichtor
Detail views
Deichtor

Dortmund, Germany

Planung
Design
Gerber Architekten, Dortmund

Bauherr und Planer reduzieren die Typologie des Bankhauses nach Umbau und Erweiterung auf die wesentlichen Bestand-teile. Während das auskragende Dach Schutz und Behausung symbolisiert, demonstriert der verglaste Kubus einladende Gastfreundlichkeit und Offenheit. Transparenz bestimmt die Szene für ein neues Rollenverständnis, das spannungsreiche Ein- und Durchblicke gestattet.

The conversion and extension undertaken by client and designer have reduced the typology of this bank to the bare essentials. The cantilevered roof symbolises a sheltered work environment, whilst the openness of the glazed cube is inviting for visitors. The unobstructed views afforded by transparency set the scene for a new understanding of the roles played by the building users.

Detailansichten
Dortmunder Volksbank
Detail views
Dortmunder Volksbank

„Nur aus dem Spannungsfeld des Gegensätzlichen können wir leben und Architektur formulieren."
„It is through conflict and diversity that we live and shape architecture."

Prof. Eckhard Gerber, Architekt

Gent, Belgium

Planung
Design
G + D Studiegroep – Arch. D. Bontnick

Die Verschmelzung eines ovalen mit einem rechteckigen Baukörper ist das eine Gestaltungsmerkmal, die betonte Rastergliederung ein anderes. Das neue Verwaltungsgebäude von Gent zeigt ca. 7000 m² Fassadenfläche aus dem System FW 50 mit Drehkipp-Fenstern aus Iskotherm 64.

The integration of an oval and rectangular building is one design feature, the emphasized grid structuring another. The new administration building in gent presents approximately 7000m² of façade in System FW 50 with turn-tilt windows in Iskotherm 64.

Außenansichten
Stedelijk Administratief
Centrum
Outside views
Stedelijk Administratief
Centrum

Dortmund, Germany

Planung
Design
Gerber Architekten,
Dortmund

Mitwirkende Sachverständige
Consultants
Dipl.-Ing. M. Lange, Hanover

Außenansichten
Arbeitsamt Dortmund
Outside views Dortmund
Employment Centre

Rund 10.000 m² Fassaden-
flächen wurden mit Schüco
Systemen gestaltet. Für die
Dächer der gläsernen
Gebäudeverbindungen wurde
das System SK 60 eingesetzt,
für die großzügig verglasten
Gebäudeflächen FW 50 mit
Fenstern aus Royal S 65.

The façade covering
approximately 10.000m² was
designed and built using various
Schüco systems. System SK 60
was used for the roofs of the
glazed connections between the
buildings, FW 50 for the large
areas of glazed façades, with
Royal S 65 windows.

Hallbergmoss, Germany

Planung
Design
Arge Maki & Associates, Tokio
mit SSP Architekten
Schmidt-Schicketanz +
Partner GmbH, Munich

Mitwirkende Sachverständige
Consultants
Richard Fuchs, Munich

Elf Häuser mit hoher Transparenz, flexibler Nutzung und
strengen, bündigen Raster-
fassaden: Pfosten-Riegel-Konstruktion aus dem Schüco
System FW 50 mit integrierten
Blockfenstern aus Royal 78BS.
Stahldächer mit Abdeckungen
aus SK 60.

Eleven buildings of high
transparency, flexibility of use
and well ordered flush grid
façades: Mullion and transom
construction of Schüco System
FW 50 with integrated block
windows Royal 78BS. Steel
roofs with SK 60 roofing.

Außenansichten
Isar Büro Park
Outside views
Isar Office Park

Warsaw, Poland

Planung
Design
Apar-Projekt Sp. z o.o. Tadeusz
Szumielewicz i Partnerzy,
Warsaw
ARCA Architects & Consultans
Ltd., Warsaw

Mitwirkende Sachverständige
Consultants
Alfa Planung sp. z o.o. Zabrze
Alfa-Plan GmbH,
Efringen-Kirchen, Germany

In der Zeichenwelt der Türme
setzt Warschaus neuer Skyscraper starke Akzente.
Spannend schildert sein
Konstrukteur das breite Spektrum des Formvokabulars in der
Architektur. Aus jedem Blickwinkel erschließt sich eine neue
Umrissfigur. Das an Höhepunk-
ten reiche Bauwerk ist von
dominanter Präsenz, wobei der
kühne Entwurf eine lebhafte
Korrespondenz mit kühlen
Fassadenmaterialien eingeht.

Warsaw's new skyscraper brings
a new emphasis to the symbolic
world of towers. Its designer
excitingly showcases a wide
vocabulary of architectural form.
Each different viewing angle
reveals new contours. This is
an imposing building rich in
highlights, the bold design
achieving a lively counterpoint
with cool façade materials.

Außenansicht Centrum
Administracyjno
Outside view Centrum
Administracyjno

„Ein Gebäude ist wie eine Hülle oder ein Gefäß, das nur dann
Vitalität, Lebensqualität und Inspiration ausatmet und die
Kommunikation unter den Nutzern fördert, wenn es selbst wie
ein Organismus erlebt werden kann."

„A building is merely a shell or vessel unless it can
come to life by projecting a sense of vitality, quality of
life and inspiration, and facilitating communication."

Vienna, Austria

Planung
Design
Prof. Wilhelm Holzbauer, Vienna

Der Andromeda-Tower war das erste Bürohochhaus in Wiens „Donau-City". Seine konvexe, elliptische Form nimmt komplementär die konkav geschwungenen Formen der UNO-Bauten in seiner Nachbarschaft auf. Die geneigten Glasfronten der „Skylobbies" auf der SW-Seite orientieren dabei den Bau eindeutig in Richtung Stadtzentrum. Die Fensterelemente der 2-schaligen Element-Fassade sind aus Sonderprofilen des Systems Royal S mit verdeckt liegenden Dreh-Kipp-Flügeln konstruiert.

The Andromeda Tower was the first multi-storey office building in Vienna's "Danube City". Its convex, elliptical shape complements the concave curves of the neighbouring UNO building. The inclined glass fronts of the "Sky lobbies" on the SW side give the building a clear orientation towards the town centre. The window units of the twin wall unitized façade is constructed from special profiles from the Royal S system with concealed turn/tilt vents.

Außenansichten
Andromeda Tower
Outside views
Andromeda Tower

Die aus dem Bau herausragende
Scheibe ist die Fortsetzung der
Achse, die das Gebäude gliedert:
in einen langen, geschlossenen
Teil und einen mit halb freiste-
henden Punkthäusern. Diesen
Teil überspannt eine Pultdach-
Konstruktion, die geschützte
Höfe schafft. Sämtliche Fassa-
den bestehen aus dem System
SK 60 V, die eingesetzten Fens-
terelemente aus Royal S 65
und Royal S 70 B.

The feature wall projecting from
the building is the extension
of the axis which divides the
building into a long enclosed
section and a section with
semi-freestanding rotundas.
A monopitch roof construction
spans the rotundas to create
sheltered atria. All façades
are system SK 60V, the
window units are Royal S 65
and Royal S 70B.

Außenansichten
Technologie- und
Gründerzentrum
Outside views
Technology and
Enterprise Centre

Berlin, Germany

Planung
Design
Architekturbüro
Reinhard Müller, Berlin

Mitwirkende Sachverständige
Consultants
PBI Planungsbüro für innovative
Fassadentechnik GmbH,
Wiesbaden

In den 30er-Jahren am Spreeufer
erbaut, entfaltet sich das Kühl-
haus nach dem Umbau zur
1. Adresse der New Economy
Offices. Die ehemals fast
geschlossene Fassade wurde
radikal zu drei Seiten geöffnet.
Hinter der vorgehängten Glas-
konstruktion herrscht wieder
Betriebsamkeit. Transparenz und
Raumhöhen bis 4 m setzen die
Lofts ins rechte Licht. Highlight:
Vom rundum verglasten Staffel-
geschoss aus wandert der Blick
über die Berliner Dachlandschaft.

Built in the 1930s on the bank
of the Spree, this cold store has
been transformed into the
prestigious headquarters of New
Economy Offices. The original
virtually closed façade has been
radically opened up on three
sides. Behind the glazed curtain
walling, the building is bustling
with activity again. The
extensive glazing and rooms up
to 4 m high show the luxury
offices in a favourable light.
Another highlight is the pent-
house, which is glazed all the
way round to offer a stunning
view over the roofs of Berlin.

Außenansicht
Die Spreespeicher
Outside view
Die Spreespeicher

„Licht und Wasser – Leben und Arbeiten in Harmonie mit der
Umgebung."
„Light and water – living and working in harmony
with the environment."

Reinhard Müller, Architekt

Centre for Enterprise and Innovation

Völkermarkt/Kärnten, Austria

Planung
Design
Prof. Arch. Dipl.-Ing.
Günther Domenig

Zwischen Betonpfeilern hängen-
de und über dem Boden schwe-
bende Aluminium-Glas-Konstruktion mit stark auskragenden
Geschossen. Verbunden mit
einem Treppenhausturm, der
das gleiche Schüco Fassaden-
System zeigt wie das
Hauptgebäude: FW 50 mit
Senkklapp-Fensterflügeln.

An aluminium-glass-construction
with cantilevered storeys
suspended between concrete
columns as if floating above
the ground. The staircase tower
connects the floors and
incorporates the same Schüco
Façade-System as the main
building: FW 50 with projected
top hung windows.

Außenansichten
Gründer-, Innovations-
und Gewerbezentrum
Outside views
Centre for Enterprise
and Innovation

Chambery, France

Planung
Design
Cabinet Guillermont,
Aix-lex-Bains

Vier Schüco Systeme wurden
für die Fassadengestaltung dieses Verwaltungsgebäudes eingesetzt: SK 60 für das geschwungene Eingangsdach, FW 50 für
Festverglasungen, Façade Lisse
für den Structural Glazing-Teil
und Royal S 55 für zweifarbige
Fenster.

The façade design for the
Hospital Administrative Building
incorporates four Schüco
systems: SK 60 for the curved
roof above the entrance, FW 50
fixed glazed curtain wall, Façade
Lisse for the structural glazing
part and Royal S 55 for two-
colour windows.

Außenansichten
Hopital de Chambery
Outside views
Hopital de Chambery

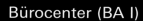

Bürocenter (BA I)

Berlin, Germany

Planung
Design
Architekten Kahlen + Partner,
Aachen

Das Attika-Geschoss, der dreigeschossige, halbrunde Erker
und der nach vorn geneigte
Frontbereich wurden mit dem
System FW 50DK errichtet, einer
Pfosten-Riegel-Konstruktion mit
integrierten und von außen nicht
sichtbaren Fensterprofilen. Die
großen Fassadenflächen sind
aus dem System FW 50.

The parapet floor, the three-
storey semi-circular bay window
and the front section sloping
forward incorporate Schüco
FW 50DK System, a mullion and
transom construction with
integrated externally concealed
window profiles.
The large facade area are in
System FW 50.

Außenansicht
Bürocenter (BA I)
Outside view
Bürocenter (BA I)

Bydgoszcz, Poland

Planung
Design
Bulanda-Mucha Architekci,
Warsaw

Die zwei tonnenförmigen
Gebäude stehen in historischer
Umgebung und demonstrieren
ihr Selbstbewusstsein durch ihre
eigenständige Architektur.
Lediglich in der Wahl der Kera-
mikpaneels gleicht man sich der
Farbe der umliegenden Bebauung an. Während der eine
Zwilling eher geschlossen konzipiert wurde, zeigt sich der
zweite voll verglaste Gebäudeteil
sehr offen. Gerade bei Nacht
wird dies durch die Beleuchtung
und der Spiegelung im Fluss
sehr deutlich und reizvoll.
Der Glasbau wurde mit dem
Schüco System FW 50 realisiert.

Two builings with barrel
vaulted roofs stand in historic
surroundings, demonstrating
their self confidence through
their original architecture.
The only similarity with the
surrounding buildings is the
coulour of the ceramic panels.
Whilst one of the two buildings
is designed to look more
enclosed, the other fully glazed
section has a much more open
appearance. At night the
combination of lighting and
the reflection in the river is
stunning. The glazed structure
was created using the Schüco
FW 50 system.

Detailansichten
Bank Rozwoju
Detail views
Bank Rozwoju

Hamburg, Germany

Bauherr
Client
Rickmers Reederei GmbH & Cie,
Hamburg

Entwurfs- und Ausführungs-
planung
Design and construction
planning
Richard Meier & Partners,
Architects, New York

Kontaktarchitekten
Contact architects
Ehrensberger & Oertz, Hamburg

Generalunternehmer
General contractor
Richard Ditting GmbH,
Rendsburg

Ausführung der Fassaden
Façade construction
FELDHAUS GmbH & Co,
Emsdetten

Für das neue Bürohaus der 1834 ursprünglich als Schiffbaubetrieb gegründeten Rickmers Reederei stand ein Grundstück mit altem Baumbestand am Westufer der Außenalster – eines großen innerstädtischen Segel- und Ruderreviers – neben dem US-Generalkonsulat zur Verfügung. Der Neubau bildet den südlichen Abschluss einer offenen Villen-bebauung und den Übergang zur geschlossenen innerstädti-schen Bebauung des Alsterufers.

Der Bau öffnet sich mit den großen Glasflächen der 2-geschossigen Eingangshalle und des Sitzungsbereiches im 2. OG zum Ufer hin, während die dem spätklassizistischen Kon-sulatsbau zugewandte Nord-seite, an der die Einzelbüros angeordnet sind, als leicht gekurvte transluzente Glaswand mit schmalen Fensterbändern in Augenhöhe ausgebildet ist und so gegenseitige Distanz und Diskretion im Verhältnis zum Konsulatsbau bietet.

The plot acquired for the new office building of the Rickmers Shipping Company, established first as a ship building company in 1834, was one with established trees on the west bank of the Aussenalster, a large city centre sailing and rowing lake, next to the US Consulate. The new building forms a southerly surround to an open aspect executive residential development and forms a transition to the closed-in inner city buildings on the banks of the Alster.

The building has an open aspect towards the banks of the Alster with the large glass surfaces of the double storey-height foyer and the conference area on the second floor. The north side which faces towards the late classical consulate building, and which houses the individual offices, is designed as a slightly curved translucent glass wall with narrow ribbon windows at eye level. This produces a sense of distance from the consulate building.

Ansicht von Nordosten (im Vordergrund das US-Generalkonsulat)
View from the north east (US Consulate in the foreground)

Ansicht von Nordosten auf die gekurvte trans-luzente Nordwand
View from the north east towards the curved translucent north wall

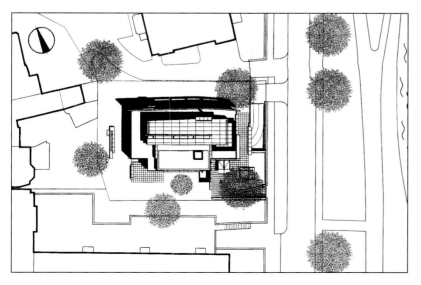

Lageplan
Location plan

Auf der Südseite liegen die Nebenräume und die Vertikalerschließung als weitgehend geschlossener Festpunkt, der auch die Horizontalaussteifung des Gebäudes übernimmt. Die nach Südwesten, d. h. in die Tiefe des Grundstücks, orientierten Gruppenbüros sind dagegen wieder voll verglast. Im zurückgestaffelten 3. OG befinden sich die Räume der Geschäftsleitung. Alle geschlossenen Außenwandflächen sind mit hinterlüfteten Aluminiumblechen in strengem Fugenschnitt und mit offenen Fugen bekleidet und – wie die Aluminium-Konstruktionen der Glasflächen – weiß pulverbeschichtet. Die äußere Erscheinung des Gebäudes mit dem zurückgestaffelten 3. OG, den relingartigen Geländern und holzbeplankten Terrassen, dem frei stehenden hohen Edelstahl-Schornstein und der leicht gekurvten Nordwand mit den schmalen Fensterbändern weckt – sicherlich nicht unbeabsichtigt – in sublimer Weise die Assoziation „Schiff".

On the south side, there are the side rooms and the vertical construction containing stair well, lift shaft and other fixed facilities, all largely enclosed, which also provides horizontal reinforcement for the building. By contrast, the open plan offices along the plot's depth facing the south west, are fully glazed. The management is accommodated in the staggered 3rd storey. The carpark is located in the basement and uses a double parking principle. All enclosed external wall surfaces are clad with rear-ventilated aluminium panelling with pronounced joint lines and open joints, white colour coated to match the aluminium frames of the glazed surfaces. The external appearance of the building with its staggered 3rd storey, railings like deck rails and wooden boarded terraces, the free-standing high stainless steel chimney and the slightly curved north wall with narrow ribbon windows give a distinct impression – clearly not unintentional – of an association with ships.

Ansicht von Südwesten auf die Gruppenbüros
View from the southwest towards the open plan offices

EG
Groundfloor

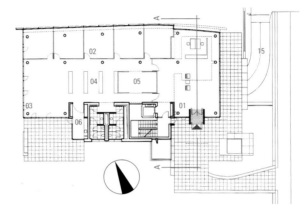

2.OG
2nd floor

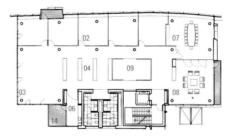

3.OG
3rd floor

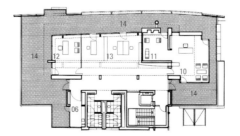

Schnitt A-A
Section A-A

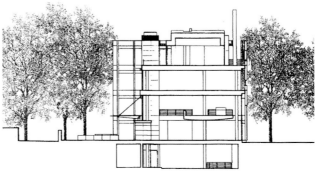

01 2-geschossige Eingangshalle
02 Einzelbüros
03 Gruppenbüro
04 Archiv
05 Raum für Post
06 Teeküche
07 Sitzungsraum
08 Lounge zu 07
09 Besprechungsraum
10 Chefzimmer
11 Ruheraum
12 Stellv. Geschäftsführer
13 Chefsekretariat
14 Terrasse
15 Zufahrt Tiefgarage

01 2 storey entrance hall with gallery on the first floor
02 Individual offices
03 Open plan office
04 Archive
05 Post room
06 Kitchen and cloakroom
07 Meeting room
08 Lounge belonging to 07
09 Consulting room
10 CEO's room
11 Relaxation area
12 Deputy Managing Director
13 Secretariat
14 Terrace
15 Entrance to the underground carpark

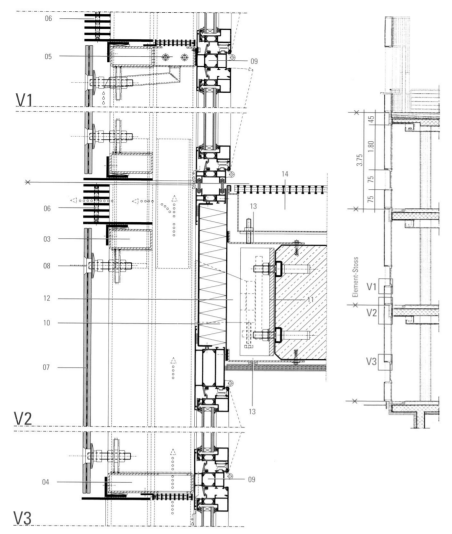

V1

V2

V3

01 Hauptpfosten der Stahlunterkonstruktion bis OK Architrav 3. OG aus 2 verschweißten Stahlrohren 100/60/8 als Doppelpfosten für Elementstoß

02 Nebenpfosten bis OK Brüstung 3. OG aus Stahlrohr 200/40/4 als Doppelpfosten wie 01

03 Zwischenriegel aus Stahlrohr 100/50/4, zwischen Pfosten eingeschweißt

04 Sturzriegel aus Stahlrohr 200/40/4, für Durchlüftung geschlitzt, mit Sturzlaibung aus Alu-Blech 5 mm und Alu-Rost

05 Regenrinne an OK Brüstung mit Alu-Rost und Brüstungsabdeckung aus Alu-Blech 5 mm

06 Lüftungsgitter mit oberer / unterer Laibung aus Alu-Blech 5 mm

07 Verbundsicherheitsgläser 2 x 8 mm mit transluzenter Zwischenfolie

08 Punkthalterung für 07

09 Geschosshohe Fensterelemente der Profilserie Schüco Royal S 70B mit Kipp- bzw. Klappflügeln, mit durchsichtiger bzw. transluzenter Isolierverglasung

10 Paneele mit MinFaser-Platten zur Wärmedämmung der Deckenvorderkante

11 Doppelagraffen aus verz. Stahl zum Einhängen der Fassadenelemente, mit Höhenjustierung

12 An den Pfosten angeschweißte verz. Stahlschwerter zum Einhängen in 11

13 Obere / untere Brandabschottung des Raumes zwischen Vorderkante Betondecken und Paneelen 10 aus verz. Stahlblech, Zwischenraum mit Perlite-Schüttung verfüllt

14 Verz. Stahlblechwanne mit Alu-Rost für Bodenkanalheizung

01 Main mullion of the steel sub-structure to the top of the 3rd floor architrave, made from 2 welded steel tubes 100/60/8 as a double mullion for the unit joint

02 Auxiliary mullion to the top edge of the 3rd floor spandrel in the form of a steel tube 200/40/4 as a double mullion like 01

03 Intermediate transom made from steel tube 100/50/4, welded between mullions

04 Intertie beam made from steel tube 200/40/4 with slots forventilation; the underside is made from 5 mm aluminium sheet and an aluminium grille

05 Guttering on the top edge of the parapet with aluminium grille and the parapet capping made from 5 mm aluminium sheet

06 Ventilation grille with the top and bottom of the reveal made from 5 mm aluminium sheet

07 Laminated safety glass panes 2 x 8 mm with translucent foil sandwiched between

08 Single point fixing for 07

09 Storey-height window units in the profile series Schüco Royal S 70B with bottom or top hung windows, with transparent or translucent insulating glass

10 Panels with mineral fibre boards for thermally insulating the front edge of the concrete floor

11 Double hook-in recesses made from galvanized steel for attaching the façade units, with facility for height adjustment

12 Steel brackets welded to the mullions for hooking into 11

13 Upper / lower fire break for the room between the front edge of the concrete floor and the galvanized steel panels 10, cavity filled with loose fill perlite

14 Galvanized sheet steel trough with aluminium grille for underfloor heating

Fassadenschnitt und -grundriss der Glasdoppelfassade Nordseite

Façade section detail and floor plan of the glazed twin wall façade on the north side

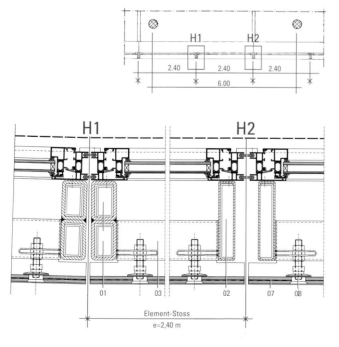

Head Office and business centre
Sofia, Bulgaria

Planung
Design
Architekturbüro „MODUS" –
Prof. Dr. D. Arch. Jeko Tilev

Der Bau stellt in seiner Erscheinung die typischen Erscheinungsmerkmale eines Bankneubaus zur Schau.
Er repräsentiert in seinem Selbstverständnis Stärke, Kraft und Dynamik, aber gibt sich auch emotional expressiv.
Am Rande einer viel befahrenen Schnellstraße wird der Bau als geometrische und starke Plastik wahrgenommen. Der emotionale Aspekt wird durch das Material Glas umgesetzt, das nicht nur Vorhangfassade ist, sondern auch durch konvex und konkave Formen, Spiegelungen und Reflexionen gut diesen Anspruch garantiert.

For the designer, this new building embodies all the archetypal values of a bank: strength, energy and dynamism, albeit with an added emotional dimension.
Built on a busy expressway, the building is designed to look like strong, geometrically formed plastic. To achieve maximum emotional impact, the architect decided to use glass, which functions as a curtain wall, whilst allowing convex and concave forms, and reflections.

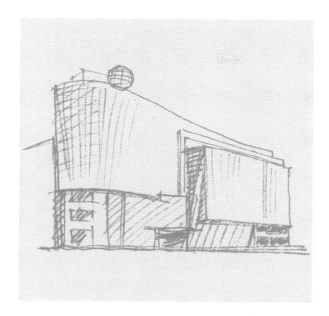

Entwurfs-Skizze
aus der Entwurfsphase
Preliminary sketch
from the design phase

Detailansichten First
East International Bank
Detail views First East
International Bank

„Architektur ist und kann nicht Skulptur sein, obwohl sie immer danach strebt. Glas, das die Trennung zwischen innen und außen aufhebt, löst diesen Widerspruch und bestätigt das Wesen der Architektur als Raumkunst."

"Architecture is not and cannot be sculpture, but always aspires to it. Destroying the boundary between interior and exterior, glass solves this contradiction and restores the essence of architecture as spatial art."

Prof. Jeko Tilev, Architekt

Katowice, Poland

Planung
Design
Pracownia Architektoniczna
„ARCH", Arch. Z. Stanik,
Arch. J. Lelatko

Der stark durchgeometrisierte
Gebäudekomplex der Bank BRE
findet seine dynamische
Ausdrucksform in der konvex
gekrümmten, aufstrebenden
Hauptfassade. Die vollflächige
Vorhangfassade mit blau ver-
spiegeltem Glas bildet den fein
wirksamen Blickfang. Das blaue
Spiegelglas steht im spannungs-
vollen Kontrast zu den warmen
Sandsteinfarben der übrigen
Gebäudeteile. Zwei 50-mm-
Systeme wurden kombiniert:
SG 50N für die Structurale
Glazing-Flächen und FW 50
für die Profilfassade. Die Fenster
sind aus dem System
Royal S 65.

The convex curved ambitious
main façade is the most
dynamically impressive part of
the geometrically challenging
building complex for the BRE
bank. The full curtain wall
façade with blue mirrored glass
creates a delicate eye-catching
appearance. The blue mirror
glass gives an exciting contrast
to the warm sandstone colours
of the rest of the building. Two
50 mm systems were combined:
SG 50N for the structural glazed
areas and FW 50 for the profile
façade. The windows are from
the Royal S 65 system.

Außenansichten
Bank BRE S.A.
Outside views
Bank BRE S.A.

Düsseldorf, Germany

Planung
Design
Gehry Partners, LLP, Santa
Monica, California, USA
Executive Architect: BM+P,
Beucker, Maschlanka und
Partner, Düsseldorf

Mitwirkende Sachverständige
Consultants
PBI, Planungsbüro für Innovative
Fassadentechnik GmbH,
Wiesbaden

Avantgardistischer Büro-Kom-
plex, Kunst- und Medienzentrum
am Düsseldorfer Rheinhafen.
Die asymmetrischen Ecken und
Kanten, Rundungen und wellen-
förmigen Fassaden mit Hoch-
glanz-Blechverkleidung sowie
die leichte Schieflage der Türme
scheinen alle Konstruktions-
gesetze zu ignorieren.
Außergewöhnlich im Konstruk-
tionsbereich, Entwurf und in
der Fertigung sind die Fassaden-
Sonderlösungen, basierend auf
dem System Royal S als
Blockfenster.

Avant-garde office complex, art
and media centre at the Rhine
port in Düsseldorf. The
asymmetric corners and curves,
the façades in the shape of
waves with highly polished plate
cladding, and the slightly
sloping position of the towers
appear to ignore all the laws of
design. The custom solutions
used for the façades based on
the Royal S block window
system are unusual in their
design, planning and fabrication.

Außenansichten
Der Neue Zollhof
Outside views
The New Zollhof

Berlin, Germany

Planung
Design
Müller Reimann Architekten,
Berlin

Mitwirkende Sachverständige
Consultants
Ing.-Büro Michael Lange, Berlin

Detailansicht
Auswärtiges Amt
Detail view
Auswärtiges Amt

Repräsentativ, selbstbewusst und gleichzeitig sehr offen präsentiert sich das Auswärtige Amt dem Besucher. Der kubische Baukörper wird an mehreren Stellen unterbrochen. Dünne Säulen, schlanke Pfeiler und Stützen verbinden die Gebäudeteile und garantieren den Erhalt der Gebäudeform.
Über dem zentralen Innenhof spannt sich ein riesiges begehbares Lichtdach, ausgeführt in der Schüco Brandschutz Konstruktion BF. Raumhohe Doppelflügelfenster als Sonderkonstruktion aus dem System Royal S und aufgeklebte Stufenisoliergläser sind weitere Bestandteile.

The new Foreign Office builing projects a distinctive and self-confident yet open appearance. The cube-shaped structure is opened up in several places. Slender columns, narrow bars and supports link the sections of the builing together and maintain its form.
A massive skylight made from Schüco BF spans the entire central inner courtyard. Other special features are: customised floor to ceiling double vent windows using a special construction of Royal S system, and surface mounted stepped double glazing panels.

International Network
Management Cente for
Deutsche Telekom AG,
Frankfurt/Main, Germany

Planung
Design
Architekten Henze + Vahjen,
Braunschweig

Mitwirkende Sachverständige
Consultants
Tragwerk Ing.-Büro grbv,
Hanover

Eine großzügige Rotunde mit
einer Doppelfassade dominiert
diese Anlage. Sie ist Anfangs-
und Endpunkt eines geschwungenen steinernen Bürorückens.
Er wird wie ein vorgelagertes
Solitärelement von einer lichten
Glashalle überdeckt. Gleichzeitig
schließt diese Halle die einzelnen Solitäre zu einem harmoni-
schen Gesamtkomplex zusammen.

A generous rotunda with a
double façade dominates this
project. It is the start and end
point of the curved stone back
wall of the office building. It is
covered by a bright glazed hall
like a detached free-standing
structure. At the same time, this
hall links the individual units
together to create a harmonious,
yet integrated whole.

Detailansichten
Internationales Netz
Management Centrum
der Deutschen
Telekom AG
Detail views
International Network
Management Cente for
Deutsche Telekom AG

The Hague, Netherlands

Planung
Design
Cesar Pelli & Associates
Architects, Newhaven,
Connecticut
Project architect: William E.
Butler III

Mitwirkende Sachverständige
Consultants
Arcadis, The Hague
Grabowski en Poort, The Hague

Jedes Gebäude dieses
Ensembles besticht durch
eigenen Charakter und Erschei-
nungsbild. Eine selbstbewusste
Erneuerung des Art-Deco-Stils
steht neben einem an Speicher-
häuser erinnerndes Nachbar-
gebäude. Als Zäsur dient das
eigenständig gestaltete Treppen-
haus zwischen den Bauten. Für
ein harmonisches Ganzes sorgen
die Auswahl der verwendeten
Materialien, deren Farbgebung
sowie das immer wiederkeh-
rende Lochfenster, ausgeführt
als Objektlösung im System
Royal S 70W.

Each building in the group has
its own captivating character
and appearance. A self-confident
renewal of Art-Deco style stands
next to another building
reminiscent of an old-style
warehouse. The individually
designed stairway forms a break
between the buildings. The
choice of building materials,
their colours and the recurring
feature of punched openings,
designed using the Royal S 70W
system produce an overall
impression of harmony.

Außenansicht
De Zürichtoren
Outside view
The Zürich Tower

Bad Oeynhausen, Germany

Planung
Design
Gehry Partners, LLP, Santa Monica, California

Das „Elektrizitätswerk Minden-Ravensberg GmbH", ein regionaler Energieversorger, hatte sein Unternehmens-Profil über ein Jahrzehnt vom Stromlieferanten hin zum Energie-Dienstleister vollzogen. Der Neubau in Bad Oeynhausen sollte Anwendungsmöglichkeiten innovativer Energietechniken wie auch das gewandelte Unternehmensimage gleichermaßen sichtbar machen. Im intensiven Planungsdialog zwischen Bauherr und Architekt entstand so das EMR (Energie-Forum-Innovation) mit seinen drei Funktionsbereichen:

- EMR-Leitstelle für das Stromversorgungsnetz
- Energie-Beratungszentrum
- Informations- und Begegnungsforum

Over the last decade "Elektrizitätswerk Minden-Ravensberg GmbH", a regional energy producer, has progressed from a supplier of electricity to a total energy service provider. The purpose of the new building in Bad Oeynhausen was to advertise both the application of innovative energy technologies and to raise the profile of the transformed company. Following intensive discussions between the client and the architect, the EMR (Energy Forum Innovation) emerged with its three functions:

- EMR control centre for mains electricity supply
- Energy Advice Centre
- Meeting place and information forum

Skizze Frank O. Gehry
Frank O. Gehry's sketch

Außenansicht Energie-Forum-Innovation
Outside view Energy Forum Innovation

Frankfurt/Main, Germany

Planung
Design
Prof. Christoph Mäckler
Architekten, Frankfurt/Main

Mitwirkende Sachverständige
Consultants
Ingenieurbüro Kannemacher,
Rath & Sturm, Frankfurt/Main
IFFT Institut für Fassaden-
technik, Frankfurt/Main

Eine neue Landmarke in der
City-West, dem Tor zur Main-
metropole. Die markante For-
mensprache und Granitstein-
Fassaden stehen für Solidität,
das Belüftungskonzept regelt
angenehm klimatisierte Büro-
welten. Zum Beispiel durch
Frischluftzufuhr über die Sonderkonstruktion der Kastenfenster.
Deren Flügel lassen sich beliebig
öffnen, während die integrierte
Blende eine direkte Sonneneinstrahlung verhindert.

This building represents a
new landmark in City West, the
gateway to the metropolis.
The striking forms and granite
façades stand for solidity, whilst
the ventilation system ensures
pleasantly air conditioned office
space. Fresh air is supplied
by means of the specially
constructed box windows. The
built-in blind excludes direct
sunlight so the individual
windows can be opened as
required.

Detailansichten Scala
Detail views Scala

„Die architektonische Auseinandersetzung mit Form und
Proportion verleiht dem Gebäude Repräsentation und
Selbstverständlichkeit."
„The architectural juxtaposition of shape and
proportion gives the building an uninhibited presence."

Prof. Christoph Mäckler, Architekt

Tallinna Bank
Administrative Building

Tallinn, Estonia

Planung
Design
Aare Saks, FFNS Arkitekter,
Stockholm

Im Erdgeschoss eine offene
Passage ohne einsichtblockie-
rende Verglasung. Im Dachbe-
reich zwei zurückgesetzte
Attikageschosse. Dazwischen
rund 2000 m² Fassade mit
reflektierender Verglasung und
feingliedrigen Aluminiumprofilen
aus Schüco FW 50 mit Fenster
aus Royal S 65.

At ground floor level is an
open passageway with clear
glazing. The two top storeys
are set back, slender columns
supporting the roof. The main
façade consists of approx.
2,000 m² reflective glazing
with fine structured aluminium
profiles using Schüco FW 50
and windows in Royal S 65.

Außenansicht
Tallinna Bank
Outside view
Tallinna Bank

Mapfre Centro Cesvimap

Avila, Spain

Planung
Design
Arquitecto
D. Manuel de Lorenzo

Drei Materialien bestimmen
die Optik dieser Fassade: „ge-
stapelte" Natursteine, silberfar-
bene Profilbleche und dunkel-
blaue Verglasung. Das Schüco
Fassaden-System FW 50 und
die Fenster aus Royal S 50 fügen
sich im Farbton der Verglasung
unauffällig ein.

Three building materials
determine the optical effects
of this façade: natural stone
masonry, silver coloured profile
metal sheeting and dark-blue
glazing. The Schüco Façade
System FW 50 and the windows
of Royal S 50 harmonize well
with the colour of the glazing.

Außenansicht
Mapfre Centro
Cesvimap
Outside view
Mapfre Centro
Cesvimap

Rostock, Germany

Planung
Design
INROS Planungsgesellschaft
Rostock,
Dipl. Ing. Klaus Gollnick +
Dipl. Ing. Katrin Friedel,
Rostock

Außenansichten
Stadtwerke Rostock
Outside view Rostock
Works Department

Office and Exhibition Centre „De Witte Dame"

Eindhoven, Netherlands

Planung
Design
Dirrix van Wylick Architekten,
Eindhoven + DHV AIB b.v.,
Eindhoven

Mit dieser Instandsetzung wird
an frühe Meisterwerke des
Industriebaus erinnert. Sachlich,
schnörkellos, geradezu asketisch
die Wirkung der Fassade. Das
Pfosten-Riegel-Prinzip zieht sich
durch die weiße Betonkonstruk-
tion und die Ausfachungen mit
den querliegenden Aluminium-
Glas-Elementen. Das Fassaden-
System FW 50 mit den schmalen Ansichtsbreiten wurde mit
Klappflügelelementen aus Royal
S 70 W kombiniert.

This renovation recaptures
early masterpieces of industrial
building. The Façade appears
functional, unadorned, almost
ascetic. The mullion and
transom principle is featured
throughout the white concrete
construction, as well as in the
infill panels with their horizontal
aluminium glass units. The
façade system FW 50 with
narrow sight lines was combined
with Royal S 70 W top hung
windows.

Außenansichten
„De Witte Dame"
Outside view
„De Witte Dame"

Klagenfurt, Austria

Planung
Design
Büro Morphosis, Architect Thom
Mayne, Santa Monica, CA

Mitwirkende Sachverständige
Consultants
Statik: DI Klaus Gelbmann,
Villach

Mit dem aufgeständerten
Ensemble bleibt Morphosis
seinem Stil treu. Durch den
zentralen verglasten Baukörper
schieben sich Rahmen, Treppen,
auskragende Balkone und
Stahldächer. Eine riesige vorgesetzte Lamellenwand filtert das
Licht. Besonders bei Nacht sind
die Lichtspiele der transluzenten
Fassade spannend. Fensterelemente aus dem System
Royal S 65, und für die Fassade
wurde das System SK 60V eingesetzt.

This raised group of buildings is
true to the Morphosis style.
Ramps, stairs, balconies and
steel canopies enter and emerge
from the central glazed
structure. A gigantic wall of slats
mounted on the side filters the
light. The play of the light from
the translucent façades is
enticing, particularly at night.
Window units were constructed
using the Royal S 65 system and
the façade using the SK 60V
system.

Außenansicht Hypo-
Alpe-Adria-Centrum
Outside view Hypo-
Alpe-Adria-Centre

Anckelmannplatz, Hamburg,
Germany

Planung
Design
BRT Architekten
Bothe Richter Teherani,
Hamburg

Mitwirkende Sachverständige
Consultants
PBI, Wertingen
DS-Plan, Stuttgart

Bürohaus
Berliner Bogen
Berlin Arch Office

Ein kraftvoller Bogenschlag vom
Wasser zur Stadt. Und ein Haus
im Haus. Kammartig umschließt
die Glashülle den massiven
Gebäudekern, dessen Decken-
platten von den mächtigen
Stahlträgern abgehängt sind.
Sechs Wintergärten sorgen als
Klimapuffer für Ausgleich zwischen Innen und Außen. Das
LowTech-Konzept lebt von den
zwei Fassadenebenen zugunsten
einer natürlichen Raumbelüftung
bei reduzierten Invest- und
Betriebskosten.

This imposing arch links water
and urban landscape whilst
allowing a building within a
building. The glass envelope
encloses the solid core of the
structure, whose slabs are
suspended from the mighty
steel girders. Six indoor gardens
provide a buffer between the
indoor and outdoor environment.
The low-tech design derives its
strength from the double façade,
which promotes natural
ventilation whilst reducing
capital costs and overheads.

„Reduktion, Leichtigkeit und Transparenz: Wir sind daran interessiert, die Schönheit von Gebäuden zu steigern, indem wir sie
ökologisch und konstruktiv effizienter gestalten."

„Minimalism, lightness and transparency: our aim
is to enhance the beauty of buildings with ever
more ecological and structurally efficient designs."

Hadi Teherani, BRT Architekten

CHG Weingarten

Weingarten, Germany

Planung
Design
Daller Huber Architekten,
Stuttgart

Mitwirkende Sachverständige
Consultants
Brecht, Stuttgart

Außenansichten
CHG Weingarten
Outside views
CHG Weingarten

88

Edificio de Oficinas y Garajes „Centro Empresarial Campo de las Naciones", Madrid, Spain

Planung
Design
Julián Franco López, Arquitecto, S.L.

Außenansichten
Campo de las Naciones
Outside views
Campo de las Naciones

Die elegante Familie von Glaskuben, Glasstelen und Türmen wirkt wie ein Ensemble aus Kristallen und Glaskörpern. Mit absolut spärlichen Mitteln wird ein Höchstmaß an Wirkung und Modernität geschaffen. Gestaltungsmittel wie zum Beispiel ein horizontaler Sonnenrost in einer ansonsten völlig glatten Spiegelfassade oder die sämtlich nicht existierenden oder nicht sichtbaren Eckprofile verleihen jedem der Baukörper sein spezielles „Outfit".

The elegant grouping of glass cubes, glass tubes and towers gives the effect of an ensemble of crystal and glass. With the minimum of materials, the maximum effect and modernist impression is created. Design elements such as the horizontal sun grilles in the otherwise smooth mirror façade, or the either non-existent or concealed corner profiles, give each section of the building its own particular "outfit".

Plauen, Germany

Planung
Design
Obermeyer Albis-Bauplan,
Plauen, Germany

Leitender Architekt
Chief architect
Dipl.-Ing. Silvio Lux

Verwaltungsbau klassischen
Formats. Klare Konturen präzi-
sieren die räumliche Ordnung.
Die Gestalt sowie wohl formu-
lierte Fassadenöffnungen und
Säulen mit rein konstruktiven
Aufgaben prägen den sachlichen
Gestus. Details veredeln das
Bauwerk, so wie die rahmenlose
Punktverglasung und filigranen
Zug-Stab-Konstruktionen bei
Flächen bis 14 m Traufhöhe.

The contours of this traditional
administrative building clearly
delineate its use of space. Its
overall style and well-formulated
structural columns and façade
openings reinforce an air of
pragmatism. The structure is
refined by details such as the
frameless glazing with retaining
clips and slender tension rods
for areas up to an eaves level
of 14 m.

Innenansicht
Sparkasse Vogtland
Inside view
Sparkasse Vogtland

„Filigranität zu erreichen, erfordert äußerste Konzentration in der
Detailplanung."
    „To create fine elegant lines in architecture requires
    the utmost concentration in detail planning."

Dipl.-Ing. Silvio Lux, Architekt

Eschborn, Germany

Planung
Design
AIC Bau-, Planungs- und
Consulting Gesellschaft mbH,
Deisenhofen

ATF-Architektur Technik
Fassade, Herr Reich,
Frankfurt/Main

Das kreisrunde Gebäude mit
dem dreigeschossigen Flachbau
und dem gläsernen Verbindungs-
trakt ist ein Beispiel für funk-
tionsgerechte Schüco Systeme:
SK 60 und SK 60V für die verglasten Dach- und Wandkons-
truktionen und Royal S 70 als
Sonderlösung für die Fassade.

The circular building with its
three-storey flatroofed annex
on the front and glazed link
is an example for functional
Schüco Systems SK 60 and
SK 60V for the glazed roof
and wall constructions,
Royal S 70 for the facade.

Außenansicht
Verwaltungs- und
Entwicklungsgebäude
Outside view Admin
and Development Centre

Pessac, France

Planung
Design
Claude Bouey und Georges
Guerin, Architecte, Bordeaux

Die Empfangs- und Erschließungshalle der Universitätsklinik
wurde als Rundbau mit zurück-
springendem Obergeschoss
gestaltet. Die Fassade ist eine
französische Variante des
Structural Glazing-Systems mit
schmalen Glasleisten. Im
Abstand von 6 Rasterfeldern stehen tragende Säulen, die die
Rundung betonen. Natürliche
Belüftung durch Klappflügel, die
geschlossen nicht sichtbar sind.

The entrance area and hall
of the University Clinic are
designed as a circular building
with the upper floor set back.
The façade is a french variation
of the structural glazing system
with narrow glazing beads.
The structural columns are
positioned at every sixth grid
bay, which emphasizes the
curvature. Natural ventilation
is provided by the top-hung
windows which are not visible
when closed.

Außenansichten
Centre hospitalo-
universitaire
Outside views
Centre hospitalo-
universitaire

Rheinbach, Germany

Planung
Design
Zacharias + Partner, Dipl.-Ing.
Architekten,
St. Augustin-Niederpleis

Ein gläserner Bau mit besonderen Energiespar-Effekten: Alle Fassaden-, Dach- und Fensterprofile entsprechen der Rahmenmaterialgruppe 1 mit erhöhtem Wärmeschutz. Die Schattierung im Bereich des Firstes und der Cafeteria erfolgte mit photovoltaischen Solarelementen zur gleichzeitigen Stromerzeugung.

A glazed building with special energy saving effects: All façade, roof and window profiles comply to frame material Group 1 with enhanced thermal protection. The shading in the ridge area and the cafeteria is facilitated by the photovoltaic solar panels which also produce electricity.

Außenansicht
Gründer- und
Technologiezentrum
Outside view
Enterprise and
Technology Centre

Samsung Boramae Complex Bulding

Seoul, South Korea

Planung
Design
Sam-Woo Architects
& Associates Inc., Seoul

Verwaltungsgebäude des koreanischen Elektronik-Konzerns mit einer zehngeschossigen Aluminium-Glas-Fassade im kräftigen Dunkelblau. Die typischen Klappflügel der weißblauen Lochfenster kehren auch in der Profilfassade wieder. Hier wurde das feingliedrige Pfosten-Riegel-System FW 50 mit vertikaler Silikonfuge eingesetzt.

Administrative building of the Korean electronics group with a ten-storey aluminium glass façade in a strong dark-blue colour. The typical top hung window of the white/blue punched openings are also repeated in the profile façade, for which the fine-membered mullion and transom system FW 50 with vertical silicone jointing was chosen.

Außenansicht
Samsung Boramae
Complex Bulding
Outside view
Samsung Boramae
Complex Bulding

Hamburg, Germany

Planung
Design
Grüntuch/Ernst
Architekten BDA, Berlin

Mitwirkende Sachverständige
Consultants
Ludwig & Mayer, Berlin

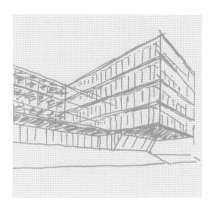

Objekt-Skizze
aus der Entwurfsphase
Preliminary sketch
from the design phase

Der viergeschossige Glaskörper kragt über dem zurückgesetzten Erdgeschoss deutlich orientiert zur Elbe hin. Hanseatisch zurückhaltend ist er reduziert auf seine wesentlichen Bestandteile wie Rundstützen, den lamellenverkleideten Stirnseiten der Geschossplatten und die Fassade. Es handelt sich um eine Doppelfassade, deren Außenhaut kaum wahrnehmbar ist. Besonders reizvoll ist der Anblick abends bei erleuchtetem Gebäude.

Außen- und
Detailansichten
Outside and
detail views

The four-storey glass structure perches on the set-back ground floor, facing towards the river Elbe. With true Hanseatic restraint, the building is pared down to its essential components, which include the circular supports, the two ends mounted with louvre blades for solar shading, and the façade. It is a twin wall façade with an almost imperceptible outer skin. The building is particularly striking when lit at night.

„Architektur ist für uns die Suche nach neuen technischen, künstlerischen und kulturellen Möglichkeiten mit der Verpflichtung zu Effizienz und Komfort."

"For us, architecture is the search for new technical, artistic and cultural possibilities, allied with a commitment to efficiency and comfort."

Almut Ernst und Armand Grüntuch, Architekten

Paris, France

Planung
Design
Arte charpentier et associés,
designed by Abbés Tahir, Paris

Die von Naturstein dominierte
Blockbebauung erhält eine
schräge Einkerbung, die eine
Eingangssituation herausbildet.
Hierbei betont eine gläserne
Rotunde die Kopfsituation des
Blocks und leitet stadträumlich
den Besucher in den Innenhof
des Gebäudes. Dieser etwas
privatere Bereich wird ab dem
ersten Obergeschoss durch
einen schwebenden gläsernen
Vorhang definiert, der sich aus
dem vorgeschobenen Glaserker
der gegenüberliegenden
Hofseite herauszuschieben
scheint. Der Glasvorhang filtert,
trennt und öffnet in einem.

This block construction,
predominantly of natural stone,
has a sloping recess at the
corner which forms the entrance
area. A glass rotunda emphasises
the block's prominent position
and guides the visitor from the
city into the inner courtyard of
the building. This more private
area is defined by a floating glass
curtain from first floor height
which appears to slide out of the
glass oriel projecting from the
other side of the courtyard. The
glass curtain is a filter, divider
and open feature combined.

Detailansicht Meunier
Detail view Meunier

Kassel, Germany

Planung
Design
Bieling & Bieling Architekten
BDA, Kassel

Systemgeber für
RGI-Doppelfassade
System provider for
RGI twin wall façade
Prof. Dr.-Ing. Ingo Grün,
Ratingen

Entlang eines langgezogenen Rückens orientiert sich eine Kammstruktur mit Betonscheiben und stählernen Nottreppenhäusern an deren Enden, die an die amerikanischen Feuertreppen erinnern.
Auf der anderen Seite stellt sich das Gebäude als Langteil mit geschwungenem Abschluss dar. Hier gliedert es sich vertikal klassisch in drei Zonen: die Sockelzone in Naturstein mit Lochfenstern, die Mittelzone als Doppelfassade für Schallschutz und zur Energieeinsparung und die abschließende, zurückgesetzte Glasfassade mit Hutkrempe. Gerade der Fassadenteil in der Mitte mit seiner angenehmen Transluzenz und Tiefe gibt dem Bau sein typisches Aussehen.

Along a lenghty spine, a comb structure has been created with concrete panels and steel emergency stairways reminiscent of American fire escapes.
On the other side, the building appears to be elongated with a curved end section. At this point it divides vertically into three classical zones: The pedestal zone in natural stone with punched openings, the middle zone, a double façade to provide noise insulation and to save energy, and the concluding recessed glass façade with brim. The middle façade section typifies the building's appearance with its attractive translucency and depth.

Außenansichten
Kali + Salz
Outside views
Kali + Salz

Munster, Westfalia, Germany

Bauherr
Client
LVM-Versicherungen, Munster

Entwurfs- und Ausführungs-
planung, Bauleitung
Design and construction
planning
HPP Hentrich-Petschnigg &
Partner KG, Düsseldorf

Fassadenplanung
Façade planning
Ingenieurbüro für Fassadentech-
nik Memmert & Partner, Neuss

Ausführung der Fassaden
Arbeitsgemeinschaft
LVM-Glasfassade, bestehend aus
Façade construction LVM glass
façade joint venture, comprising
Feldhaus GmbH & Co.,
Emsdetten
Scheffer GmbH, Sassenberg
WPS Metallbau GmbH, Munster

Modell des Gebäude-
komplexes der LVM
vor der Erweiterung
Model of LVM building
complex before the
new extension

1 Kolde-Ring
2 Stauffenberg-Straße

Der Gebäudekomplex der LVM-
Versicherungen in Münster
bestand bis 1996 im Wesentlichen aus
• einem 1967 errichteten
  10-geschossigen Hochhaus
  (jetzt als „Bauteil B" bezeichnet) mit vorgelagertem
  Vorstandspavillon,
• dem 4- und 6-geschossigen
  kreuz- bzw. kammförmigen
  Erweiterungsbau von 1977
• und dem U-förmigen 6-ge-
  schossigen Erweiterungsbau
  von 1987 nach Plänen des
  Büros HPP Hentrich-Petschnigg & Partner, Düsseldorf
  (aufgrund eines Gutachter-
  wettbewerbs). 1994 kam der
  dreiecksförmige 4-geschossi-
  ge Bau westlich der Stauffenberg-Straße hinzu, ebenfalls
  nach Plänen von HPP.

Up until 1996, the LVM
Insurance building complex
consisted mainly of the
following sections:
• a ten storey block built in
  1967 (referred to here as
  building section B) with a
  management suite in a
  pavilion projecting out from
  the rest of the building,
• a four storey extension in the
  shape of a cross and a six
  storey extension shaped like
  a comb, built in 1977, and
• a U-shaped six storey
  extension built in 1987 to
  design by Messrs HPP
  Hentrich-Petschnigg &
  Partners from Düsseldorf
  (who won the tender bid).
  A triangular four storey
  building was added in 1994
  to the west of Stauffenberg-
  Straße, again to a design
  from HPP.

Die Aufgabenstellung
des Bauherrn

Das Projekt der Erweiterung umfasste eine grundlegende Sanierung und gleichzeitige Aufstockung des Hochhauses von 1967 sowie einen turmförmigen 20-geschossigen Erweiterungsbau (jetzt als „Bauteil A" bezeichnet) anstelle des Vorstandspavillons. Der Vorstand sollte in den obersten beiden Geschossen der Aufstockung des Bauteils B untergebracht werden; der Haupteingang von der Stauffenberg-Straße her in den Erweiterungsbau von 1977 mit der von HPP ebenfalls neu gestalteten Eingangshalle sollte erhalten bleiben.

Das Entwurfskonzept
der Architekten

Die Architekten versahen die 4-geschossige Aufstockung des Bauteils B mit einem weitgehend verglasten Pultdach, unter dem im 13. und 14. OG die Arbeits- und Sitzungsräume des Vorstandes angeordnet wurden. Die darunter liegenden Geschosse und das 2. bis 18. OG des turmförmigen Bauteils A enthalten normale Büroräume.

Um den Haupteingang an der Stauffenberg-Straße vom Kolde-Ring sichtbar zu lassen, wurden die untersten beiden Geschosse des Turms als verglaste, aber ansonsten offene „Luftgeschosse" ausgebildet. Im Hinblick auf
- den Schutz gegen Außenlärm vom Kolde-Ring und der Stauffenberg-Straße her,
- die natürliche, von Wind und Wetter unabhängige Belüftung der Büroräume und
- einen optimalen, d. h. „äußeren" beweglichen Sonnenschutz in Form von Horizontal-Lamellenstoren wurden die Bauteile A und B mit einer sog. Doppelfassade, d. h. mit einem für Wartungs- und Reinigungszwecke begehbaren Luftraum zwischen deren innerer und äußerer Schale versehen, der mit der Außenluft in Verbindung steht und hohe Winddrücke bzw. Druckdifferenzen (Böen) so stark dämpft, dass die Büroräume über Öffnungen der inneren Schale natürlich belüftet werden können.

Modell des Gebäudekomplexes mit der Erweiterung
Model of the building complex with the extension

1 Kolde-Ring
2 Stauffenberg-Straße

Außenansicht der Doppelfassade des Bauteils A
Outside view of the double façade, building A

Innenansicht der Doppelfassade des Bauteils A mit geöffnetem Drehflügel zum Lüften und Betreten des Raumes zwischen den beiden Schalen
View of the double façade from inside building A, showing the glazed side hung vents open for ventilation and for access to the space between the two skins

102

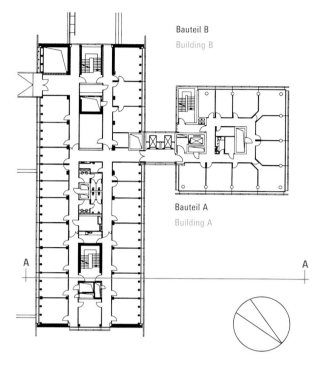

Bauteil B
Building B

Bauteil A
Building A

Normalgeschoss –
Grundriss der Bauteile
A + B und Schnitt A-A
Floor plan of a normal
storey in building
sections A + B and
section detail A-A

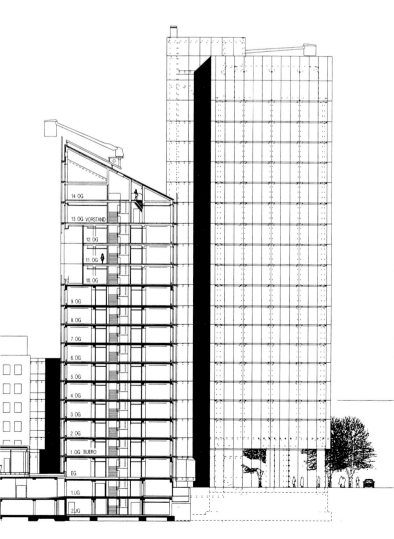

The client's terms of reference

The extension project included extensive renovation work and an addition to the top of the block built in 1967, as well as a 20 storey block in the shape of a tower (referred to here as building section A) instead of the pavilion containing the management suite. The management would be moving into the top two storeys of the extension on the top of building section B; the main entrance from Stauffenberg-Straße into the 1977 extension and the new entrance hall created by HPP would remain the same.

The architect's design concept

The architects envisaged a four storey extension on the top of building section B with a predominantly glazed mono-pitch roof above the working areas and conference rooms for the management on the 13th and 14th floors. The floors below and the second to 18th floors of the tower (building section A) were to contain normal offices.

To ensure that the main entrance on Stauffenberg-Straße is visible from the Kolde-Ring, the bottom two floors of the tower were glazed, but otherwise designed to be open.

In order to ensure
• a low level of external noise intruding from the Kolde-Ring and Stauffenberg-Straße
• natural ventilation in the offices, independently of actual wind and weather conditions
• optimum „externally" adjustable solar shading in the form of horizontal slats, building sections A and B were constructed using a so-called double façade. This type of construction provides an air space between the external and internal skins which can be entered for maintenance and cleaning purposes, and which is connected to the outside air, but has such a strong damping effect on high wind pressures and pressure differences (gusting), that the offices can be ventilated naturally via openings in the internal skin.b.

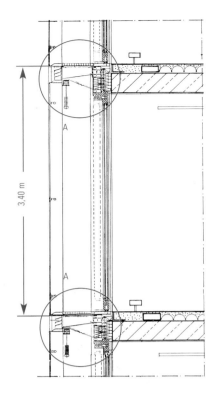

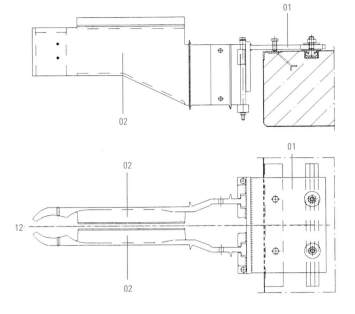

Fassadenschnitt
Bauteil B
Façade section,
building B

Seitenansicht und
Draufsicht der
Doppelschwerter
Side view and top view
of the double brackets

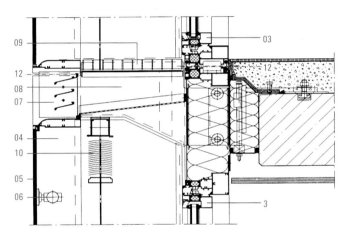

01 abgewinkelte Ankerplatte
02 Schwerter aus Alu-Guss
03 innere Schale mit raumhohen Drehflügeln
   bzw. Festverglasung
04 Alu-Lisenenprofile mit integrierter Führung
   für Außenbefahranlage
05 randlose Verglasung mit
   ESG d = 12 mm
06 Punkthalterung aus Edelstahl
07 horizontales Lüftungsband mit Regenlamellen
   und Insektengitter
08 Luftkasten mit ober-/unterseitiger Lochung
   für Zu-/Abluftstrom
09 verzinkter Gitterrost
10 Horizontal-Lamellenstore
   mit Elt-Antrieb
11 fakultatives Glasschott d = 6 mm
   gegen Luftschall- und Rauch-Längsleitung
12 Elementstoß

01 curved anchor plate
02 cast aluminium brackets
03 inner skin with floor to ceiling
   side hung vents and fixed glazing
04 aluminium palister strips with
   integrated guide rails for external walkways
05 frameless glazing in 12 mm
   toughened safety glass
06 stainless steel retaining clips
07 horizontal ventilation strip with rain-proof slats
   and insect mesh
08 ventilation boxes with holes in top/bottom
   for air inlet/outlet
09 galvanized grille
10 electrically operated solar
   shading with horizontal slats
11 6 mm thick glazed partition
   to prevent permeation of noise
   and smoke
12 unit joint

Vertikaler
Detailschnitt
im Punkt A
Vertical detail
section in point A

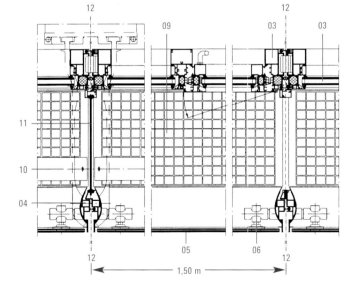

Horizontale
Detailschnitte
Horizontal
detail sections

Konstruktion und Montage der Fassade als vorgefertigte Kastenelemente

Die innere Schale der Elemente besteht aus wärmegedämmten Profilen auf Basis der Serie Schüco Royal S 70.1 mit raumhohen Drehflügeln, die zum Lüften und Betreten in den Zwischenraum öffnen, bzw. mit Festverglasung. Die äußere Schale besteht aus randlosen ESG-Scheiben d = 12 mm, die mit Punkthalterungen an vertikalen Alu-Lisenenprofilen befestigt sind.

Beide Schalen sind am oberen Rand durch Schwerter aus Alu-Guss zu geschosshohen 1,50 m breiten Elementen verbunden, am unteren Rand durch die Gitterroste zum Begehen des Zwischenraumes.

Diese Elemente wurden komplett mit Verglasung und Sonnenschutz am Bau aufgezogen, mittels der Alu-Schwerter in die abgewinkelten Ankerplatten an den Deckenvorderkanten eingehängt und mit den Nachbarelementen verschraubt. Je nach innerer Raumaufteilung, i. d. R. in jedem 3. Elementstoß, können vertikale Glasschotten montiert werden, die die Luftschall- und Rauch-Längsleitung im Zwischenraum verhindern.

Durchlüftung und Wärmedurchgangskoeffizient der Doppelfassade

Luftkästen mit äußeren Regenlamellen, in der rechten Hälfte jedes Elements oberseitig und in der linken Hälfte unterseitig gelocht, bewirken eine diagonale Luftströmung im Raum zwischen den beiden Schalen. Die Lufteintritts- bzw. -austrittsöffnungen der Elemente liegen also jeweils seitlich versetzt übereinander, sodass die sog. Rezirkulation (d. h. das Eintreten verbrauchter Raumluft in die jeweils darüber liegenden Elemente) weitestgehend verhindert wird (Rezirkulationsrate nach Laborversuchen ca. 15 %).

Der zu erwartende winterliche Mittelwert des Wärmedurchgangskoeffizienten der Doppelfassade $k_{aequiv. Fassade}$ beträgt 1,2 W/m².K.

Construction and assembly of the façade using pre-fabricated box units

The internal skin of the unit is made of thermally broken profiles based on the Schüco Royal S 70.1 series. It has floor to ceiling glazed side hung vents which can be opened for ventilation and to gain access to the air space between the skins, or fixed glazing. The external skin is made of 12 mm thick frameless single pane toughened safety glass secured to vertical aluminium palister strips by means of retaining clips.

The two skins are connected at the top to 1.5 m wide, storey-height units by means of cast aluminium brackets, and at the bottom by the grilles which form the walkways in the air space.

These units are delivered to the site, complete with glazing and solar shading, where they are hoisted into place, hooked, by means of the aluminium brackets, into curved anchor plates on the front edge of the ceiling, and screwed onto the adjoining units. Vertical glazed partitions can be installed to divide up the area – usually one every third unit – to prevent noise and smoke permeating through the air space.

Ventilation and heat transfer coefficient of the double façade

Ventilation boxes with external rain slats, with punched holes in the right half of the top of each unit and in the left half of the bottom, effect a diagonal air flow in the air space between the two skins of the façade. In other words, the inlet and outlet ventilation holes in the unit are offset from one another to prevent, as far as possible, what is known as recirculation (i.e. used air entering the rooms above). In laboratory tests the recirculation rate was 15 per cent.

The expected winter mean of the double façade $k_{equiv. façade}$ is 1.2 W/m².K.

Montage der Elemente der Doppelfassade
Assembling the units of the double façade

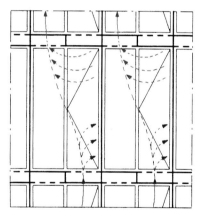

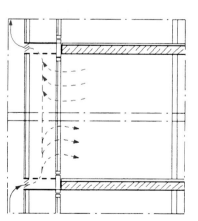

Schema der Durchlüftung der Doppelfassade und der dahinter liegenden Räume (Ansicht und Schnitt)
Diagram showing the ventilation of the double façade and the rooms behind (face and sectional view)

Offenbach, Germany

Planung
Design
Novotny Mähner Assoziierte,
Offenbach

Mitwirkende Sachverständige
Consultants
a + f, Frankfurt/M.

Elegante Landmarke für Offenbach mit interessanten verschiedenen Ansichten. Das Aufstre-
ben des polygonal endenden
Glasturmes wird durch das
Einstellen einer Blechlisene in
seiner Spitze noch betont.
In die Ganzglas-Elementfassade
sind zur horizontalen Gliederung
Bleche eingeklemmt worden.
Im Kontrast dazu das feste
Rückgrat mit der Lochfassade
in Naturstein aus Dorfer-Grün.

This building, with its many
intriguing perspectives,
represents an elegant new
landmark on the Offenbach
skyline. The soaring height of
the glass tower, which ends in a
polygon, is further emphasised
by the metal pilaster strip running
down the front. Metal sheets
have been inserted in the
structurally glazed unitised
façade, dividing the tower
horizontally. These contrast
with the solid backbone made
of green natural stone with
punched openings.

Außenansicht
City Tower
Outside view
City Tower

Objekt-Skizze
aus der Entwurfsphase
Preliminary sketch
from the design phase

„Hochhäuser sind für uns Architekten eine Herausforderung,
aber kein Grund zur Aufregung."
"For us architects, office blocks are a challenge, but
nothing to get excited about."

Professor Fritz Novotny

Düsseldorf, Germany

Planung
Design
BM + P Beucker Maschlanka
und Partner GbR, Architekten
Stadtplaner, Düsseldorf

Mitwirkende Sachverständige
Consultants
Fassadenberatung Ingenieurbüro
Memmert

Im alten Rheinhafen-Gebiet von
Düsseldorf siedeln sich die
modernen Medien an. Die gläserne Eingangs- und Verteiler-
halle sowie die geschosshohen
Ausfachungen sind SK 60-Kons-
truktionen. Die Fenster bestehen
aus Royal S 70B und bilden mit
den Fassadenprofilen eine
Einheit.

The modern media are
establishing themselves in
the old Rhine harbour area.
The glazed entrance and main
hall as well as the storey-high
cladding are in SK 60V
construction. The windows
are in Royal S 70B and form
a homogeneous whole with
the façade profiles.

Außen- und
Innenansichten
Medienzentrum
Düsseldorf
Outside and inside
views Düsseldorf
Media Centre

AOK Head Office

Chemnitz, Germany

Planung
Design
SSP Architekten Schmidt-
Schicketanz und Partner GmbH,
Munich

Mit dem Sächsischen Staats-
preis für Architektur ausgezeich-
neter Neubau, der mit dem vor-
handenen Altbau verbunden ist.
Feingegliedertes Gesamtbild
durch horizontal profilierte
Bleche und das schmale Schüco
Profilsystem FW 50, das die Vertikale betont bzw. große Glasflächen einrahmt.

The extension of an existing
building was awarded the
"Sächsische Stattspreis für
Architektur" (State of Saxony
Prize for Architecture). A fine
structured overall picture is
produced by the use of
horizontal formed aluminium
sheeting and the narrow Schüco
Profile System FW 50 which not
only emphasizes the vertical
lines but also provides frames
for large glazed areas.

Außenansichten
AOK Haupt-
geschäftsstelle
Outside views
AOK Head Office

Lippischen Landes-
Brandversicherungsanstalt

Detmold, Germany

Planung
Design
GWB Planen + Bauen,
Robert G. Busl, Munich

Filigranes Fassadenbild aus
Lisenen, Service-Balkonen,
geschosshohen Pfosten-Riegel-
Konstruktionen in Himmelblau
und Fensterflügeln in Schwefel-
gelb. Dieses heitere Ensemble
wurde mit den Systemen SK 60,
FW 50 und Royal S 65 realisiert.

Filigree elevation treatment
consisting of pilaster strips,
access balconies, storey-
height mullion and transom
construction in light-blue and
window frames in yellow. This
cheerful ensemble is made of
Systems SK 60, FW 50 and
Royal S 65.

Außen- und
Innenansichten
Lippischen Landes-
Brandversicherungs-
anstalt
Outside and inside
views Lippischen
Landes-Brandversiche-
rungsanstalt

110

Berlin, Germany

Planung
Design
Karres · Hartmeyer · Dreyer
Dipl.-Ing. Architekten BDA,
Hamburg
MBB – Deutsche Aerospace-
Hochfrequenztechnik Dr. Frye

Außenansicht
Axel Springer
Verlag AG, Erweiterung
Outside view
Axel Springer
Verlag AG extension

Der bekannte Hochhaus-Bau
aus den 60er-Jahren wurde in
der bereits damals geplanten
T-Form erweitert. Die Neubau-
Fassade sollte sich in Material
und Struktur absetzen und die
Architektur der Jahrtausend-
wende signalisieren. Die hier
eingesetzten Systeme: aus der
Fenster-Konstruktion Iskotherm
und SG 50 für den Giebel.

The famous high-rise building
of the 60s has been extended
to form the T-shape as originally
designed. It was intended to set
in contrast the façade of the
extension by the use of modern
materials and structuring
in order to demonstrate the
architecture of the turn of the
millenium. Systems applied:
Iskotherm for windows and
SG 50 for the narrow side.

Die gebogene Vorhangfassade,
flankiert von zwei Gebäudeflügeln
in Ziegelmauerwerk mit Lochfenstern, zeigt von der Eingangsan-
lage bis zum obersten Stockwerk
Schüco Systemtechnik.

The curved curtain wall façade,
flanked by two wings in
brickwork with individual
windows, demonstrates Schüco
systems from the entrance up
to the top floor.

Hamburg, Germany

Planung
Design
Dipl.-Ing. Architekten Uwe
Hohaus + Partner, Hamburg

Mitwirkende Sachverständige
Consultants
GFI – Gesellschaft für
Ingenieurleistung, Hamburg

Außenansicht
Umweltbehörde –
Landesamt für
Informationstechnik
Outside view
Regional IT Centre for
Environment Dept.

Hamburg, Germany

Planung
Design
BRT Architekten
Bothe Richter Teherani,
Hamburg

Mitwirkende Sachverständige
Consultants
AMP-Albrecht Memmert &
Partner, Neuss

Der ABC-Bogen in Hamburg
besteht aus drei gläsernen
Baukörpern: einem wellenförmi-
gen Riegel, einem „Glashinter-
haus" und dem bogenförmigen
11-geschossigen Hochhaus.
Trotz einer Vielzahl von bau-
physikalischen Maßnahmen
wie Energiesparfassade, außen
liegendem Sonnschutz, Bauteil-
kühlung etc., stellt sich der Bau
als markante humane Glasarchi-
tektur dar. Bei der Außenfassade
handelt es sich um eine objekt-
bezogene Sonderkonstruktion
mit integrierten Fenstern auf
Basis des Systems Royal S.

The ABC Arch in Hamburg
consists of three glazed
structures: an undulated
transom, a glazed rear section
an an arc-shaped eleven storey
block. Despite its many special
structural requirements such
as an energy saving façade,
external solar shading, sectional
climate control etc., the building
is still a strikingly human piece
of glazed architecture. The
external façade is a customised
projekt design with integrated
windows based on the Royal S
system.

Detailansichten
ABC-Bogen
Detail views
ABC Arch

Düsseldorf, Germany

Planung
Design
Ingenhoven Overdiek
Architekten, Düsseldorf

Mitwirkende Sachverständige
Consultants
DS-Plan, Stuttgart

Der Komplex besteht aus zwei treppenförmig zum Wasser hin abgestuften Gebäudeteilen mit einem gemeinsamen festen Kern. Der Neubau wirkt wie eine neu interpretierte Version eines Speichergebäudes, des „gläsernen Speichers". Durch die Transparenz der durchgehenden Verglasung von Fußboden bis Decke sind Waren und Exponate für jedermann sichtbar, quasi ein Schaufenster.
Die stirnseitige auskragende und sich verjüngende Deckenverkleidung unterstützt diesen Eindruck, gliedert gleichzeitig die Horizontale und bindet schließlich die Fassade in ihrer Ganzheit.

The complex consists of two structures that step gradually down to the water, joined together by a fixed core. This new building is a modern interpretation of a storage facility – a glass warehouse. Glazed throughout, its transparency from floor to ceiling means that goods and exhibits are visible to all, almost like a shop window.
The projecting and tapering cladding at the front underlines this impression, at once dividing the building horizontally and binding the façade as a whole.

„Bei unserer Herangehensweise hat die Nachhaltigkeit die erste Priorität, d. h. die Frage ist, wie lange und wie nachhaltig lässt sich ein Gebäude nutzen."

"Since sustainability is our number one priority, our approach is based on how long a building can be used."

Christoph Ingenhoven, Ingenhoven Overdiek Architekten

AOK Bayern Head Office, Aschaffenburg Branch

Aschaffenburg, Germany

Planung
Design
Architekten BDA KOSIG +
KOSIG, Würzburg

Mitwirkende Sachverständige
Consultants
Ing.-Büro R + R Fuchs, Munich

Ein stark strukturiertes Gefüge
aus unterschiedlichen Baukörpern mit einer Rotunde als domi-
nantem Eckpunkt bildet die neue
Krankenkassen-Hauptverwal-
tung. Alle Vertikal-, Rund- und
Schrägverglasungen werden von
dem Profilsystem FW 50 getragen. Die Fensterbänder und integrierten Fensterelemente sind
aus Royal S 70.

A well-structured complex
of various buldings with a
rotunda dominating the corner
site where the new health
insurance headquarters is
located. All vertical, curved
and sloped glazing is supported
by the profile system FW 50.
The ribbon windows and
integrated window elements
are Royal S 70.

Außenansichten
AOK Hauptverwaltung
Outside views
AOK Head Office

Multi-purpose office
and services centre
Berlin-Reinickendorf, Germany

Planung
Design
HPP Hentrich-Petschnigg
& Partner KG, Düsseldorf

Mitwirkende Sachverständige
Consultants
IFB-Institut für Bauphysik,
Dipl.-Ing. Horst R. Grün,
Mühlheim a. d. Ruhr

Der zehngeschossige, halbrunde
Büroturm wirkt wie ein Schutz-
schild für die sich daran anschlie-
ßenden, gestaffelten Gebäude.
Horizontale Betonung der
Geschosse durch querformatige
Glasfelder und Sonnenschutz-
einrichtungen. Eingesetzt
wurden die Schüco-Systeme
FW 50 und SG 50N, für die
Fenster Royal S 70.

The ten-storey semi-circular
office tower forms a protective
shield to the staggered buildings
adjoining. The square glass
fields and solar shading create
horizontal emphasis at each
floor. The systems used were
Schüco's FW 50, SG 50N, and
Royal S 70 for the windows.

Außenansichten
Anthropolis
Outside views
Anthropolis

Amsterdam, Netherlands

Planung
Design
Meyer en van Schooten
Architecten, Amsterdam

Ein typisch unverwechselbarer
Solitär, der seinen Platz braucht
und deutlich beansprucht.
Scheinbar gerade gelandet oder
auf dem Sprung. Vorne gibt das
riesige Panoramafenster den
Blick frei wie von einer Kom-
mandobrücke. Seitlich finden
sich die Laubengänge und
Erschließungstreppen, die zu
den „Kajüten" führen. Der
Rumpf ist natürlich verkleidet.
Die Hydraulikstoßdämpfern
nachempfundenen Füße deuten
auf weiche Landung. Ihre
Schrägstellung suggeriert Start-
bereitschaft und Dynamik.

Like a distinctive solitaire, this
building needs and clearly
occupies its own space. It looks
as if it has just landed or is
ready for take-off.
The large window at the front
affords a panoramic view,
rather like the bridge of a ship,
whereas the rear houses the
decks, as in the galleons of old.
Walkways and staircases on
the sides lead to the "cabins".
Naturally, the main body is
cladded.

Detailansichten
ING Group
Detail views
ING Group

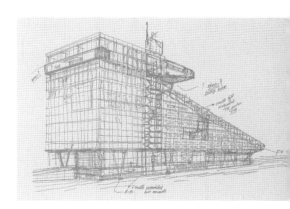

„Themen aus der gegenwärtigen Gesellschaft wie Zugänglichkeit,
Transparenz und Beständigkeit sind für uns Themen, die zusammen mit dem gestellten Auftrag einen Leitfaden für unsere
Entwürfe bilden."
"Modern concerns about accessibility, transparency
and sustainability are additional factors that play a key
role in our designs."

Roberto E. Meyer und Jeroen W. van Schooten, Meyer en van Schooten, Architecten

Munster, Germany

Der Gebäudekomplex der LVA Münster ist als kreisförmiger Zweispänner konzipiert, gegliedert durch sehr filigran gehaltene Treppenhäuser. Der vorgesetzte Fluchtbalkon bzw. Wartungsgang erfüllt gleichzeitig Sonnenschutzfunktion. Der durch die kreisförmige Anordnung gebildete Innenhof ist gärtnerisch gestaltet und dient als Rekreationszone. Die sehr transparent wirkende Fassade ist im System Royal S als Sonderkonstruktion ausgeführt, die Eingangslage in dem System Royal S 65.

The LVA building complex in Münster was designed as a circular double span, subdivided by staircases with fine construction lines. The emergency balcony and maintenance walkways also serve to protect against the sun. The circular layout creates a courtyard which is laid out like a small garden and serves as a recreational area. The façade, which appears to be transparent, was built using the Royal S system in a customized design. The entrance building uses Royal S 65.

Planung
Design
Dipl.-Ing. Architekt
Michael Knoche, Munster

Mitwirkende Sachverständige
Consultants
Dipl.-Ing. Mosbacher,
Friedrichshafen

Außenansicht
LVA Münster
Outside view
LVA Münster

Hanover, Germany

Planung
Design
gmp-Architekten von Gerkan,
Marg und Partner, Hamburg

Als sichtbarer Bezug zum Auf-
traggeber ist der kammerartige
Betonskelettbau mit Wellblech
verkleidet worden. Dazwischen
sind hohe mit Galerien ausge-
stattete, großzügig verglaste
Innenhöfe angeordnet, die sich
mit den geschlosseneren
Büroflügeln abwechseln. Die
Fensterfelder haben – durch
die in Holz ausgeführten
Fensterflügel – eine dezente
Akzentuierung erfahren.

As a visible reference to the
client, the comb-like concrete
skeleton structure has been clad
using corrugated metal panels.
In between, inner courtyards
with high ceilings, galleries
and generously proportioned
glazing alternate with more
enclosed office tracts. The
window modules are
accentuated by the use of
wooden vent frames.

Außenansicht Metall-
Berufsgenossenschaft
Outside view Metall-
Berufsgenossenschaft

Ku'damm Office Building

Berlin, Germany

Planung
Design
Murphy/Jahn, Chicago

Auf einem nur raumbreiten Grundstück entstand hier ein weiteres Wahrzeichen am Kurfürstendamm. Die Konstruktion der gläsernen Hülle basiert dabei auf dem Schüco System SG 50N. Die jeweils zwei Geschosse übergreifende Gliederung der gläsernen Hülle und die sichtbare Stahlkonstruktion machen die Abhängung der auskragenden Bauteile für den Betrachter spürbar. Die Gliederung des Kerns und großer Teile des oberen Technikgeschosses mit starren Alu-Lamellen ist eine bewusste Hommage an den expressionistischen Baustil des Architekten Erich Mendelsohn.

On a plot only the width of a single room, a new landmark has been created on the Kurfürstendamm. The structure of the all-glass envelope is based on the Schüco SG 50N system. The division of the all-glass envelope into sections, each spanning two storeys, and the visible steel construction give the observer the impression that the projecting building components are suspended. The structure of the main section and large parts of the upper hi-tech layer, with its fixed aluminium large louvre blades, pay deliberate homage to the expressionistic architectural style of Erich Mendelsohn.

Außenansichten
Bürohaus am Ku'damm
Outside views
Office block
on the Ku'damm

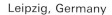

Leipzig, Germany

Planung
Design
Koch + Partner Architekten und
Stadtplaner, Munich/Leipzig

Der Neubau für die Postbank in Leipzig liegt im nordöstlichen Randbereich der Innenstadt. Er schloss die bis dahin offene Westseite eines dreieckigen Platzes und schirmt durch seine Lage den nördlich gelegenen Mariannenpark vom Verkehrslärm des südlichen Bahngeländes ab. Die Architekten haben bewusst die für Leipzig typische 4- bis 5-geschossige Blockrandbebauung aufgenommen. Über dem Gesims des massiven, durch Fenstergruppen strukturierten Baukörpers erheben sich, als Pendant zur umgebenden Dachlandschaft, zwei weit zurückgesetzte Attika-Geschosse mit einer filligranen Alu-Glas-Fassade. Der in dem Baublock entstandene Innenhof ist zum Teil als glasüberdeckte Halle mit einem Tonnengewölbe ausgebildet und zum Mariannenpark hin aufgebrochen.

The new building for the Postbank in Leipzig is located on the north-eastern edge of the city centre. It has closed off the previously open west side of a triangular plaza and by its position shields the Mariannenpark to the North against traffic noise from the railway to the South. Architects intentionally recreated the look of a typical Leipzig 4 to 5-storey block on the edge of the development. A two storey roof parapet with a slimline aluminium-glass façade rises above the cornice of the massive building, constructed from windows and window groups, as a counterpart to the surrounding skyline. The inner courtyard created by the building partly consists of a glass covered hall with a barrel vault, and it opens out towards the Mariannenpark.

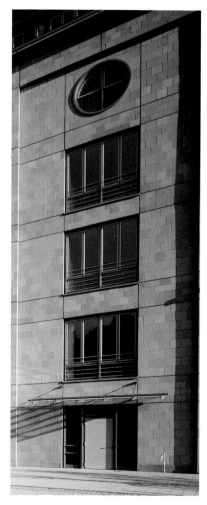

Außenansichten und
Innenhof Postbank
Outside views
and inner courtyard
Postbank

Warsaw, Poland

Planung
Design
Kohn Pedersen Fox Associates,
New York
Biuro Projektów Architektury,
Warsaw
A. Epstein and Sons Int. Inc.,
Chicago

Das Warschau-Finanz-Zentrum, ein Gebäude für finanzdienstleistende Firmen im Zentrum der Stadt, steht in unmittelbarer Nähe zum „Palast der Kultur und der Wissenschaften". Das von der Grundstücksform her rechteckige Hochhaus wendet sich mit seiner gekurvten Kontur der oberen Stockwerke und der, auf die Altstadt weisenden, bis zum Straßenniveau durchgehenden Spitze, diesem Palast zu. Die Fensterflächen und die mit poliertem Granit verkleideten Wände wurden als komplette Elemente von der österreichischen Metallbaufirma vorgefertigt, nach Warschau transportiert und montiert!

The Warsaw Finance Centre, a building for finance companies in the centre of the city, is immediately next to the "Palace of Culture and Science". Taking its shape from the plot, this rectangular building, with the curved lines from its top storeys and its nose inclined towards the old town and carrying on through to street level, appears to be turning towards the palace. The window surfaces and the polished granite-clad walls were prefabricated as complete units by the Austrian fabricator, transported to Warsaw and installed on site.

Außenansichten
Warschau-
Finanz-Zentrum
Outside views
Warsaw Finance Centre

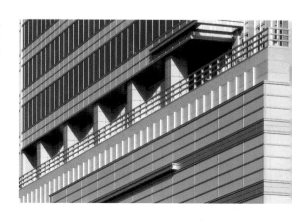

Copenhagen, Denmark

Planung
Design
Dissing + Weitling
Architekten, Copenhagen

Detailansichten
DaimlerChrysler
Detail views
DaimlerChrysler

Wunderschön klarer Glaskubus mit vorgestellter Scheibe aus dunklem Stein in der Tradition der Moderne. Über dem Ganzen ein papierdünnes Dach, unter dem sich der Glaskörper wie ein Schiff herausschiebt. Die Verglasung geht ohne sichtbaren Rahmen in den Boden und betont damit die Transparenz des Gebäudes und den Übergang von Außen- und Innenraum. Die Konstruktion ist innenliegend, wodurch der Charakter des Glaskubus erhalten bleibt. Für die Fenster kam das System Royal S als Sonderkonstruktion mit integrierten Klappflügeln zum Einsatz.

This is an exquisite clear glazed cube with a slice of dark stone at the front in the modern tradition. An ultra-fine projecting roof covers the entire structure, whilst the glazed structure beneath looks like a ship. The glazing without any visible frame appears to run into the ground, thus emphasizing the transparency of the building and the transition from the outside to the inside. There is an internal supporting structure, maintainig the character of the glass cube. The windows were made to a special specification using the Royal S system with integrated top-hung vents.

Ørestaden, Denmark

Planung
Design
Henning Larsens Tegnestue A/S

Mitwirkende Sachverständige
Consultants
Arkitekt Jan Besiakov,
Nacharkitekt Carsten
Hyldebrandt

Größe beweisen. Die Reduktion der Formen und Farben trifft mit einer Wucht und Nachhaltigkeit, die dem Gebäude Monumentalität verleihen. Die eindringliche Architektursprache tradiert das Erbe nordamerikanischer Hochhaus-Konzepte. Im Renaissance-geprägten Kopenhagen setzt der 20-Geschosser mit den angegliederten Flachbauten ein sichtbares Zeichen bis weit ins Schwedische.

This building is a true embodiment of size. Restricted use of shape and colour enhances its impact and lends the building a monumental, timeless quality. The intensity of its architectural language reflects inherited North American concepts of the skyscraper. In Renaissance-influenced Copenhagen, the 20-storey building, with linked low-rise blocks, is a landmark visible from well into Sweden.

Außenansichten Ferring
International Center
Outside views Ferring
International Center

Objekt-Skizze aus der
Entwurfsphase
Preliminary sketch
from the design phase

„Die Harmonie von Kopf und Herz ist wichtig
in der Architektur."
    „The right balance of heart and mind is crucial in
    architecture."

The head office building, Seoul,
South Korea

Planung
Design
D.M.J.M., USA
Heerim Architects & Engineers

Mit bildhauerischer Kraft setzt
sich das Bankgebäude in Szene.
Dynamische Formen künden von
Macht und Expansion. Die
Funktionen sind ablesbar. Das
Gebäude öffnet sich seinen
Gästen, das Dachgeschoss
beschirmt. Die leicht erhöhte
Lage der Baukörper verstärkt
den Eindruck nach der Einzig-
artigkeit und Besonderheit des
Ortes.

This bank dominates the
landscape like a sculpture. Its
dynamic form signifies power
and expansion and is a clear
expression of function. The
building opens up to welcome
visitors under the shelter of the
roof storey. Its slightly elevated
position reinforces the
impression of uniqueness and
distinctiveness.

Außenansicht Korea
Development Bank
Outside view Korea
Development Bank

Malmö, Sweden

Planung
Design
KHR AS Arkitekter,
Jan Söndergaard,
Mikkel Beedholm, Virum

Mitwirkende Sachverständige
Consultants
Skanska Stålteknik, Malmö

Das Bauen im Bestand gewinnt an Bedeutung. Aufgaben für die Sanierung, Umnutzung und Unterhaltung der Gebäude rücken in den Blickpunkt. Unorthodoxe Lösungen können die Brücke zwischen Alt und Neu schlagen. Prachtvoller Stuck neben kristallin reinen Glasfassaden? – Eine Frage der architektonischen Meisterschaft. Die Entwurfsverfasser haben jedenfalls diese Frage im schwedischen Malmö für sich entschieden.

Blending new constructions with the existing building stock is becoming increasingly important, with attention focusing on renovation, changes in use and maintenance. Unorthodox solutions can bridge the gap between old and new. To set the crystalline purity of glazed façades against a fine period piece demands considerable architectural mastery. The confident decision taken by the designers in Malmö in Sweden is a case in point.

Detailansichten
Butterickshuset
Detail views
Butterickshuset

Bülach, Switzerland

Planung
Design
Atelier ww, Dipl. Architekten,
Zürich

Zwei langgestreckte
Gebäudetrakte, mit streng
gegliederten Fassaden und auf
Stützen „schwebend", sind mit
einer 17 m breiten und 45 m
langen Lichtdachkonstruktion zu
einer Einheit verbunden. Die
Außenhaut des Daches ist aus
SK 60, die vertikalen Giebel- und
Fassadenflächen aus SK 60 V.
Für die Fensterbänder wurden
Verbundflügelelemente auf Basis
des Systems Royal S gebaut.

Two long building complexes
with clearly structured façades
appear to 'float' on columns and
are linked by a skylight roof
construction 17 m wide and
45 m long. The outer skin of
the roof is system SK 60, the
vertical gable and the façade
areas are SK 60V. Composite
windows based on the system
Royal S were used for the ribbon
windows.

Außen- und
Innenansichten
Vetropack Holding AG
Outside and
inside views
Vetropack Holding AG

Dresden, Germany

Planung
Design
Planungsring Ressel GmbH,
Dresden

Der repräsentative und interessanteste Teil des Gebäudes besteht aus einem zurückhaltenden ruhigen Glaskörper mit eingestellten, herausgeschobenen und durchgesteckten Elementen. Dies ergibt ein reizvolles Spiel, welches durch die farbigen Akzentuierungen noch verstärkt wird. Die vorgehängten Alu-lamellen gliedern den Bau zusätzlich, wie auch die abschließende und auskragende Hutkrempe als Sonnenschutz.

The most impressive feature of the building is its understated glass structure with inset and protruding units. This creates a stunning effect, accentuated by the striking use of colour. The façade-mounted aluminium blades provide relief to the building, as does the projecting brim on the top, which offers solar protection.

Detailansichten
Handwerkskammer
Detail views Chamber
of Crafts and Trade

„Farbakzente und unterschiedliche Stufen von Transparenz im spannungsreichen Dialog."
"Accentuated colour and different levels of transparency in an exhilarating dialogue."

Planungsring Ressel GmbH

Prague, Czech Rep.

Planung
Design
Atelier Pak, Pata & Frydecký
Architekti

Mitwirkende Sachverständige
Consultants
Sipral a.s., Fassadenplaner und
MB

Außenansichten
Hadovka Office Park
Outside views
Hadovka Offive Park

St. Denis, France

Planung
Design
Atelier 4A

Konzeption
Conception
Cabinet Claude Parent
Cabinet Reichen et Robert

Das Verwaltungsgebäude der Electricité de France präsentiert sich als langgestreckter plastisch durchgearbeiteter Baukörper, klar strukturiert mit dynamischer Ecklösung. Der Gebäudekomplex umschließt einen imposanten glasüberdeckten Innenhof, der ein gegen die Außenwelt abgeschirmtes großflächiges Recreationscenter darstellt. Für die Fassade wurde das System Royal S65 eingesetzt.

The Electricité de France head office builing is a long three-dimensional structure, clearly defined with dynamic corners. The building complex includes an imposing glass covered inner courtyard used as a large recreational area, screened off from the outside world. The Royal S65 system was used in the façade.

Außenansichten
EDF St. Denis
Outside views
EDF St. Denis

Hamburg, Germany

Bauherr
Owner
Bundesrepublik Deutschland
unter Beteiligung der Freien und
Hansestadt Hamburg, vertreten
durch den Bundesminister für
Verkehr, Bau- und Wohnungs-
wesen, vertreten durch die
OFD/LBV Hamburg, vertreten
durch das Finanzbauamt
Hamburg

Nutzer
Client
International Tribunal for the law
of the Sea, vertreten durch den
Bundesminister der Justiz

Planung
Design
Alexander Freiherr v. Branca
Emanuela Freiin v. Branca,
Munich

Bauleitung
Site-management
WGK Planungsgesellschaft mbH,
Hamburg

Fassadenplanung
Façade design
Planungsbüro für Fassaden-
technik Erich Mosbacher,
Friedrichshafen

Luftaufnahme von
Süden
Aerial photograph
from the south

Die 3. Seerechtskonferenz der
UN wählte 1981 die Freie und
Hansestadt Hamburg zum Sitz
des neuen „Internationalen
Seegerichtshofes", der damit zur
ersten UN-Einrichtung in der
Bundesrepublik wurde. Sie stellte – im Hinblick auf die
Bedeutung dieses Gerichts – ein
repräsentatives Parkgelände an
der Elbchaussee mit einer denk-
malgeschützten Villa von 1871
und altem Baumbestand zur
Verfügung und übernahm auch –
mit substanzieller Beteiligung
Hamburgs – die Baukosten.

In einem internationalen
Wettbewerb unter 15 namhaften
Architekturbüros erhielt der
Entwurf der Architekten
Alexander Freiherr von Branca
und Emanuela Freiin von Branca
den 1. Preis und den Auftrag zur
Ausführung. Die gesamte
Anlage wurde im Juli 2000 im
Beisein von UN-Generalsekretär
Kofi Annan eingeweiht.

In 1981 the 3rd UN Conference
on maritime law chose the
Hanseatic city of Hamburg for
the seat of the new
"International Tribunal for the
Law of the Sea", which became
the first UN building in the
Federal Republic. On account
of the importance of the court,
a prestigious area of parkland
on the Elbchaussee was
chosen with a listed mansion
constructed in 1871 set in
mature woodlands. The Federal
Republic also took responsibility
for the building costs, with
substantial help from Hamburg
itself.

15 prominent architect's
practices competed in an
international competition where
architects Alexander Freiherr von
Branca and Emanuela Freiin von
Branca won first prize and were
commissioned for the design.
The completed complex was
officially opened in July 2000 in
the presence of UN Secretary
General Kofi Annan.

Luftaufnahme
von NO
Aerial photograph
from the NE

Gesamtansicht
von Süden
Overall view
from the south

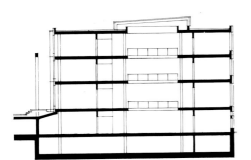

Schnitt A-A
Section detail
A-A

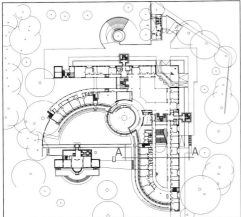

Grundriss
Erdgeschoss
Ground floor
plan

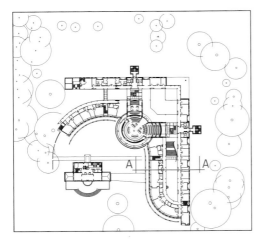

Grundriss
1. Obergeschoss
First floor plan

Die Aufgabenstellung des Nutzers

Das Raum- und Funktionsprogramm wurde zwischen Auswärtigem Amt, Bundesjustizministerium und einer UN-Kommission abgestimmt und umfasst im Wesentlichen

- einen großen und zwei kleine Sitzungssäle,
- eine Bibliothek,
- Beratungszimmer für Gericht und Streitparteien,
- die Dienstzimmer für Präsidium, Kanzler, 23 Richter und ca. 100 Mitarbeiter aus unterschiedlichen Erdteilen und Rechtssystemen und
- ein Kasino.

Das Entwurfskonzept der Architekten

Im Wesentlichen ging dieses maßgeblich von der Villa, dem Baumbestand und der Sichtverbindung der wichtigen

Räume zum Park und zur Elbe aus. Das Resultat:
Der Neubau öffnet sich in einem geschwungenen Trakt mit Glasdoppelfassade zum Park. Der weiße Außenputz und die vorgestellte Arkade markieren den Material- und Höhenbezug zur Villa; die Rotunde des großen Sitzungssaales – als geistiges und funktionelles Zentrum der ganzen Anlage – bildet formal den Kontrapunkt zur Villa.

Die Bürotrakte an der N- und O-Seite sind dagegen eher geschlossen und streng linear ausgebildet. Sie sind mit dem geschwungenen Trakt durch eine glasüberdeckte Halle bzw. einen Gartenhof mit verglasten Brücken verbunden.

Die Funktion des Kasinos wurde der Villa zugewiesen.

Die äußere Erschließung des Neubaus erfolgt von der gedeck-

The client's terms of reference

The spatial and functional specification was coordinated by the German Foreign Office, the Federal Ministry of Justice and a UN commission and comprised:

- One large and two small courtrooms
- Library
- Consultation rooms for court and litigating parties
- Chambers for the Presiding Council, the Chancellor, 23 judges and about 100 employees from different regions of the world and different legal systems
- Coffee lounge

The architect's draft concept

The architect's draft concep took the villa, woodland setting and views of the park and the Elbe from the most important rooms as a starting point.

The new building has an open aspect onto the park in the sweeping lines of a glazed twin wall façade. The white exterior render and the forward arcade emphasise the relationship between the materials and the height; the rotunda housing the

large courtroom – as the intellectual and operational centre of the entire complex – constitutes a formal counterpoint to the villa.

The offices on the North and East side by contrast are more enclosed and of a strict linear design. They are joined to the main section by a glass covered hall and courtyard with glazed bridges.

The villa has been given over to the coffee lounge.

The external section of the new building emerges from the covered driveway in the North East corner through the impressive foyer, which extends over three floors, to the staircases, lifts and access to the corridors.

The function of the glazed twin wall façade

The function of the glazed twin wall façade was selected with a view to energy optimisation:

- No air-conditioning (only cooling ceilings)
- Natural, draft-free ventilation (even in the strong and gusty winds in the Elbe Valley)

ten Vorfahrt an der NO-Ecke her über die durch drei Geschosse gehende repräsentative Eingangshalle, an der die Treppen, Aufzüge und Anbindungen der Flure liegen.

Die Funktion der Glasdoppelfassade

Im Hinblick auf eine energetische Optimierung wurde diese Fassadenart gewählt, denn daraus resultiert
- Verzicht auf Klimaanlagen (nur Kühldecken),
- natürliche, zugfreie Belüftung (auch bei starkem bzw. böigem Wind im Elbetal),
- Nachtauskühlung ohne Verzicht auf Einbruchschutz und
- optimaler, beweglicher Sonnenschutz (Lamellenstoren) vor der inneren, klimatrennenden Schale.

Diese innere Schale besteht aus einer Aluminiumkonstruktion mit

Öffnungsflügeln zum Lüften und Reinigen als Sonderkonstruktion auf Basis der Profilserie Schüco Royal S 75, die äußere Schale aus einer festverglasten Pfosten-Riegel-Konstruktion mit achsweise angetriebenen Glaslamellen für die Durchlüftung. Beide Schalen sind in geschosshohen, i. M. 2,50 m breiten Elementen vorgefertigt und montiert. Im Zuge der Montage wurde die Durchlüftungszone durch horizontale und vertikale Glasschotten zur Unterbindung von Schall- und Rauchausbreitung in „Kastenfenster" unterteilt.

In jeder Fensterachse wurde ein geschlossener, wärmegedämmter Öffnungsflügel bis zur äußeren Schale „vorgestülpt" zur direkten Belüftung und akustischen Verbindung nach außen (soweit gewünscht).

Innenansicht der Fassade mit geöffnetem Lüftungsflügel
Inside view of the façade with vent open

- Night ventilation without compromising security against break-in
- Optimal, adjustable sunblinds (slats) in front of the internal façade skin.

This internal skin consists of an aluminium structure with opening vents for ventilation and cleaning. It is a special design based on the profile series Schüco Royal S 75. The external skin consists of a fixed glazed mullion transom construction with pivoting glass slats for air circulation.

Both skins are manufactured and installed as floor to ceiling units of 2.5m, measured at the centre. The air circulation space was divided into "box windows" by horizontal and vertical glazed partitions during the installation, to prevent the spread of sound and smoke.

Each opening window has an enclosed, thermally insulated opening vent with "front meeting stile" which meets the inner façade wall to provide direct ventilation and sound transmission to the outside (if desired).

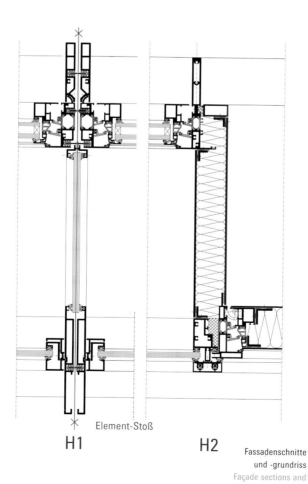

Element-Stoß

H1   H2

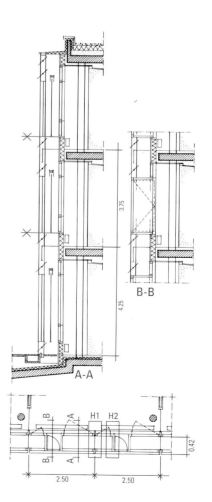

Fassadenschnitte und -grundriss
Façade sections and floor plan

B-B

A-A

Budapest, Hungary

Planung
Design
Puhl Antal Építész Irodája,
Budapest

Mitwirkende Sachverständige
Consultants
ATF-Architektur Technik
Fassade, Frankfurt/Main,
Germany

Objekt-Skizze
aus der Entwurfsphase
Preliminary sketch
from the design phase

Neue Arbeitswelten fordern
Raum, Licht und ein Ambiente,
das motiviert. In diesem Zeichen
stand der Bau einer Büro-City im
ungarischen Budapest, ein
Komplex von der Größe eines
Ortsteils. Glas, Naturstein und
Metall als Materialien sowie
begrünte, Schatten spendende
Innenhöfe spiegeln den
Anspruch der Baubeteiligten
nach einem erstklassigen
Umfeld wider – Architektur für
die Gemeinschaftsbedürfnisse
der Stadt.

Progressive work environments
demand space, light and an
ambience that engenders
motivation. A new commercial
district built in the Hungarian
capital of Budapest fits the bill
exactly. Glass, stone, metal
and shady courtyards reflect
the stakeholders' right to a
first-class built environment
meeting the needs of the urban
community

Außenansichten
Mom-Park
Outside views
Mom-Park

„Im Leben des Menschen spielen sich Tragödien und Komödien
ab, die Architektur ist nur die Begleitmusik dazu."
„Human life is suffused with comedy and tragedy.
Architecture merely provides the accompaniment."

(Alvar Aalto)

145

Warsaw, Poland

Planung
Design
Autorska Precownia Architectury
Kurylowicz & Associates Ltd.,
Warsaw

Mitwirkende Sachverständige
Consultants
Georg Tuscher – Biuro
Techniczne, Sopot

Das Gebäude präsentiert sich als dominanter, steinerner Kubus mit klarer Ausrichtung. Der Haupteingang und die riesige Sonnenlamelle auf dem Dach dokumentieren klar, welche Fassade die wichtigste ist. Im Gegensatz zu den übrigen Lochfensterfassaden mit Glasvorbauten und Erkern als Gliederungselement erhält die Hauptfassade eine vollflächige Planarglashaut. Diese verleiht der dahinter liegenden zweiten Haut den Charakter eines Bühnenbildes, was durch die bewusste Betonung der Mitte mit Öffnung nach innen eine zusätzliche zentrale Akzentuierung erfährt.

Detailansichten
Budownictwa Focus
Detail views
Budownictwa Focus

The building presents itself as a dominating, stone cube in clear alginment. The main entrance and enormous sunblinds on the roof clearly show which façade is the most important. In contrast to the other façades with punched openings, glass canopies and oriels, the main façade is joined together by a planar glass skin over its entire surface. The second skin, located behind it, takes on the character of a stage set, the deliberately emphasised inward opening producing additional accentuation of the centre.

Moscow, Russia

Planung
Design
Häussler Gruppe, Stuttgart

Entwurfs- und
Ausführungsplanung
Design and construction
planning
Weidleplan Consulting GmbH,
Stuttgart

Zwei Hochhaus-Scheiben mit
26 und 16 Geschossen sind
durch verglaste Brücken auf
allen Ebenen verbunden. Die
streng gegliederten Fassaden
haben gleiche Abmessungen im
Brüstungs- und Fensterbereich.
Hierfür wurde eine Sonderkonstruktion aus Royal S Profilen
und für die Blockfenster das
System Royal 78 BS eingesetzt.

Two slender high-rise buildings
of 26 and 16 storeys are
linked on all floors by glazed
passageways. The distinctly
structured façades have spandrel
and windows sections of
equal dimensions. A special
construction of Royal S
profiles and block windows
in Royal 78 BS was specified.

Außenansicht
Kreditinstitut der
Russischen Föderation
Outside view
Russian Federation
Credit Institute

Green Island Administrative Building

Brussels, Belgium

Planung
Design
Atelier d´Art Urbain, Brussels

Die postmoderne Gestaltung dieses Verwaltungsgebäudes mit einer Fülle klassischer Architektur-Zitate setzt klare Kontraste zwischen weißen Stein- und blaugrauen Metallflächen. Die darin integrierten Fenster sind aus Royal S 65, in besonderen Sicherheitsbereichen aus Royal S 70DH, der durchschusshemmenden Ausführung.

The post-modern design of this administrative building with a multitude of classic architectural allusions sets clear contrasts between the white stone and the blue-grey metal areas. The integrated windows are Royal S 65 and in the special security areas Royal S 70DH, which is a bullet-resistant construction.

Außenansichten
Green Island
Verwaltungsgebäude
Outside views
Green Island
Administrative Building

Chemnitz, Germany

Planung
Design
Dipl.-Ing. Architekt
Dieter Punckt, Berlin

Mitwirkende Sachverständige
Consultants
ANGA, Ing.-Büro für
Fassadentechnik GmbH,
Dresden

Ein rechteckiger Turm als Eckbebauung, daran anschließend
zwei Seitenflügel. An der Ge-
bäude-Rückseite vorgesetzte
Treppenhäuser und Verbindungs-
brücken. Alle Glasfassaden sind
aus dem schmalen Profilsystem
FW 50, für die langgezogenen
Fensterbänder wurde eine Sonderkonstruktion des flächenbündigen Blocksystems
Royal S 70B eingesetzt.

A rectangular tower on a
corner development with two
adjacent wings. Staircases
and connecting bridges adjoin
the rear side of the building.
All glass façades are of the
narrow profile System FW 50.
A special construction of the
flush-mounted block window
system Royal S 70B was
used for the extensive ribbon
windows.

Außenansichten
Technisches Rathaus
Outside views
Technical City Hall

Jules Destrooper

Lo-Reminge, Belgium

Planung
Design
Architekt Jo Rabaey, Veurne

Außenansichten
Jules Destrooper
Outside views
Jules Destrooper

Berlin, Germany

Planung
Design
BHLM Architekten Stadtplaner
Beucker · Haider · Lang-
hammer · Maschlanka,
Düsseldorf
Prof. Polonyi & Fink GmbH,
Berlin

Ein Wintergarten von 24 m
Durchmesser belichtet und
belüftet die Büros auf natürliche
Weise und erlaubt das Arbeiten
bei geöffneten Fenstern ohne
Geräuschbelästigung mitten in
der Stadt. Klima-Pufferzone statt
Klima-Anlage – gebaut aus den
Schüco Systemen SK 60 und
SK 60V.

A rotunda measuring 24 m
in diameter provides natrual
light and ventilation for the
surrounding office and allows
people to work with the
windows open in the midst
of a city without being disturbed
by traffic noise.
A climate buffer effect instead
of air-conditioning – designed
using Schüco Systems SK 60
and SK 60V.

Außen- und
Innenansichten
Verwaltungsgebäude
Schering AG
Outside and inside
views Schering AG
Administrative Building

Twin Square

Diegem, Belgium

Planung
Design
Bureau d'Architecture Emile
Verhaegen

Ühispank

Tallinn, Estonia

Planung
Design
Architekt Raivo Puusepp

Mitwirkende Sachverständige
Consultants
AS Merko Ehitus

Aus der Stadtlandschaft Tallinns
erhebt sich das neue Gebäude
der Ühispank wie ein über-
dimensionaler Eiskristall. Der
kristallin gegliederte Baukörper
mit großflächigen Schrägverglasungen und die lichtgrau
spiegelnde Glasfassade schaffen
diesen Eindruck.
Für die Glasfassade wurde das
System FW 50 eingesetzt, teils
als Sonderkonstruktion. Die
großflächigen Lichtdächer wurden im System SK 60 realisiert,
die Eingangshalle im System
Royal S 65.

The new Ühispank building rises
up from the urban surroundings
of Tallinn like an oversized ice
crystal. The crystalline structure
with large areas of sloped
glazing and the light grey
mirrored glass façade encourage
this impression.
The FW 50 system, partly in a
special design, was used for the
glass façade. The large-scale
glass roofs were fabricated
using SK 60 system, the
entrance building is Royal S 65.

Außenansicht
Twinsquare
Outside view
Twinsquare

Außenansicht
Ühispank
Outside view
Ühispank

Bielefeld, Germany

Planung
Design
Dipl.-Ing. Hans-Hermann Seydel,
Bielefeld

Mitwirkende Sachverständige
Consultants
Dipl.-Ing. H. Windmöller
Ingenieurbüro für Bauwesen

Die symmetrische Anlage, die
halbrund angeordneten Säulen
verleihen dem Gebäude eine
klassizistische Anmutung.
Die voll verglaste Baukörperecke
wird gekrönt von einem aufge-
lösten, teilverglasten Spitzen-
haubendach. Das System FW 50
mit schmalen Profilen sowie
SK 60 für die Schrägverglasung
verleihen der Fassade eine
Transparenz, die zusammen mit
den davorgesetzten kräftigen
runden Säulen eine spannungs-
volle Komposition bilden.

The symmetrical structure with
semi-circular columns gives the
building a classic air.
The fully glazed corner of the
building structure is topped
with a separate partially glazed
pointed curved roof. The FW 50
system with narrow profiles and
the SK 60 system used for the
sloped glazing give the façade a
transparency which, together
with the sturdy round columns
in front, form an exciting
composition.

Außenansichten
Outside views

Berkshire, Great Britain

Planung
Design
Aukett Europe – Architecture &
Landscape Design

Mitwirkende Sachverständige
Consultants
Whitby Bird – Structure, Mott
MacDonald
Sub-Structure & Civils, Rybka –
M & E

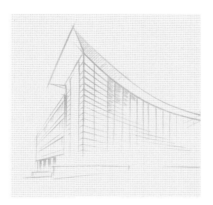

Objekt-Skizze
aus der Entwurfsphase
Preliminary sketch
from the design phase

Flügeldächer markieren den
neuen europäischen Stützpunkt
nach Silicon Valley-Vorbild. Die
Nähe zu London und Heathrow
nährt den Business Park mit
florierender Geschäftigkeit. Rund
40 000 qm Nutzfläche stehen
bereit. Dachform, Glaskonstruk-
tionen und Freiraumgestaltung
sind Ausdruck für den Wandel
in der Industriegesellschaft.
Das von Stahl und Bergbau
gezeichnete Landschaftsbild ist
verblasst.

Wing-shaped roofs mark a new
European trend based on the
architecture of Silicon Valley.
The proximity to London and
Heathrow means this business
park is flourishing. Around
40,000 m² of floor space is ready
for occupation. The roof form,
glazing and freeform design
reflect the changes in industrial
society. The landscape
associated with steel and mining
is giving way to something new.

Außenansichten
Reading International
Business Park
Outside views
Reading International
Business Park

„Architektur hat ihren Sinn erfüllt, wenn sie Besitzer, Bewohner,
die gegenwärtigen und zukünftigen Gesellschaften zu inspirieren
vermag."

„Architecture fulfils its purpose when it inspires
owners, occupiers and the society of today and
tomorrow."

Stuart W. McLarty, Architekt

Potsdam, Germany

Planung
Design
Pysall – Starenberg & Partner,
Braunschweig,
Projektleitung: Dipl.-Ing.
M. Mombeck

Mitwirkende Sachverständige
Consultants
Ing.-Büro K. Krüger, Kiel

Die Akademie- und Verwaltungsgebäude liegen in einer weitläufigen Parklandschaft. Die Verbindung zu dem LBS-Gebäude
erfolgt durch eine vollverglaste
Brücke und einem zwei
Geschosse hohen Hallengang –
beides FW 50-Konstruktionen.
Die Fassade des Gebäudes mit
seinen Treppenhaustürmen und
Erkern ist eine Demonstration
der Vielseitigkeit des Systems
Royal S 65.

The academic and
administration buildings are
situated in an extensive park
landscape. The connection to
the LBS building is formed by
a fully glazed bridge and a
hallway two stores high – both
of FW 50 construction. The
façade of the building with its
staircase towers and oriel bays
demonstrates the versatility
of the Royal S system.

Außenansichten
Sparkassenakademie
und Verwaltung
LBS-Ost
Outside views LBS East
Sparkassenakademie
Administrative Building

Berliner Bank

Poznan, Poland

Planung
Design
STUDIO ADS Sp. z o.o., Arch.
Piotr Z. Barełkowski

Eine Gebäudesanierung mit
Hilfe von Aluminium-Systemen,
aus denen kleinteilige Konstruk-
tionen gefertigt wurden.
Die Fenster in den oberen
Geschossen sind Dreh-Kipp-
Elemente mit feststehenden
Oberlichtern aus Royal S 65.
Die Verglasungen im 1. und
2. OG bestehen aus FW 50 DK-
Konstruktionen, deren Mittelteile
ebenfalls zu Drehkipp-Elementen
ausgebildet wurden.

This building was renovated
using aluminium systems
from which small units were
fabricated. The windows in the
upper floors are Royal S 65 tilt
and turn units with fixed top-
lights. The glazing on the first
and second floors consists of
FW 50 DK constructions, the
central section of which also
features tilt and turn units.

Außen- und
Geschäftshaus
Berliner Bank
Outside and
inside views
Geschäftshaus
Berliner Bank

LEGO Korea Co., Ltd.

I-chon, South Korea

Planung
Design
Ktm. Kwang Sung + Soren

Ein großes Tor lädt ein ins blau-
weiße Lego-Land. In den
Fassaden aus Metallkassetten
sind Fensterelemente aus dem
System Iskotherm bündig eingesetzt. Der Eingangsbereich wird
durch eine vorgesetzte
Konstruktion aus dem Fassaden-
System SK 60 V betont.

An enormous gate invites
visitors to blue-white Legoland.
Windows elements in Schüco
System Iskotherm are
fitted flush into the metal
panel facades. The entrance
area is emphasized by a
projecting construction in the
façade System SK 60 V.

Außenansicht
LEGO Korea Co.
Outside view
LEGO Korea Co.

Brussels, Belgium

Planung
Design
Michel Jaspers & Atelier d´Art
Urbain, Brussels

Ein Bank-Neubau wie für die Ewigkeit errichtet: Granit, Glas und Aluminium sind die dominanten Baustoffe für Fassade und Haupthalle. Bestechend ist die souveräne Handhabung der Aluminiumprofile in verschiedenen Ansichtsbreiten, die sich zu einem stilsicheren Ganzen fügen. Lichtdach aus dem System SK 60, die Fassade aus FW 50.

A new bank building seemingly intended for eternity: granite, glass and aluminium are the dominant materials for façade and main hall. An outstanding feature is the masterly application of the aluminium profiles in various face widths, which create a uniform style. Skylight in SK 60, façade in FW 50.

Außen- und Innenansichten Hoofdkantoor Kredietbank
Outside and inside views Kredietbank Head Office

Vienna, Austria

Planung
Design
Architekturbüro Thomas Feiger,
Vienna

Über einer sich zur Straße
abtreppenden und in Höhe der
Nachbarbebauung vermittelnden
Sockelbebauung erhebt sich
dieser eigenwillige Riese.
Entschlossen strebt er empor
und endet markant in einer auf-
kragenden fünfgeschossigen
Erkernase, die dem Gebäude
Richtung und Bewegung und
einen unverwechselbaren Eigen-
charakter verleiht.
Sämtliche Fassaden differenzie-
ren sich durch plötzliche Rück-
sprünge, schräges Einklappen
oder einfach durch den Wechsel
im Farbton der Brüstungs-
paneele. So erhält das Hochhaus
und jede der vier Fassaden für
den Betrachter ein immer unter-
schiedliches Gesicht.

A unique giant soars above a
pedestal construction, rising
to the height of neighbouring
buildings from steps to the
street at its base. The building
soars above resolutely and ends
pointedly in a projecting
five-storey oriel, which lends
it movement, direction and an
unmistakeably individual
character.
All the façades are differentiated
by unexpected recesses, sloping
recesses or simply by a change
in tone of the spandrel panel
colour. This allows the high-rise
and each of its four façades to
present a constantly changing
face to the observer.

Außenansichten
IZD-Office Center B
Outside views
IZD-Office Centre B

Sonderegger AG

Wil, Switzerland

Planung
Design
ecolo architekten GmbH
Benno und Cornelia Bisegger,
Mörschwil

Mitwirkende Sachverständige
Consultants
Grünenfelder + Lorenz,
Ing. Büro, St. Gallen

Außenansichten
Sonderegger AG
Outside views
Sonderegger AG

Cologne, Germany

Planung
Design
Prof. Erich Schneider-Wessling,
Dipl.-Ing. Hanno Lagemann,
Cologne

Mitwirkende Sachverständige
Consultants
Michael Kraus, Birgit Schlösser,
Dirk Scherdin

Außenansichten
Deutsche Caritas
Outside views
Deutsche Caritas

Das Entwurfskonzept lässt, durch Gliederung, Abstufung und Transparenz, das Verwaltungsgebäude sensibel auf die Maßstäbe der Umgebung reagieren. Die drei in Winkelform angeordneten, ineinander übergehenden Zylinder nehmen mit ihren ein- und ausschwingenden Formen Rücksicht auf den reichhaltigen Baumbestand des Grundstücks. Die Außenhaut der Baukörper setzt sich selbstbewusst von den konventionellen Fassaden der umliegenden Gebäude ab und stellt zugleich durch die facettierte Spiegelung dieser Gebäude den baulichen Kontext auf raffinierte Weise wieder her.

Die markanten Gitterroste sind zugleich Reinigungs- und Fluchtbalkone wie auch Sonnenschutz.

The design concept means that the office is not out of scale with the surrounding environment due to its terraced layout and its transparency. The three cylinders merge together at an angle, showing respect for the abundance of trees on the site with the ebb and flow of their shapes. The outer skin of the building confidently stands out from the conventional façades of nearby buildings and by producing the faceted reflection of these buildings recreates their structural context in a sophisticated way.

The prominent grilles serve both as balconies for cleaning and emergencies, as well as providing solar shading.

Ankara, Turkey

Planung
Design
A Tasarım / Ali Osman Öztürk,
Ankara

Mitwirkende Sachverständige
Consultants
GMW und Vecihi Yıldız

Objekt-Skizze
aus der Entwurfsphase
Preliminary sketch
from the design phase

Alles an diesem Zentrum ist rund, radial oder dreht sich scheinbar um einen anderen Körper. Dem hellen dünneren Pfeiler, der wiederum in einer metallenen Antennensäule endet, ist ein spitz zulaufender elliptischer Hochhausturm vorgestellt. An der Basis tritt die Konstruktion sichtbar nach außen, in Form von zweigeschossigen Säulen. Flankiert werden die Türme von einem Basisbau, dessen Pultdach ebenso bogenförmig gewölbt ist. Die Verwendung von verspiegeltem Sonnenschutzglas verstärkt die Volumenhaftigkeit der einzelnen Gebäudeelemente.

Detailansichten
Armada
Detail views Armada

Everything about this building seems to be round, radial or to rotate around another structure. A tapering, elliptical high-rise tower stands in front of a light, slender pillar, which in turn is completed by a metal antenna column.
At the base, the construction projects outwards in the form of a series of two-storey pillars. Adjacent to the towers is a low-rise building, whose curved monopitch roof complements the circular shapes of the tower. The use of mirrored solar protection glass gives the individual building components a greater sense of volume.

„Kreativ sein, um herausragende Formen zu schaffen, kreativ sein, um die öffentliche Entwicklung zu fördern, kreativ sein, um der Technologie zu huldigen."
„Being creative for outstanding forms, creative for public development and creative for technology."

Ali Osman Öztürk, Architekt

Berlin, Germany

Planung
Design
Prof. Dr.-Ing. Arno Bonanni,
Architekten, Berlin, Germany

Mitwirkende Sachverständige
Consultants
Dipl.-Ing. S. Köhler
Akustik-Labor, Berlin, Germany

Gelungene Ecklösung: Wie ein
Schiffsbug ragt die Spitze des
Gebäudes in den Straßenraum.
Große Bullaugen in der aufge-
ständerten Sockelpartie sowie
die ausgestellten aufgespannten
Sonnensegel unterstützen die-
sen Eindruck. Die auskragenden
Sonnenschutz-Lamellen geben
dem Bau Geschwindigkeit.

A successful solution for a
corner location: The front of the
building rises into the space
above the street like the bow of
a ship. Large portholes in the
raised plinth and sunshades like
unfurled sails continue the
theme. The brise soleil gives the
impression of speed.

Detailansicht Klinik
Hohenzollerndamm
Detail view clinic on
Hohenzollerndamm

Agiplan Group Consultancy and Planning Centre

Mühlheim a. d. Ruhr, Germany

Planung
Design
Foster and Partners, London

Projektsteuerung
Project supervision
agiplan AG,
Mühlheim a. d. Ruhr

Der Fassadenschwung leitet
die Besucher in das Innere des
Gebäudes, zunächst in ein 18 m
hohes Atrium, das Alt- und Neubau verbindet. Das außergewöhnlich großformatige Fassadenraster von 2,70 m, bei
3,60 m Geschosshöhe, nimmt
die Proportionen des Altbaus
auf. Die Gebäudehülle aus
dem System FW 50 ist mit 100
großen, in die Fassade integrierten Senk-Klapp-Lüftungsflügeln
ausgestattet.

The curvature of the façade
leads the visitor to the inner
part of the building, initially
into an 18 m high atrium which
connects the old with the new
building. The unusually large
grid of the façade – 2.70 m in
width by 3.60 m storey height –
adopts the proportions of the
old building. The outer skin of
the building in System FW 50
is fitted with 100 extremely large
top hung-vents integrated into
the façade.

Außenansichten
Beratungs- und
Planungszentrum der
agiplan-Gruppe
Outside views
Agiplan Group
Consultancy and
Planning Centre

Doxford, Great Britain

Planung
Design
Studio E Architects, London

Mitwirkende Sachverständige
Consultants
Rybka Battle Consulting
Engineers, London

Newcastle Photovoltaics
Applications Centre,
Newcastle upon Tyne

Eine der größten Photovoltaik-
Fassaden Europas wurde im
Business Park Doxford installiert.
Die Solarbänder sind 60 m lang,
3 Geschosse hoch und mit
52.000 poly-kristallinen Solar-
zellen bestückt. Von den insgesamt 900 m² Fassadenfläche
sind 532 m² solaraktiv und
erzeugen 55.100 kWh Jahres-
leistung. Das für den konventionellen und photovoltaischen
Bereich eingesetzte System ist
SK 60V.

One of the largest photovoltaic
façades in Europe was installed
in the Business park at Doxford.
The bands of solar units are 60
m long. 3 storeys high and fitted
with 52,000 polycrystalline
solar cells. Of the façade's
900m² surface area, 532 m² is
made up of solar panels,
producing 55,100 kWh per year.
The system SK 60V is used
for both the conventional and
photovoltaic areas.

Außen- und
Innenansichten
The Solar Office
Outside and
inside views
The Solar Office

Fornebu, Norway

Planung
Design
NBBJ-HUS-PKA architects,
Joint venture: NBBJ architects,
USA
HUS arkitekter, Norway
Per Knudsen arkitektkontor,
Norway

Futuristisch anmutende Architekturlandschaft. Mit einem großen Schwung wird ein weiter Raum geschaffen, der begrenzt wird durch diese wegkippenden, stürzenden schiefen Formen, die ihrerseits unter einem weit überdeckenden Dach Schutz finden. Viele Formen scheinen direkt und schief aus dem Erdreich herauszubrechen. Das Auge findet ständig neue Nischen und Kanten. Insgesamt aber streben die Bauteile nicht in die Höhe, sondern scheinen eher von der Weite der norwegischen Natur inspiriert zu sein, der sie entgegen zu streben scheinen.

A futuristic architectural landscape. The broad, sweeping construction creates a vast space, contained by irregular tilting and plunging shapes, themselves protected by a generously overhanging roof. Many of the shapes seem to burst forth from the soil – directly and at an angle. The eye constantly finds new niches and edges.
However, the overall impression is one of width rather than height, the building stretching out towards its apparent inspiration – the expanse of the Norwegian countryside.

Außenansichten
Telenor Fornebu
Outside views
Telenor Fornebu

„Die Architektur verleiht der Firmenzentrale und ihren Arbeitsräumen eine neue Realität und Überschwenglichkeit – ein vorher kaum zu erahnendes Gefühl der Inspiration."
"The architecture has transformed the headquarters and working spaces with a new reality and exuberance – an inspired spirit scarcely imagined before."

Bjørn C. Sørum, Peter Pran, Architekten

Die vorangegangenen Objekte sowie die Bauwerke dieser Doppelseiten sind nur eine Auswahl perfekter Antworten auf die Frage nach Büro- und Verwaltungsgebäuden von hoher Gestaltungs- und Umsetzungsqualität.

The projects shown on the previous page and the buildings on this double page are just a selection of perfect solutions to requests for high quality office and administrative buildings.

Hötorgscity, Höghus
Stockholm, Sweden

Hanseforum Hamburg
Germany

Office Building
Vienna, Austria

Löwentor centre
Stuttgart, Germany

Residential and office building
Valentinskamp
Hamburg, Germany

WMF-Building
Berlin, Germany

Public prosecutor's office
Naples, Italy

Warnowtherme
Rostock, Germany

Refacing development
Berliner Tor
Hamburg, Germany

New library building
Bernburg, Germany

DEBITEL Building 4
Stuttgart, Germany

Kreissparkasse Riesa,
Germany

BILLA AG Centre
Vienna Neudorf,
Austria

Plange Mühle
Düsseldorf, Germany

VEDIOR BIS
St. Denis, France

Kreuzeckbahn
Garmisch-Partenkirchen,
Germany

Dorottya-Hof
Budapest, Hungary

Salim Al Sayegh
Building
Sharjan, UAE

Mapo Inhabitants Hall
Seoul, Korea

Hamar town hall
Hamar, Norway

Oficinas en „La
Florida"
Madrid, Spain

Dutch embassy
Ankara, Turkey

Eon-Zentrale
Düsseldorf, Germany

Bergisel ski-slope
Innsbruck, Austria

MPD-Microelectronic
Packaging Dresden,
Germany

National Bank of
AbuDhabi, UAE

Moskovit AG
cultural centre
Moscow, Russia

Liesbosch
Neuwegein,
Netherlands

Etisalat
Telecommunications
Ajman, UAE

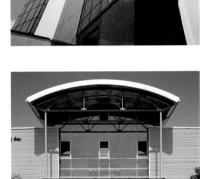

Tobit
Ahaus, Germany

Samsung Noble
Country
Kyounggi-do, Korea

Solaris
Capelle a/d Ijssel,
Netherland

Fortis
Brussels, Belgium

Channel Tower
Hamburg, Germany

Munich City Tower
Munich, Germany

Business Avenue
Dubai, UAE

Savings bank
Neubrandenburg,
Germany

Public and
research library
Kelsterbach, Germany

Handelsblatt
publishing house
Frankfurt/Main,
Germany

Federal press and
information office
Berlin, Germany

science museum
Freiburg, Germany

Centrum Nord
office building
Munster, Germany

Pharmexa
Hørsholm, Denmark

177

Gewerbe- und Industriebauten
sind Bauten, die besonderen
funktionalen Bedingungen für
die Herstellung von Produkten
sowie deren Verteilung dienen.
Optimierte logistische Ablauf-
prozesse bestimmen den Workflow und damit die funktionale
Grundrissstruktur sowie die
Gesamtarchitektur.

Industrial buildings are buildings
that provide the particular
functional conditions required
for both manufacturing products
and their distribution. Optimised
logistic processes define the
workflow and therefore also the
basis of the outline structure
and the overall architecture.

Gewerbe- und Industriebauten
Industrial buildings

Woking, Great Britain

Planung
Design
Foster and Partners, London

Projektmanagement
Project management
Arlington Securities Ltd, London

Fachingenieure
Specialist engineers
Ove Arup & Partners, London

Die Planung und Ausführung des McLaren Technology Centers ist das Ergebnis eines interaktiven Expertenteams. Unter Berücksichtigung der Kriterien Kosten- und Risikominimierung sowie Qualitätssteigerung unter Beibehaltung der gestalterischen Flexibilität war Schüco als Teil dieses Teams für Planung und Realisierung der Gebäudehülle zuständig.

The planning and development of the McLaren Technology Centre was the result of work by an expert team working closely together. Giving due consideration to the criteria of cost, risk management and quality whilst retaining design flexiblity, Schüco was part of this team, responsible for planning and creating the building envelope.

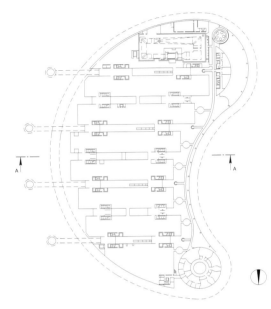

Schnitt Erdgeschoss
Section ground floor

Detailansichten McLaren
Technology Centre
Detail views McLaren
Technology Centre

Detailansichten McLaren
Technology Centre
Detail views McLaren
Technology Centre

Schnitt A-A
Section A-A

Gerade Linien, ausschließlich
rechte Winkel, Glas und
schwarzer Stahl verleihen dieser
kubischen Anlage eine Anmutung von Klarheit und Einfach-
heit.
Gemäß dem Prinzip von Mies
van der Rohe: „Weniger ist
mehr" besticht das Objekt durch
zweckorientierte Zurückhaltung
und einer beeindruckenden
Geradlinigkeit.
Die Structural Glazing Fassade
mit filigranen, vertikalen
Windverbänden gliedert das
Gebäude großflächig.

With straight lines, right angles
everywhere, glass and black
steel this cuboid building gives
and impression of clarity and
simplicity. Following the Mies
van der Rohe principle: "less is
more", its deliberate restraint
and magnificent rectilinear
appearance makes the builing
impressive. The stuctural glazing
façade with fine vertical bracing
divides the building into large
sections.

Detailansichten Boots
Detail views Boots

Valkenswaard, Netherlands

Planung
Design
Meyer Adviesburo
Bouwprojekten
Architekt Rien van Luyt

Außenansichten
Pool Quip
Outside views
Pool Quip

Neoplan Omnibus GmbH

Plauen, Germany

Planung
Design
Herbert Gergs
Freier Architekt
Stuttgart-Möhringen

Mirae High Technology Research Center

Dongtan-myun, Hwasung-gun,
Kyunggi-do, South Korea

Planung
Design
ATEC Architects & Associates
Inc.

Außenansichten
Neoplan
Outside views
Neoplan

Detailansichten
Mirae Center
Detail views
Mirae Center

Dresden, Germany

Bauherr
Client
Volkswagen AG
Wolfsburg

Architekt und Gesamtplaner
Architect and overall planner
Henn Architekten,
Munich/Berlin

Fassadenplanung
Façade design
Hussak Ingenieurgesellschaft,
Lauingen

Ausführung der Fassaden des
Manufakturbereichs
Façade construction for the
production area
Mero GmbH & Co. KG,
Würzburg

Ausführung der Fassaden
des Erlebnisbereichs
Design of the façades on
the activity zone
Anders Metallbau GmbH,
Fritzlar

**Aufgabenstellung
und Programm**
der Automobilmanufaktur
Dresden GmbH, einer Tochter-
gesellschaft des Volkswagen-
Konzerns, war die bauliche
Realisierung eines innovativen
Konzepts, bei dem die – weitgehend von Hand erfolgende –
Endmontage des neuen Ober-
klassemodells „Phaeton" für den
Kunden, aber auch für das Auto-
interessierte Publikum allgemein
zur Schau gestellt werden sollte.
Auch die Auslieferung an den
Kunden sollte „inszeniert"
werden.

Project requirements
The Dresden GmbH car plant,
a subsidiary of the Volkswagen
Group, was the culmination
of an innovative plan to open
the final assembly line of the
hand-built luxury Phaeton both
to potential customers and to
the general public. It was also
designed to "stage" the roll-out
to the customer.

Der Bau sollte zu diesem Zweck außen und innen völlig verglast sein. Ein spezieller „Erlebnisbereich" sollte nicht nur der Auslieferung an den Kunden dienen, sondern mit Ausstellungen, technischen Simulationen usw. über das Thema „Auto" und „VW-Konzern" informieren, zugleich aber auch den Rahmen bieten für allgemeine kulturelle Veranstaltungen wie z.B. das „Philosophische Quartett" des ZDF.

Das Land Sachsen als eine der Wiegen des deutschen Autobaues und die Stadt Dresden als eine der „Weltkultur-Städte" erschienen für die Realisierung dieses Konzepts besonders prädestiniert.

Städtebauliche Situation
Der quadratische Gesamtkomplex der Manufaktur steht in Sichtweite des Stadtzentrums am Straßburger Platz auf dem kriegszerstörten Messegelände und grenzt an den „großen Garten", eine ausgedehnte barocke Parkanlage um das ehemalige „Gartenpalais" von 1680. Voraussetzung für den Standort

war allerdings u.a. die Zusage einer emissionsfreien Produktion und einer verkehrsfreundlichen Anlieferung der vorgefertigten Autoteile vom Logistikzentrum am Stadtrand mittels speziell entwickelter „Cargo-Tram-Züge" auf den Gleisen der Straßenbahn.

Die Manufaktur ist damit ein Symbol für die partielle Abkehr von der „Charta von Athen", die die räumliche Trennung von

Wohnen und Industriearbeit postulierte. Dresden wird auf diese Weise um eine neue identitätstiftende Sehenswürdigkeit bereichert.

Entwurfskonzept
Die Mehrgeschossigkeit des eigentlichen Manufakturbereiches sowie die Anordnung des Erlebnisbereiches ergeben sich einerseits aus dem Grundstückszuschnitt und der städtebaulichen Situation, andererseits aus

The building therefore needed to be fully glazed inside and outside. As well as for rolling out new vehicles, a special "activity zone" was designed to provide information about cars and the VW Group through exhibitions and technical simulations, and also to serve as a venue for general cultural events, for example, the discussion forum "The Philosophical Quartet" broadcast on ZDF.

The state of Saxony, cradle of the German automotive industry and Dresden, international city of culture, seemed the natural choice for this project.

City location
The rectangular complex lies on Straßburger Platz, within view of the city centre, on the site of the exhibition centre destroyed in the war. It borders the "great garden", an extensive baroque park around the former "garden palace" which dates back to 1680.

Before this site could be approved for the project, however, emission-free production had to be guaranteed. Special "CarGoTrams" which run on the tramlines had to be developed to ensure that transportation of prefabricated parts from the logistics centre on the outskirts of the city would not cause traffic congestion.

The plant thus heralds a departure from the "Charter of Athens", which advocated keeping residential and industrial areas apart. As a result, the Dresden skyline has been further enriched with another unique landmark.

Design
The shape of the site, its urban location and a desire to make the production processes involved in final assembly accessible to the public all influenced the design of the multi-storey production area and the layout of the "activity zone".

Straßburger Platz, more an intersection of two busy streets, is now completed at its southeast corner by the 22 m high production area, which fronts the whole complex on the north-east and south-east sides.

On the corner, the "activity zone" nestles on a large terrace over the basement. Its large glass walls offer views of the city centre and great garden, and are subdivided by the 40 m high "vehicle cylinder", the extensively enclosed building structure for vehicle roll-out, a customer lounge and small administration section.

The entrance to this terrace and the "activity zone", and also the roll-out area for new cars have been created using lightweight bridges over the water features. The prefabricated automotive parts are delivered to a bay at basement level on the south-east side of the production area.

den Funktionsabläufen der Endmontage und den Einblicksmög-
lichkeiten in diese Endmontage
vom Erlebnisbereich aus.

Der Straßburger Platz – eher
eine Kreuzung zweier stark
befahrener Straßen – erhält an
seiner SO-Ecke jetzt einen Halt
durch den ca. 22 m hohen Baukörper des Manufakturbereiches,
der den Gesamtkomplex auf der
NO- und SO-Seite winkelförmig
begrenzt.

In diesen Winkel „schmiegt"
sich auf einer großen Terrasse
über dem UG der „Erlebnisbereich". Seine großen Glaswände
öffnen sich zum Stadtzentrum
und zum großen Garten, sind
aber durch den 40 m hohen
„Fahrzeug-Zylinder" und die
weitgehend geschlossenen Baukörper der Fahrzeug-Ausliefe-
rung und Kunden-Lounge sowie
eines kleinen Verwaltungs-
Traktes durchbrochen und
gegliedert.

Den Publikumszugang zu dieser
Terrasse und zum Erlebnisbereich bzw. die Abfahrt für die
ausgelieferten Wagen bilden

leichte Brücken über die vorgelagerten Wasserflächen. Die
Anlieferung der vorgefertigten
Autoteile und die sonstige
Andienung erfolgt in einem
auf UG-Ebene liegenden Hof an
der SO-Seite des Manufakturbereiches.

Konstruktion der äußeren und inneren Glaswände
Im Erlebnisbereich sind die
1-schaligen äußeren Glaswände
in einer serienmäßigen Schüco-
Aufsatzkonstruktion mit Isolierverglasung auf „konventioneller"
Stahlrohr-Unterkonstruktion ausgeführt.

Im Manufakturbereich sind die
äußeren, i.d.R. nicht-Klima-
trennenden Schalen in Schüco-
Aufsatzkonstruktion mit Einfachverglasung ausgeführt. Sie sind
an massiven Stahl-Flachprofilen
von den Stahl-Kragarmen auf
der Dachdecke abgehängt
und zur Aufnahme seitl. Kräfte
gegen das Tragsystem des
Baukörpers bzw. im Bereich

Design of internal and
external curtain walling
In the activity area, the single
glazed outer curtain walling
is a standard Schüco add-on
construction with insulated
glazing on a "conventional"
steel tube substructure.

In the production area, the
external skins, which do not
constitute a climate barrier, are
a Schüco add-on construction
with single glazing. They are
attached to the massive steel
flats of the steel cantilevers on
the roof and reinforced to
support lateral forces against
the load-bearing system of the
building structure and then
against the inner skin of the
glazed twin wall façades.

The inner skin, which divides
the outside temperature from
the interior environment, and the
glass wall to the "activity zone"
feature special Schüco profiles
with insulation glazing. These
are fixed to pre-tensioned

Gesamtansicht
von Westen
Overall view from
the west

Blick aus dem
Manufaktur-Bereich
nach NW
View from the
manufacturing area
to NW

Schnitt A-A
Selection A-A

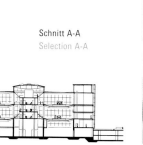

Grundriss
2. Obergeschoss
Floor plan
2nd floor

01 Montage auf Schuppenband
02 Montage an Gehängebahn
03 Karosserielager
04 PKW-Rampe
05 Betriebsbüros (in glasüberdachtem Lichthof)
06 Fahrzeugzylinder für 300 PKW
07 Erlebnisbereich
08 Auslieferung und Kunden-Lounge
09 Büros der Verwaltung
10 Sitzungsraum

01 Assembly on conveyor belt
02 Assembly on hanging conveyor
03 Car body warehouse
04 Car ramp
05 Offices (light well)
06 Vehicle cylinder for 300 cars
07 Activity area
08 Roll-out area and customer lounge
09 Administrative offices
10 Conference room

Ansicht von
Nordosten bei Nacht
View from the
north-east at night

der Glas-Doppelfassaden gegen die innere Schale ausgesteift.

Die Klima-trennenden inneren Schalen und die Glaswand zum Erlebnisbereich sind in Schüco-Sonderprofilen mit Isolierverglasung ausgeführt, die zur Abtragung der vertikalen und horizontalen Kräfte an vorgespannten Edelstahlseilen befestigt sind.

Die äußere und innere Schale sind auf diese Weise jeweils mit einem Minimum an statischem Querschnitt konstruiert und wirken dadurch sehr elegant und transparent!

Die durchlüfteten Glas-Doppelfassaden

wurden an der SO- und SW-Ecke des Manufakturbereiches angeordnet, wo Arbeitsbereiche mit geregelten Temperaturen direkt an das Außenklima grenzen (vergl. Grundriss 2.OG). Ihr Gesamt-k-Wert beträgt 1,2 W/m² K, ihr Gesamtenergiedurchlassgrad g bei heruntergelassenen Sonnenschutzlamellen 0.11.

Diese Glas-Doppelfassaden sind in den folgenden Detailzeichnungen dargestellt.

stainless steel cables to transfer the horizontal and vertical loads. This means that the outer and inner skins are each constructed with a minimum of structural cross section, giving an impression of transparency and elegance.

Ventilated glazed twin wall façades

The south-east and south-west corners of the production area

are twin wall façades, where working areas with regulated temperatures are directly adjacent to outside air (see floor plan of 2nd floor). The total k value is 1.2 W/m²K, its total energy transmission level with the solar shading louvres down is 0.11.

The details of these glazed twin wall façades are shown in the following drawings.

Detailschnitte V4 und
H durch Profile der
Glas-Doppelfassade
V4 and H section
details through
the profiles of the
glazed twin wall façade

Schnitt und Grundriss
Glas-Doppelfassade
Section and floor plan
of the glazed twin wall
façade

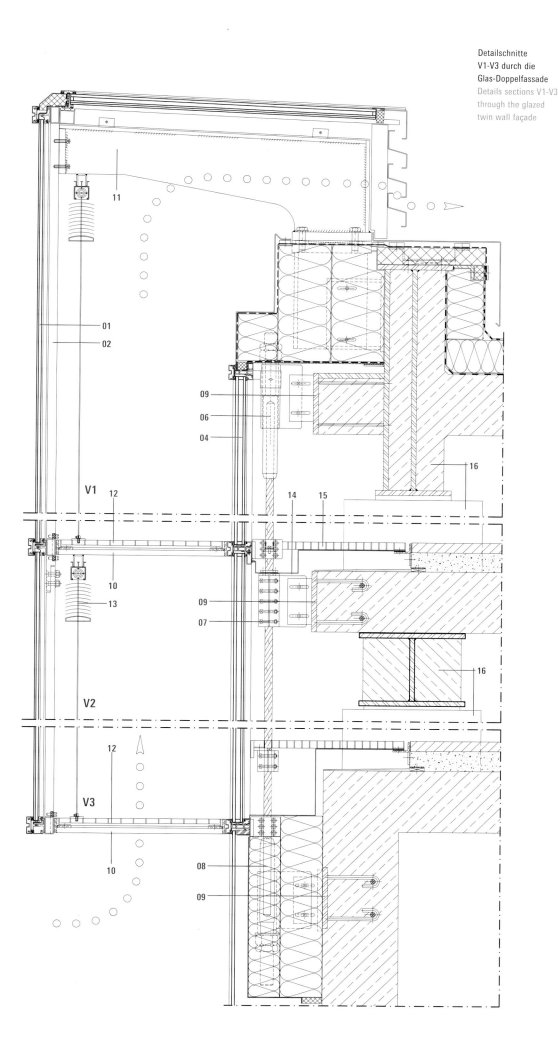

Detailschnitte
V1-V3 durch die
Glas-Doppelfassade
Details sections V1-V3
through the glazed
twin wall façade

Legende zu den Detailschnitten H und V1-V4:

01 Einfachverglasung in VSG mit vertikalem
   Stufenfalz, d nach stat. Erfordernis, mit glasbün-
   digen Aluminium-Deckschalen
02 vertikale Stahl-Flachprofile 60/40, e = 2,00 m
   mit Aluminium-Aufsatzprofilen
03 horizontale Riegel aus Stahlrohr 70/40
04 Isolierverglasung mit Argongas-Füllung, außen
   ESG mit Reflexbeschichtung, innen Floatglas
   LZR 12 mm, d nach stat. Erfordernis
05 thermisch getrennte Aluminium-Sonderprofile
   an vorgespannten Edelstahl-Seilen Ø 30 mm,
   Seilklemmen aus Edelstahl-Guss
06 oberer Fixpunkt der Seile
07 Seilklemmen aus Edelstahl-Guss zur
   Seilhalterung und -führung
08 untere Spannschlösser der Seile
09 einbetonierte Stahlverankerungen zu 06–08
10 Stahl-Flachprofile 20/60 zur Aussteifung der
   äußeren Schale und als Auflager für
   Gitterrost 12
11 verz. Stahl-Kragarme e = 2,00 m mit
   oberseitiger Isolierverglasung zur Abhängung
   von 02
12 verz. Gitterroste für Glasreinigung und Wartung
13 Aluminium-Lamellenstoren b = 100 mm
14 rauchdichte Abschottungen aus verz.
   Stahlblech
15 Aluminium-Gitterroste
16 Tragsystem des Gebäudes aus vorgefertigten
   ausbetonierten Stahlrohrstützen und Profilstahl-
   Unterzügen

Key to the section details H and V1 to V4:

01 Single glazing in laminated safety glass with
   vertical stepped rebate to suit structural
   requirements, with aluminium cover caps fitted
   flush to the glass
02 Vertical steel flats 60/40, e = 2.00 m with
   aluminium add-on profiles
03 Horizontal transom made of steel tube 70/40
04 Twin wall argon gas-filled glazing, external toughened safety glass with reflex
05 Thermally broken special aluminium profiles on
   pre-tensioned Ø 30 mm stainless steel cables,
   swaged cable ends made of die-cast stainless
   steel
06 Top cable fixing point
07 Swaged cable ends made of die-cast stainless
   steel for cable brackets and guides
08 Cable turnbuckles at the base
09 Steel anchor points embedded in concrete for
   06–08
10 Steel flats 20/60 for bracing the outer skin and
   as support for grille 12
11 Galvanised steel cantilevers e = 2.00 m, with
   insulated glazing over the top, for attaching 02
12 Galvanised grilles for cleaning glass and
   maintenance
13 Aluminium louvre blinds, b = 100 mm
14 Smoke-proof dividers made of sheet steel
15 Aluminium grilles
16 Structural support system made from
   prefabricated steel tube supports with concrete
   and steel girders

Erfurt, Germany

Planung
Design
IFB Planungsgruppe Dr. Braschel
GmbH, Stuttgart

Mitwirkende Sachverständige
Consultants
Stephan Schiller, Büro für
Fenster- und Fassadentechnik,
Kornwestheim

Ein strenges Raster aus großflächigen, querformatigen
Glasfeldern bestimmt das
Fassadenbild der neuen Messe.
Dahinter liegt eine Stahlkonstruktion, die den technischen
Charakter betont. Die Fassaden-
systeme SK 60V und FW 50
wurden im Fenster- und Türen-
bereich mit Royal S 65 kombiniert.

An exact grid of large horizontal
glass panels determines the
elevational treatment of the new
exhibition centre. Behind the
façade is the steel construction
which emphasises the technical
character of the building.
The façade systems SK 60V
and FW 50 are combined in the
window and door sections with
Royal S 65.

Außenansichten
Messe Erfurt
Outside views
Erfurt exhibition centre

Kirchheim, Germany

Planung
Design
Fiebiger GmbH,
Architekten u. Ingenieure,
Kaiserslautern

Außenansicht Keiper
Outside view Keiper

Alcina Cosmetic

Bielefeld, Germany

Planung
Design
Blum/Spornitz Architekten,
Bielefeld

Kraftwerk Schwarze Pumpe

Schwarze Pumpe, Germany

Planung
Design
Angerer & Feuser, Architekten,
Munich

Außenansicht Alcina
Outside view Alcina

Außenansichten Kraft-
werk Schwarze Pumpe
Outside views
Kraftwerk Schwarze
Pumpe

Chemnitz, Germany

Planung
Design
Dipl.-Ing. Arch., Dipl.-Ing. Geod.
Peter Henkel, Geislingen

Der sich auf 16 Geschosse auf-
türmende Gebäudekomplex ist
ein anschauliches Beispiel für
die Vielseitigkeit der Schüco
Systeme. FW 50DK für die
Vertikal- und Polygon-Fassaden,
Royal S 65 für Lochfenster.

The building complex rising up
to 16 storeys is a typical
example demonstrating the
flexibility of Schüco systems.
FW 50DK for the vertical and
polygon façades, Royal S 65 for
the individual windows.

Außenansichten
Solaris-Tower
Outside views
Solrais-Tower

Berlin-Adlershof, Germany

Bauherr
Client
Wista-Management GmbH,
Berlin (im Auftrag des Berliner
Senats)

Entwurf und Ausführungs-
planung
Design and construction
planning
sauerbruch hutton architekten,
Berlin

Projektleitung
Project management
Klaus de Winder,
Holger Frielingsdorf

Ausschreibung und Objekt-
überwachung
Specifications and
project supervision
Harms & Partner,
Berlin/Hannover

Fassadenberatung
Façade consultant
Michael Lange, beratender
Ingenieur VBI Berlin/Hannover

Technische Gebäudeausrüstung
und Simulation der Wärme-
und Strömungsverhältnisse in
der Doppelfassade
Fixtures and fittings, and
simulation of heat and air flow
in the twin wall façade
Zibell, Willner & Partner,
Berlin/Köln

Ausführung der Fassaden
Façade design
Radeburger Fensterbau GmbH,
Radeburg-Bärwalde (Sachsen),
Gebr. Schneider, Stimpfach

Das „Innovationszentrum für
Optik, Optoelektronik und
Lasertechnologie" – kurz
„Photonikzentrum" – gehörte zu
den ersten Neubauten, die nach
den Vorstellungen des Berliner
Senats auf dem Gebiet des ehe-
maligen Flughafens Johannisthal
realisiert wurden. Hier sollte
zwischen und mit den heterogenen baulichen Relikten der
Technik- und Wissenschaftsent-
wicklung eine neue „Stadt für
Wirtschaft und Wissenschaft"
entstehen. Der Planungsauftrag
für 2 Bauten des Photonik-
zentrums – ein 3-geschossiger
Labor- und Bürobau und ein
1-geschossiger Hallenbau – war
das Ergebnis eines Einladungs-
wettbewerbs.

The "innovation centre for
optics, opto-electronics and
laser technology" (known as the
Photonics Centre) is one of the
first new buildings on the site of
the former Johannistal Airport,
based on an idea from the Berlin
senate. Here, between and
alongside the heterogeneous
relics of technology and
scientific development, a new
"City for Economics and
Science" is planned. The
winning design from the
competition held consisted of
two buildings for the Photonics
Centre: a three storey laboratory
and office block, and a single
storey hall.

Das Entwurfskonzept der
Architekten mit zwei transparent
wirkenden amöbenförmigen
Bauten und dem diagonalen
Verlauf der Gasse zwischen diesen beiden Bauten, wie auch der
Erschließungsflure als Rückgrat
des Laborbaues, nutzt die zur
Verfügung stehende Grund-
stücksfläche optimal ohne einen
sich anschließenden alten
Baumbestand zu beeinträchti-
gen. Der Entwurf nimmt dabei
das Thema der funktionsbedingt
freien Bauformen älterer wie
auch neuer Forschungsein-
richtungen in dem Gelände auf
und wirkt – im Verein mit der
oszillierenden Farbigkeit der
Fassaden – damit zugleich für
die künftigen Nutzer identitäts-
bildend.

The architect's draft concept –
with two transparent amoeboid
buildings linked by a diagonal
passageway, and development
floors forming the backbone
of the laboratory – makes the
best possible use of the space
available, without impacting
on the stock of mature trees
nearby. The design underlines
the theme of unrestricted
building shapes for old and new
research facilities on the site
and, allied with the oscillating
colour of the façades, also
builds an identity for the future
user.

The load-bearing system for the
laboratory building consists of
different depths of the building
structure (as required for dark

Ansicht der
1-geschossigen
Versuchshalle von
Südwesten
View single storey
hall from south-west

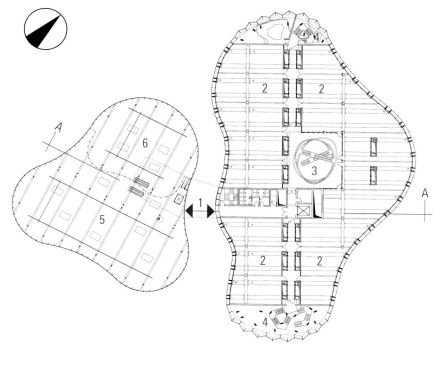

Das tragende System des Laborbaues ergibt sich aus den diffe-
rierenden Tiefen des Baukörpers
(entsprechend den Anforderungen an Dunkellabors), sowie aus
dem mäanderförmigen Profil der
Geschossdecken, deren trogför-
mige Betonfertigteil-Unterzüge
die Versorgung der Labors mit
Medien aus dem Boden ermöglichen. Im Bereich der hochlie-
genden Deckenfelder erfolgt die
Versorgung dagegen von oben.

Aus diesen trogförmigen Unterzügen resultieren dann die
Betonfertigteil-Doppelstützen,
die in der Flurzone die Schächte
für Steig- und Fall-Leitungen
und außen die Auftriebs-
schächte für die Doppelfassade
flankieren.

Grundriss
und Schnitt A-A
Floor plan
and section A-A

rooms) and the meandering
profile of the ceilings, whose
trough-shaped concrete girders
allow the laboratory to be
supplied with media from the
ground. The upper intermediate
floors are supplied from above.

These trough-shaped girders
then form the prefabricated
concrete double supports. In the
floor area, the supports flank the
shafts for rising and falling
cables; outside, they flank the
ventilation shafts for the twin
wall façade.

Prinzip-Schnitt
durch das Labor
Principal section
through the laboratory

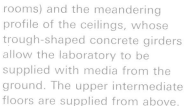

Axonometrie des
tragenden Systems
Axonometry of the
support system

Vertikal-Schiebefenster
als Kastenfenster
mit seitlichem
Auftriebsschacht
Vertical sliding window
as a box window with
side ventilation shaft

Raumhohe Drehflügel
ermöglichen den
Zugang zu den
Auftriebsschächten
Room-height side hung
vents allow access to
the ventilation shafts

Das Prinzip einer Doppelfassade, in diesem Fall mit allseitiger Abschottung des Luftzwischenraumes vor den Fenstern jedes Geschosses (also „Kastenfenstern"), die durch Abluftöffnungen mit einem seitlich angekoppelten Auftriebsschacht verbunden sind (also eine „Kasten-Schacht-Fassade"), wurde aus folgenden Gründen gewählt:

- Verringerung der Wärmeverluste im Winter durch die Pufferzone zwischen innerer und äußerer Schale,
- Möglichkeit natürlicher Fensterlüftung infolge reduzierter Windanströmung auf die innere, klimatrennende Schale,
- dadurch auch Möglichkeit der Nachtlüftung zur Auskühlung der Gebäude-Speichermassen (bei gleichzeitigem Einstiegschutz) und damit deutliche Verringerung der Betriebszeiten von stationären Kühlflächen bzw. raumlufttechnischen Anlagen,
- Verbesserung des Schutzes gegen Außenlärm bei geöffneten Fenstern und gleichzeitige Unterbindung der Schall-Längsleitung im Luftzwischenraum.

A twin wall façade – with cross-walls in the interspace on all sides of the windows in each storey (i.e. "box" windows), which are linked by air outlet openings to a side ventilation shaft (i.e. a "box shaft façade") – was chosen for this project for the following reasons:

- Reduction of heat loss in winter, due to the buffer zone between the inner and outer skins
- Option of natural ventilation through the windows as a result of reduced wind impact on the inner skin
- Option of night cooling to cool down the storage mass of the building, thus significantly reducing the operating times of stationary cool areas
- Improved protection from outside noise when windows are open and simultaneous prevention of noise transfer in the air space

Die Glasfassadenkonstruktion des Hallenbaues
The glass façade construction of the hall

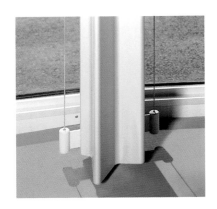

Horizontalschnitt
durch Pfosten der
Glasfassade
Horizontal section
through the mullion of
the glass façade

Fußpunkt des Pfostens
der Glasfassade
Base point details for
the mullion of the glass
façade

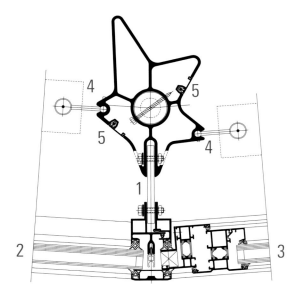

1 Schwerter zur
  Halterung der
  Glasfassade
2 Festverglasung
3 Klappflügel für Zuluft
4 Spannhalter für
  Lamellenstoren
5 Kanäle für elektr.
  Zuleitungen zu
  Stellmotoren

1 Brackets for fixing
  the glass façade
2 Fixed glazing
3 Top hung vent for
  incoming air
4 Clamping bracket
  for louvre blinds
5 Channels for
  electrical cables to
  servo-motors

Die Konstruktion der Doppel-
fassade des Laborbaues
Twin wall façade construction
for the laboratory

Vertikalschnitt in
Ebene Kastenfenster
Vertical section
at box window level

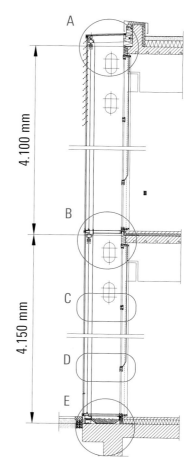

4.100 mm

4.150 mm

Vertikalschnitte A-E
Vertical sections A-E

1 Vertikal-Schiebefenster mit 2Scheiben-IV
2 Pfosten-Riegel-Konstruktion mit 1Scheiben-VSG
3 1Scheiben-Sonnenschutz-VSG
4 Stahlrohr 40/40/5 als Aussteifung zwischen den
   beiden Schalen
5 Zuluftschlitze h = 30 mm
6 Abluftöffnungen zu Auftriebsschacht
7 Horizontal-Abschottung aus Warzenblech
8 Gitterrost über Tauwasser-Auffangrinne mit
   Kiesschüttung
9 raumhoher Drehflügel

1 Vertical sliding window with 2 panes of
   insulation glazing
2 Transom/mullion construction with 1 pane of
   laminated safety glass
3 1 pane of solar protection laminated safety glass
4 Steel tube 40/40/5 as reinforcement between
   the two skins
5 Air inlet holes, h = 30 mm
6 Air outlet openings for ventilation shaft
7 Horizontal cross-walls made of warted plate
8 Grille across condensation water collection gully
   with loose-fill gravel
9 Room-height side hung vent

Horizontalschnitte
durch Doppelstützen =
Auftriebsschacht (li)
und Fensterfelder =
Kastenfenster (re)
Horizontal sections
through double
supports = ventilation
shaft (left) and glazed
areas = box window
(right)

Merryhill, Great Britain

Planung
Design
Percy Thomas, Birmingham

Ein Gebäudekomplex mit vielen attraktiven Details, dessen Dach von ringsum angeordneten, silberfarbenen Säulen „getragen" wird. Das Schüco System FW 50 dient für die Festverglasungen, Iskotherm für interessante Klapp- und Schwingflügel-Fenster.

A building complex full of attractive details, the roof being "supported" by silver-coloured pillars arranged around the building. Schüco system FW 50 was chosen for the fixed glazing, Iskotherm for the interesting of top hung and horizontal pivot windows.

Außenansichten
Point North
Outside views
Point North

Edificio del I.N.S.S.

Madrid, Espana

Planung
Design
Arquitecto José Antonio Galea
Fernández, Madrid

Eine Fassaden-Konstruktion der
außergewöhnlichen Art: Frei-
stehende Betonpfeiler tragen ein
gläsernes Schutzschild zur
Straßenseite und zugleich die
Geschosse des Gebäudes:
raumhoch, dunkelblau verglast
auf Basis des Schüco Systems
SK 60V.

A very unusual kind of façade
construction: free-standing
concrete columns support a
glazed screen facing the street,
while the storeys of the building
are clad with room-high dark-
blue glazing based on Schüco
system SK 60V.

Detailansichten
Edificio del I.N.S.S.
Detail views
Edificio del I.N.S.S.

Viborg, Denmark

Planung
Design
Arkitektfirmaet Kjelgaard &
Pedersen, Viborg

Mitwirkende Sachverständige
Consultants
Kjølhede, Mammen & Serup

Die fortschrittliche Technologie
der Kraft-Wärme-Kopplung in
einer angemessenen architektonischen Präsentation. Zwei
gewölbte Schalen mit beschich-
teten Blechen umschließen den
technischen Kern, den eine
Aluminium-Glas-Konstruktion
schützt und zugleich offenlegt.
Gearbeitet wurde mit den
schmalen Systemen FW 50 und
FW 50S, die großflächige
Fassadenraster erlauben.

The progressive technology of
thermal power presented in an
appropriate architecture. Two
vaulted shells with coated metal
sheeting surround the technical
core, which is protected and
at the same time made
transparent by an aluminium
glass construction. The narrow
face width systems FW 50 and
FW 50S were used, allowing
large facade module widths.

Munich, Germany

Planung
Design
Architekten BDA/DWB
Prof. Kaup, Dr. Scholz
Dipl.-Ing. Jesse + Partner,
Munich
Obermeyer Planen + Beraten,
Munich

Mitwirkende Sachverständige
Consultants
Dipl.-Ing. Michael Lange,
Hanover

Überall wo auf dem Münchener
Messegelände Gebäude mit
Fassaden, Fenstern und Türen
aus Aluminium-Systemen zu
sehen sind, handelt es sich um
Schüco Konstruktionen. Für die
Fassaden, die die große Ost-
West-Achse abschließen, wurde
eine Sonderausführung des
Systems SK 60V entwickelt. Für
die Fenster und Türen entschied
man sich für Royal S 65.

At the Munich exhibition
centre, all the aluminum system
façades, which align the main
east-west axis, a special
construction of system SK 60V
was developed. System
Royal S 65 was chosen for the
windows and doors.

Außenansichten
Messe München
Outside views Munich
exhibition centre

Hotels sind Beherbergungs-
stätten, die mit unterschied-
lichstem Komfort in der Raum-
qualität und Ausstattung dem
Gast den Aufenthalt angenehm
gestalten. In Hoteltypen, wie
First Class-, Art- oder Design-
Hotels, wird das Raumangebot
und das umgebende Ambiente
in besonderer Weise inszeniert.

Hotels provide accommodation
and are designed with a range
of comfort levels in the quality
of the room and the amenities,
to ensure the guest has a
comfortable stay. In some types
of hotel, such as first class
hotels and art or design hotels,
the selection of rooms and the
surrounding ambience are
presented in a particular way.

Hotels
Hotels

Zacharias+Partner
Dirrix van Wylick
WS Atkins & Partners
Wörrlein & Partner
Derek Walker Associates Waser, Achermann
Wartiainen Architects Lunde & Lövseth
Engin Ünal and Ibrahim Öztürk Verhaegen
Prof. Dr. Jeko Tilev Csaba Tompos Pierre Traversier
Studio ADS Sp Studio E Architects Percy Thomas
Arch. Z. Stanik, Arch. J. Lelatko Tadeusz Szumielewicz i Partnerzy, ARCA Architects & Consultans
SIAT Architektur Siklósi és Társa Skovgaard Sørensens, Friis & Moltke, P. Andersen
Schaub+Partner Schmidt-Schicketanz Prof. Schneider-Wessling Hans-Hermann Seydel
RMJM Cabinet Roth Hartmut+Ingeborg Rüdiger Sam-Woo Architects Scholl Architekten
RKW Rhode Kellermann Wawrowsky Renner Hainke Wirth Planungsring Ressel RHWL Architects M. Papanikolaou, S. Sakelaridou Sauerbruch Hutton
Florian Riegler & Roger Riewe Leonardo Proli Puhl Antal Építész Irodája Dieter Punckt Pysall-Starenberg & Partner
Raivo Puuseep Reinhardt+Sander Obermeyer Albis-Bauplan Planteam West Renzo Piano
Jo Rabaey John Portman & Associates Reinhard Müller Müller Reimann Ollertz & Ollertz Cesar Pelli J.S.K. Perkins & Will
Richard Meier & Partners van Mierop & Belaieff Müller-Hartburg ZT Novotny Mähner NPS NHP
Kosig+Kosig Kresing Architekten Arn. Meijs Mills, Beaumont, Leavey Murphy/Jahn NBBJ-HUS-PKA Architects
Prof. Mäckler Marki and Associates Kjelgaard & Pedersen Kwang Sung+Soren Mengler KG Meyer, Awiesburo Meyer en van Schooten
Kohn, Pedersen, Fox Kaci Archiplan Prof. Kada Kahlen+Partner Karres Harmneyer Helmut Kriegbaum Daniel Libeskind Morphosis Architects
Koch und Partner Michael Knoche Hyvämäki-Karhunen-Parkkinen Karres Harmneyer IFB Planungsgruppe Meyer, Awiesburo Michaelsen und Michaelsen
Klever, Kobitz Kister Scheithauer Gross Michel Jaspers Henning Larsens Henze+Vahjen Hochter Ingenhoven Overdiek Julián Franco Lopez
KHR AS Arkitekter Michel Architekten Prof. Holzbauer José Antonio Galea Fernández Gatermann+Schossig Prof. Kaup, Dr. Scholz, Jesse+Partner, Obermeyer D. Manuel de Lorenzo
J/V GEK S.A.-Themeliodomi S.A. Peter Henkel Henn Architekten Prof. Fehringer Thomas Feiger Ingenhoven Overdiek Inros Planungsgesellschaft
Häussler Gruppe Dissing+Weitling Prof. Domenig Klaus-M. Hoffmann Holder Mathias
Daller, Huber Dieckmann & Partner Alexander Freiherr v. Branca Dorin Stefan Fiebiger Gerber Architekten Giuliani, Hönger HPP
BM+P Prof. Bonanni Claude Bouney and Georges Guerin Bieling & Bieling Ecolo Architekten Gehry Partners Hohaus+Partner
Baum and Kwiecinski, Stepa, Siudowski BHLM Architekten Autorska Precownia BRT Architekten Dr. Finta Gruttner Architekten Herbert Gergs
Arte charpentier et associés ASW ATEC Atelier 4A Architectury, Aviaplan Blum/Spomitz Foster and Partners Gerber Architekten GWB Planen+Bauen
AGS Architekten AIC Bau-Planungs GmbH Allmann Atelier d'Art Urbain Biuro Projektowe Wolfgang Brunnbauer Bruno Gerosa gmp Grumuch/Ernst Architekten
3xNielsen A Tasarim, Ali Osman Öztürk Sattler, Wappner Anderegg Architekten Basssenge, p-unan-Schulz, Heinrich, Schreiber de Architekten Cie Bulanda-Mucha Architekci G+D Studiegroep
Aare Saks Atelier Pak Angerer & Feuser ATP Auker Europe Alec French Cabinet Guillermont
Uri Blumenthal Atelier WW Architekt DEGW D.M.J.M. Cabinet Guillermont
D.M.J.M.

Ein weiterer Solitär mit Schüco Systemkonstruktionen, von denen es in den Vereinigten Arabischen Emiraten bereits eine ganze Reihe gibt. Bei dem Beach-Hotel wurden für die Vorhangfassade 21.260 m² des Systems SK 60V verarbeitet, für Balkone und Suiten 2.330 m² Royal 54 sowie für Palm Court und Coffee Colonnade 1.685 m² Schüco Sonderkonstruktionen auf Basis SK 60V.

Yet another gem designed with Schüco system constructions, of which a whole range already exist in the United Arab Emirates. The curtain wall façade of the Beach Hotel required 21,260 m² of the system SK 60V, the balconies and suites – 2,330 m² of system Royal 54, and 1,685 m² of Schüco special constructions based on SK 60V make up the Palm Court and the Coffee Colonnade.

Außenansichten
Jumeirah Beach
Outside views
Jumeirah Beach

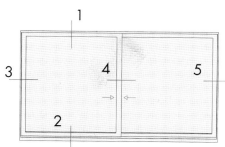

1

2

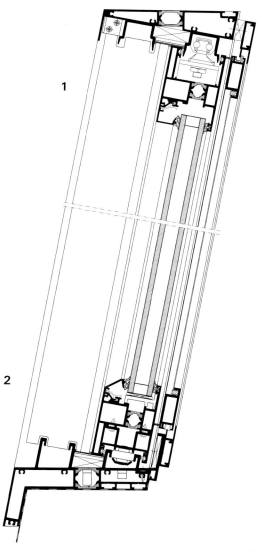

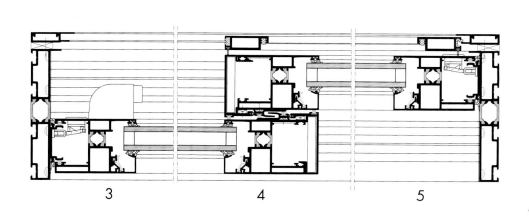

3   4   5

Budapest, Hungary

Planung
Design
Architekt Dr. Finta und
Fa. Lakoterv, Budapest

Mitwirkende Sachverständige
Consultants
Dr. Buch, Vienna, Austria

Ein Fassadensystem mit zwei
verschiedenen Ansichtsbreiten:
FW 50, in den Obergeschossen
mit schmaler 50-mm-Optik, im
Erdgeschoss/Foyer mit 80 mm
Ansichtsbreite.

A façade system with two
different face widths: FW 50, on
the upper floors thin members
of 50 mm and on the ground
floor/foyer of 80 mm face width.

Gesamtansicht
Grand Hotel Corvinus
Outside view
Grand Hotel Corvinus

Außenansichten
Grand Hotel Corvinus
Outside views
Grand Hotel Corvinus

Oestrich-Winkel/Rheingau,
Hessen, Germany

Planung
Design
Architektenbüro Dipl.-Ing.
Michaelsen und Michaelsen,
Wiesbaden

Mitwirkende Sachverständige
Consultants
Stefan Michaelsen
Dipl-Ing. Architekt

Außenansicht
Restaurant Orangerie
Outside view
Restaurant Orangerie

London, Great Britain

Planung
Design
Uri Blumenthal, Tel Aviv, Israel

Außenansicht
Victoria Plaza
Outside view
Victoria Plaza

Darmstadt, Germany

Planung
Design
Mengler Kommunal- und
Gewerbebau KG, Darmstadt

Schräg vorgezogene Glasflächen
setzen Akzente am Eingang dieses Hotelgebäudes. Eingesetzt
wurden hier die Profilfassaden
FW 50 sowie für die Kalt-/Warm-
fassade Fenster auf Basis
Iskotherm 74 Block.
Für die der nahe gelegenen
Bahntrasse zugewandten Seite
waren besondere schalldäm-
mende Konstruktionen erforder-
lich.

Sloping projecting glazed areas
emphasised the entrance of
the hotel building. The pofiled
façades are composed of FW 50
as well as the ventilated/non-
ventilated façade window based
on Iskotherm 74 Block.
Special sound insulating
constuctions are necessary for
the side facing the nearby
railway track.

Außenansicht Maritim
Rhein-Main Hotel
Outside view
Rhein-Main Hotel

Hanover-Langenhagen,
Germany

Planung
Design
Reinhardt + Sander GmbH
Planung und Baubetreuung,
Bad Salzuflen

Vorentwurf
Preliminary design
Dipl.-Ing. Heinz Wilke, Arch.
DWB, Hanover

Außenansicht
Maritim Airport Hotel
Outside view
Maritim Airport Hotel

In Flughafen-Nähe, deshalb
hohen Schallschutz-Anforderun-
gen gerecht werdend. Kalt-
Warm-Fassade mit Schallschutz-
Kastenfenstern. Gleichbleibende
Profilansichten im Festvergla-
sungs- und Fensterbereich.
Kalt-Warm-Profilfassaden mit
gleicher Brüstungs- und Fenster-
Optik. Die äußeren Profilan-
sichtsbreiten betragen 80 mm.

Due to the proximity of the
airport, it was necessary to
adopt high sound insulation
construction. A ventilated/non-
ventilated façade constuction
with sound insulating windows.
Equal profil faces in both fixed
glazing and window areas.
Ventilated/non-ventilated profiled
façades with same sight lines
for vision and spandrel areas.
The outer profile face widths are
80 mm.

Gesamtansicht
Maritim Airport Hotel
Outside view
Maritim Airport Hotel

Hamburg, Germany

Planung
Design
gmp Architekten von Gerkan
Marg und Partner, Hamburg

Mitwirkende Sachverständige
Consultants
Statik: Windels, Timm + Morgen

Außenansicht
Hotel Steigenberger
Outside view
Hotel Steigenberger

227

Hörnitz, Germany

Planung
Design
Wörrlein & Partner GmbH,
Nürnberg

Mitwirkende Sachverständige
Consultants
Herr Porlein und Herr Bauer

Außenansicht
Hotel Althörnitz
Outside view
Hotel Althörnitz

Warsaw, Poland

Planung
Design
John Portman & Associates,
Atlanta, USA
B. Proj. Kazimierski, Warsaw
Derk Fraser, Sweden

Mitwirkende Sachverständige
Consultants
Inpro Projekt Brodaczewski &
Hulewicz Sp. J.

Detailansichten
Hotel Westin
Detail views
Hotel Westin

Helsinki, Finland

Planung
Design
Arkkitehtitoimisto Hyvämäki-
Karhunen-Parkkinen, Helsinki

Detailansichten
Scandic Hotel
Detail views
Scandic Hotel

Istanbul, Turkey

Planung
Design
Architekten Engin Ünal und
Ibrahim Öztürk

Das im Istanbuler Stadtteil
Maslak liegende Hotel stellt sich
als segmentierte Hochhaus-
scheibe mit großflächigen
Fassadenverglasungen dar. Alle
Glasfassaden sind mit dem
schmalen Profilsystem FW 50
und dem System SG 50N mit
flächenbündigen Isolierglas-
Elementen gestaltet.

The hotel situated in the
Maslak part of Istanbul has the
appearance of a segmented slice
of skyscraper with large area
façade glazing. All the glass
façades are designed using the
narrow FW 50 profile system
and the SG 50N system with
flush-fitted double glazed units.

Außenansicht
Park Plaza
Outside view
Park Plaza

Berlin, Germany

Planung
Design
gmp Architekten von Gerkan
Marg und Partner, Hamburg

Mitwirkende Sachverständige
Consultants
E. Mosbacher, Friedrichshafen
DS-Plan GmbH, Mülheim/Ruhr

In der Tradition seines Vorgängerbaus stellt sich das Gebäude als Durchdringung eines quadratischen Sockels mit einem zylindrischen Oberteil dar, das sich nach oben hin abtreppt. Der Sockel wiederum nimmt die Höhe der Nachbarbebauung auf und definiert städtebaulich die Ecke am Ku'damm-Eck. Diese Geometrien werden verstärkt durch die verwendeten Materialien. Der metallisch glänzende Klinker sowie die vorgesetzten vertikalen Alulamellen unterstützen den radialen Verlauf dieser Eckbebauung. Den Eingangsbereich betont eine portalähnliche Auflösung, die Videowand zum Ku'damm hin war schon am früheren Bau das markante Erkennungszeichen.

In the tradition of its predecessor, the building represents the fusion of of a square pedestal with a cylindrical upper section which is stepped towards the top. The pedestal matches the height of neighbouring buildings and, in urban development terms, defines the corner at Ku'damm-Eck. The geometry is intensified by the materials used. The bright metallic bricks and protruding vertical aluminium slats underline the radial curve of this corner construction. The entrance is emphasised by a portal-style opening, and the video wall on the Ku'damm side, which was the distinguishing feature of the previous building.

Detailansichten
Ku'damm Eck
Detail views
Ku'damm Eck

Kulturbauten sind Museums-,
Theater- und Ausstellungsgebäude für die Präsentation
von Kultur und Kunst. Mit
besonderen Anforderungen an
die allgemeine Zugänglichkeit
und Sicherheit, an Kunst- und
Tageslicht, Akustik und technische Gebäudeausrüstung.

Centres for the Arts are
museums, theatres and
exhibition buildings for staging
cultural and artistic events. They
have special requirements as
regards general accessibility and
safety, daylight and artificial
lighting, acoustics and the
technical fixtures and fittings.

Kulturbauten
Centres for the arts

Parma, Italy

Planung
Design
Renzo Piano
Building Workshop

Mitwirkende Sachverständige
Consultants
D. Hart, Partner in charge

Klassisch konsequente Organisation der Funktionen in einer einschiffigen basilikalen Gebäudehülle. Unter einem unterspannten Satteldach sind die Bereiche Vorhalle, großzügige Freitreppe, Zuschauerraum und Bühne angeordnet. Zwei eingestellte Glasfassaden bilden den klimatischen Filter zum Außenraum und betonen gleichzeitig das Durchfließen von Innen- und Außenraum. Durch die beidseitig flankierenden Fensterreihen wird dieser Eindruck noch unterstrichen.

This single-nave basilican building envelope is characterised by a classical organisation of functions. The entrance hall, generously apportioned steps, auditorium and stage are all set under a braced gable roof. Two inset glass façades provide a climatic filter to the outside and emphasise the transition from interior to exterior. This is further reinforced by the rows of windows on either side of the building.

Außen- und
Innenansichten
Auditorium
„Niccolo" Paganini
Outside and
inside views
Auditorium
"Niccolo" Paganini

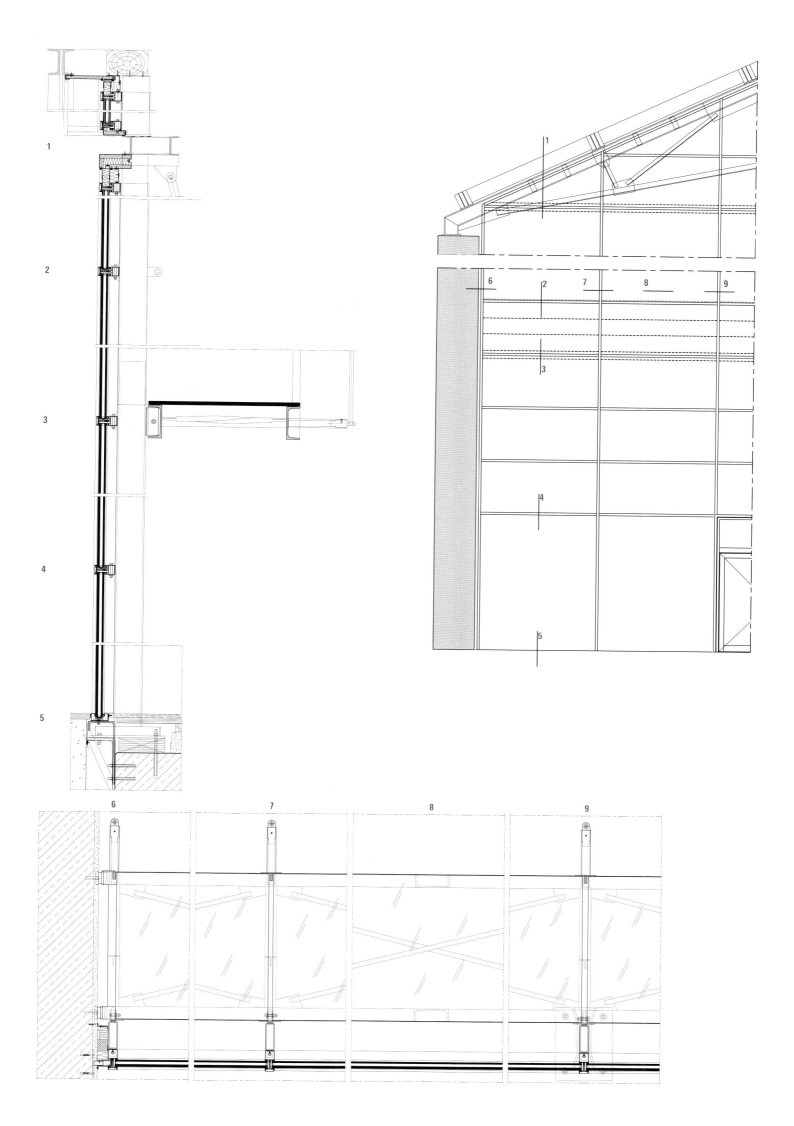

Durch die spektakulären Granit-
riegel erhält die Fassade ihre eindringliche Eigenständigkeit. Die
großzügig gerundeten Ecken –
auch im Eingangsbereich – verleihen diesem Gebäude den Charakter der klassischen Weltoffen-
heit.

The spectacular granite
transoms lend the façade a
vivid originality. The generous
curved corners, even in the
entrance hall, give the building
a classical, cosmopolitan air.

Außenansichten
Metroplitan
Outside views
Metropolitan

MISERICORDIARUM PATRI DICATUM
A.D. MMIII · PONTIFICATUS XXV

Rome, Italy

Planung
Design
Richard Meier & Partners,
Architects, New York

Mitwirkende Sachverständige
Consultants
John Eisler
Matteo Pericoli
Alfonso D'Onofrio
Nigel Ryan

Die Jubiläumskirche ist ein prägnantes Beispiel moderner Architektur in einer überaus geschichtsträchtigen Stadt und ein leuchtendes Vorbild im internationalen Kirchenbau. Die gekrümmten Außenwände ragen wie geblähte weiße Segel 26 m in die Höhe, und die sich nach oben reckende Dachverglasung ist eine deutliche Bereicherung der römischen Architekturlandschaft. Für die Fassade dieses Meisterwerks entwickelte Schüco besondere Teleskopprofile, die imstande waren, mit den Formen der beweglichen, überhängenden Segel zu kommunizieren.

One of the leading examples of contemporary architecture in one of the most historic cities, the Jubilee Church sets an important precedent in international church design. The curved white shells up to 26 m high, evoking gliding white sails, and the soaring glass skylights are a significant addition to the architectural landscape of Rome.
For the façades of this masterpiece Schüco developed special telescopic profiles, capable of conversing with the concrete of the moving overhanging sails.

Leeds, Great Britain

Planung
Design
Derek Walker Associates,
Buckinghamshire

Außenansichten
Royal Armories
Museum
Outside views
Royal Armories
Museum

Bonn, Germany

Planung
Design
Dipl.-Ing. Hartmut + Ingeborg Rüdiger, Architekten BDA, Braunschweig

Das Haus der Geschichte der Bundesrepublik Deutschland, weniger ein traditionelles Museum als Dokumentations- und Informationszentrum über die jüngere deutsche Geschichte, ist das Ergebnis eines Wettbewerbs unter 172 Architekturbüros. Die Offenheit der bis zu 7,50 m hohen Glas-, Stahl-, Alukonstruktionen im Bereich des Foyers steht in bewusstem Kontrast zur „Introvertiertheit" der nur von oben belichteten Dauerausstellungsflächen. Alle senkrechten Verglasungen wurden in Schüco Profilsystemen ausgeführt.

The building which houses the "History of the German Federal Republic" which is less of a traditional museum, more of a document and information centre relating to recent German history, is the result of a competition in which 172 architects' practices took part. The open aspect of the 7.5 m high glass, steel and aluminium construction of the foyer stands in marked contrast to the "introspective" nature of the exhibition areas which are only lit from above. All the vertical glazing used Schüco profile systems.

Außen- und Innenansichten
Haus der Geschichte
Outside and inside
views House of History

Copenhagen, Denmark

Planung
Design
C. F. Møllers Tegnestue

Außenansichten
Statens Museum
for Kunst
Outside views
Danish National Gallery

Helsinki, Finland

Planung
Design
Wartiainen Architects, Finland

Mitwirkende Sachverständige
Consultants
Evata, Finland

Norwegian Oil Museum

Stavanger, Norway

Planung
Design
Lunde & Lövseth Arkitekter AS, Oslo

Mitwirkende Sachverständige
Consultants
Nyland Byggadministrasjon AS, Stavanger

Außenansichten
High Tech Center
Outside views
High-Tech Centre

Das Ölmuseum in Stavanger präsentiert sich als hervorragendes Ensemble in wunderschöner Umgebung. Getreu dem Thema finden sich die Elemente aus dem unmittelbaren Umfeld von Bohrinseln und artverwandten Plätzen. So durchstreift man eine Ansammlung von Ölplattformen, Tanks und Bohrtürmen in diesem Technikpark. Besonderen Wert legten die Architekten auf die Textur der Oberflächen, die sie bewusst zueinander in Kontrast setzten.
So wechseln geschlossene Fassaden mit transluzenten Bereichen und vermitteln insgesamt einen überzeugenden Eindruck eines modernen Technologiemuseums.

Außenansicht
Norwegisches
Ölmuseum
Outside view
Norwegian Oil Museum

The oil museum in Stavanger is an outstanding ensemble in beautiful surroundings.
True to its theme, there are elements directly connected to oil rigs and related buildings. This technology park provides an array of oil platforms, tanks and derricks. The architects paid particular attention to the surface textures which they used intentionally to create contrasts. Opaque façades alternate with tanslucent areas which together convey an appropriate impression for a modern technological museum.

Berlin, Germany

Planung
Design
Daniel Libeskind, Berlin

Mitwirkende Sachverständige
Consultants
Ludwig + Mayer, Berlin

Außenansichten
Jüdisches Museum
Outside views
Jewish Museum

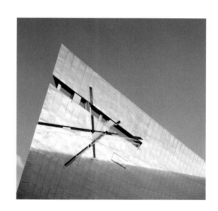

Ingolstadt, Germany

Planung
Design
Henn Architekten, Munich/Berlin

Mitwirkende Sachverständige
Consultants
Hussak Ingenieurgesellschaft,
Lauingen

Getreu der Eleganz, Sachlichkeit
und Schnörkellosigkeit ihrer
Produkte präsentiert sich die
Audi AG mit dem museum
mobile in Ingolstadt.
Die Transparenz des Glaszylin-
ders korrespondiert geschmack-
voll mit der Geschlossenheit der
sich darüber schiebenden und
drehenden Aluminiumhaut.
Gerade bei Nacht wird dieses
Wechselspiel zwischen offenen
und geschlossenen Flächen
noch deutlicher. Die radiale Betonung suggeriert die Bewegung
und Rotation aus dem Motoren-
bau und lässt letztendlich den
Namen des Bauwerkes nur allzu
logisch erscheinen.

True to the elegant, objective
and unembellished nature
of their products, the museum
mobile in Ingolstadt represents
Audi AG.
The clarity of the glass cylinder
harmonises tastefully with the
obscuring effect provided by
the sliding and rotating
aluminium skin fitted to the
upper section. Especially at
night, the alternating view
between visible and concealed
areas is more apparent. The
emphasis on the radial structure
suggests the movement and
rotation of a car engine and
makes the name of the building
all the more obvious.

257

Die Aluminiumhaut
dreht sich um den
gläsernen Baukörper
The aluminium skin
rotates around the
glass structure

Außenansichten
museum-mobile
Audi-Forum
Outside views
museum-mobile
Audi-Forum

Außenansichten
museum-mobile
Audi-Forum
Outside views
museum-mobile
Audi-Forum

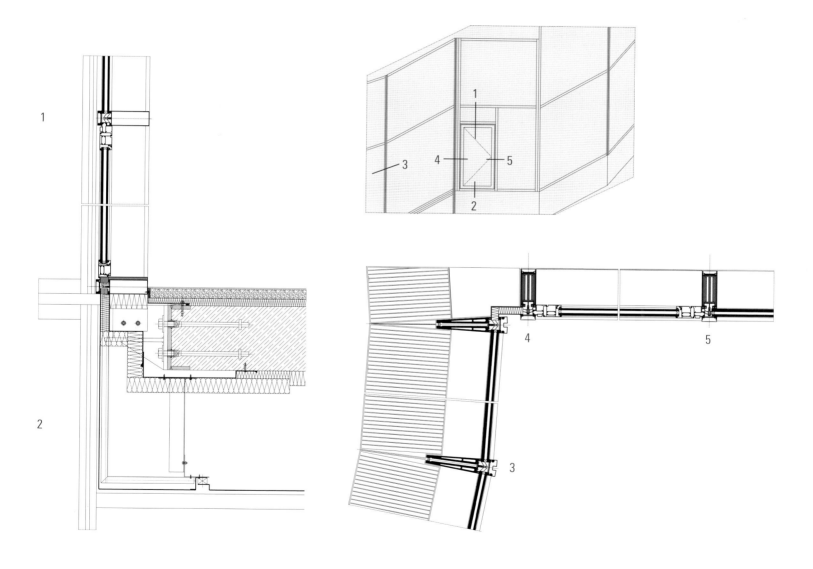

Budapest, Hungary

Planung
Design
Siklósi és Társa Kft

Außenansichten
Nationaltheater
Budapest
Outside views
Budapest National
Theatre

Außen- und
Innenansichten
Conference Center
Outside and
inside views
Conference Centre

Valencia, Spain

Planung
Design
Foster and Partners, London

Die minimalisierte und organisch geschwungene riesige Dachschale wird im Frontbereich von wenigen hohen Säulen getragen. Zusammen mit der transparent gehaltenen Fassade integriert sich das leicht wirkende Bauwerk in die flache Landschaft und setzt einen bemerkenswerten Akzent.

The minimalist and enormous organically flowing roof shell is supported at the front by just a few tall columns. Together with the transparent façade, the light and airy structure is integrated into the flat landscape, which emphasises its striking appearance.

Außen- und
Innenansichten
Conference Center
Outside and
inside views
Conference Centre

Gesamtansicht
Conference Center
Aerial view
Conference Centre

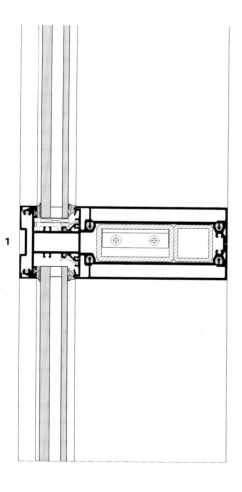

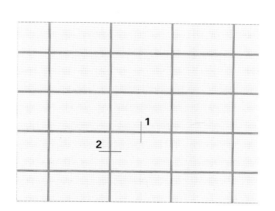

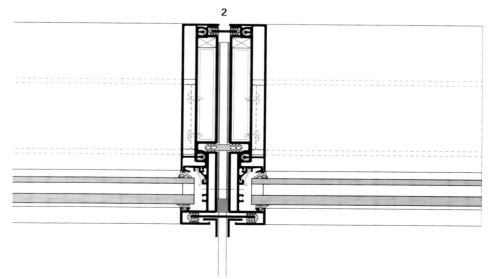

Freizeitbauten umfassen ein
breites Spektrum von Bauten
wie Stadien, Sporthallen,
Wettkampfstätten, Schwimm-
bäder, Kinoanlagen, Unter-
haltungs-Zentren etc. Primäre
Aufgabe von Freizeitbauten ist
die Förderung der Kommunikation in Kombination mit einer
hohen Funktionalität und architektonischen Qualität.

Leisure complexes encompass a
wide range of buildings, such as
stadia, sports halls, competition
arenas, swimming pools,
cinemas, entertainment venues
etc. The primary function of
leisure complexes is to support
communication in combination
with a high degree of functionality and architectural quality.

Freizeitbauten
Leisure complexes

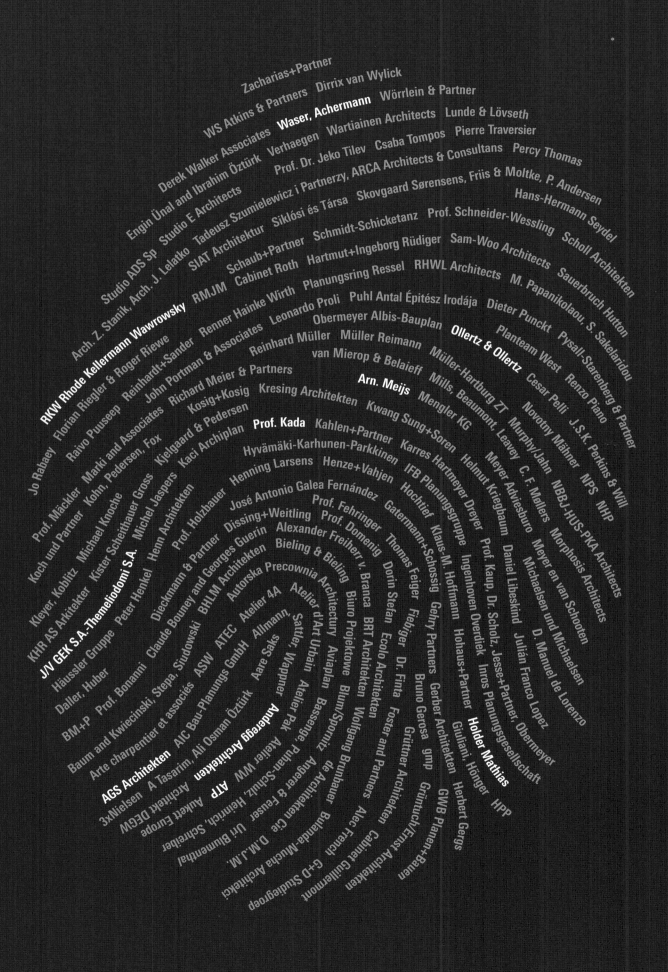

Zacharias+Partner
WS Atkins & Partners Dirrix van Wylick
Waser, Achermann Wörrlein & Partner
Derek Walker Associates Wartiainen Architects Lunde & Lövseth
Engin Ünal and Ibrahim Öztürk Verhaegen Pierre Traversier
Studio ADS Sp Studio E Architects Prof. Dr. Jeko Tilev Csaba Tompos Percy Thomas
Tadeusz Szumielewicz i Partnerzy, ARCA Architects & Consultans
SIAT Architektur Siklósi és Társa Skovgaard Sørensens, Friis & Moltke, P. Andersen
Arch. Z. Stanik, Arch. J. Lelatko Schmidt-Schicketanz Prof. Schneider-Wessling Hans-Hermann Seydel
RMJM Cabinet Roth Hartmut+Ingeborg Rüdiger Sam-Woo Architects Scholl Architekten
Schaub+Partner Planungsring Ressel RHWL Architects M. Papanikolaou. S. Sakelaridou
RKW Rhode Kellermann Wawrowsky Renner Hainke Wirth Puhl Antal Építész Irodája Dieter Punckt Pysall-Starenberg & Partner
Reinhardt+Sander Leonardo Proli Obermeyer Albis-Bauplan Planteam West Renzo Piano
Florian Riegler & Roger Riewe Reinhard Müller Müller Reimann Ollertz & Ollertz Cesar Pelli J.S.K.
Raivo Puuseep John Portman & Associates van Mierop & Belaieff Müller-Hartburg ZT Novotny Mähner NPS NHP
Jo Rabaey Marki and Associates Richard Meier & Partners Arn. Meijs Mills, Beaumont, Leavey Murphy/Jahn Perkins & Will
Kohn, Pedersen, Fox Kosig+Kosig Kresing Architekten Mengler KG C. F. Møllers NBBJ-HUS-PKA Architects
Prof. Mäckler Kjelgaard & Pedersen Kwang Sung+Soren Meyer Adviesburo Meyer en van Schooten
Koch und Partner Michael Knoche Kaci Archiplan Karres Hartmeyer Dreyer Helmut Kriegbaum Morphosis Architects
Kleyer, Koblitz Kister Scheithauer Gross Hyvämäki-Karhunen-Parkkinen IFB Planungsgruppe Prof. Kaup, Dr. Scholz, Jesse+Partner, Obermeyer Michaelsen und Michaelsen
KHR AS Arkitekter Michel Jaspers Prof. Kada Kahlen+Partner Hochtief Ingenhoven Overdiek Daniel Libeskind D. Manuel de Lorenzo
Peter Henkel Henn Architekten Henning Larsens Henze+Vahjen Gatermann+Schossig Julián Franco Lopez
J/V GEK S.A.-Themeliodomi S.A. Prof. Holzhauer José Antonio Galea Fernández Thomas Feiger Klaus-M. Hoffmann Inros Planungsgesellschaft
Häussler Gruppe Dieckmann & Partner Prof. Fehringer Prof. Domenig Dorin Stefan Gehry Partners Hohaus+Partner
Daller, Huber Claude Bouney and Georges Guerin Dissing+Weitling Alexander Freiherr v. Branca Ecalo Architekten Bruno Gerosa gmp Holder Mathias
BM+P Prof. Bonanni BHLM Architekten Bieling & Bieling BRT Architekten Dr. Finta Gerber Architekten Giuliani, Hönger HPP
Baum and Kwiecinski, Stepa, Siudowski Autorska Precownia Architectury Biuro Projektowe Wolfgang Brunbauer Herbert Gergs
Arte charpentier et associés ASW ATEC Atelier 4A Allmann, Biuro Projektowe de Architekten Cie Alec French Grüttner Architekten GWB Planen+Bauen
AGS Architekten AIC Bau-Planungs GmbH Atelier d'Art Urbain Bassenge, Angerer & Feuser Cabinet Guillermont Grüntuch/Ernst Architekten
A Tasarim, Ali Osman Öztürk Aare Saks Sattler, Wagoner Aviaplan de Architekten Cie Cabinet Guillermont G+D Studiegroep
3x Nielsen Anderegg Architekten Atelier Pak Aviaplan Blum/Sportico Uri Blumenthal
Auken Europe Atelier WW Angerer & Feuser Puhan-Schulz, Heinrich, Schreiber D.M. J.M.
ATP Bulanda-Mucha Architekci
Architekt DE&W

Valkenburg, Netherlands

Planung
Design
Arn. Meijs Architekten b.v.,
Maastricht

Die gewisse Eleganz in der
Ausstrahlung, die ein Casino
erfordert, wird durch die Kombination von Materialien und
Formen erreicht. Ein Rundbau,
verbunden mit einem zurück-
geneigten länglichen Baukörper.
Feiner, heller Naturstein im
Kontrast mit getönter Verglasung und dunklen FW 50-Profi-
len. Die Fenster aus Royal S 65.
Am Tage und auch nachts von
anziehender Wirkung.

The certain elegance which a
casino requires is achieved by
this combination of material and
shape. A circular building
together with an rectangular
wing sloping backwards. Fine
pale natural stone contrasts with
the tinted glazing and dark-
coloured FW 50 profiles. The
windows are Royal S 65. An
attraction by day and also by
night.

269

Außenansichten
Casino Valkenburg
Outside views
Valkenburg Casino

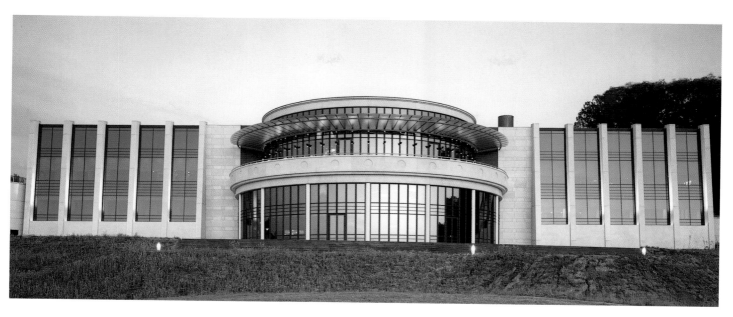

Gesamtansicht
Casino Valkenburg
Aerial view
Valkenburg Casino

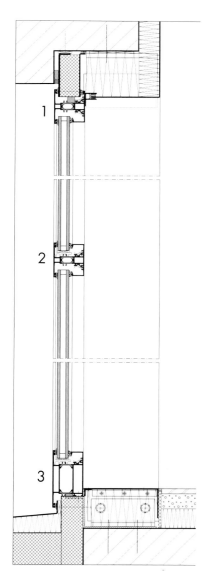

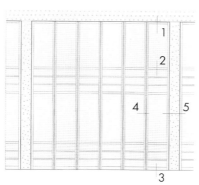

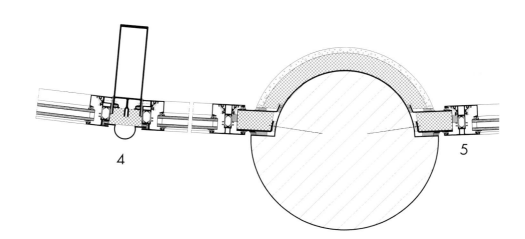

Innsbruck, Austria

Planung
Design
ATP Achammer-Tritthart &
Partner, Innsbruck

Eine Structural Glazing Fassade
der besonderen Art: geschoss-
weise auskragend, volle Transparenz, freie Sicht auf die
Konstruktion. Die großen Glas-
elemente werden von der
Fassaden-Konstruktion SK 60V
gehalten.

Structurally glazed facade of a
distinct type: storey-high
pojections, fully transparent with
clear views of the substructure.
The large glass elements are
mounted and secured to the
facade construction SK 60V.

Außenansichten
Casino Innsbruck
Outside views
Innsbruck Casino

Penrith, Great Britain

Planung
Design
Holder Mathias, Alcock plc,
Cardiff

Ferienvillen in einer Wald-Oase laden zur Erholung ein. Das Ziel war, hohe Transparenz der Außenwände durch maximalen Glas- und minimalen Profilanteil zu erreichen. Das System FW 50, das bei nur 50 mm Ansichtsbreite schlank gerahmte, große Scheibenfelder zulässt, ist dafür ideal.

Holiday villas in a forest oasis are an inviting place for recreation. The aim was to achieve a high degree of transparency of the external walls by a maximum area of glass an a minimum amount of profiles. The system FW 50, with its 50 mm narrow face width allowing large slender framed areas of glazing, is ideal for this purpose.

Gesamtansicht Oasis
Forest Holiday Village
Aerial view Oasis
Forest Holiday Village

Außenansichten Oasis
Forest Holiday Village
Outside views Oasis
Forest Holiday Village

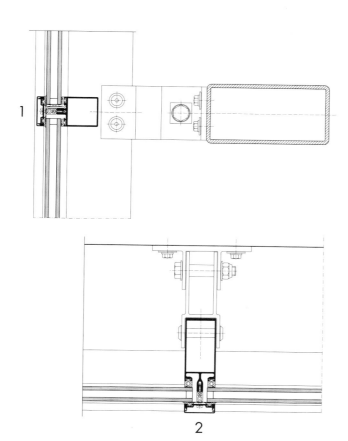

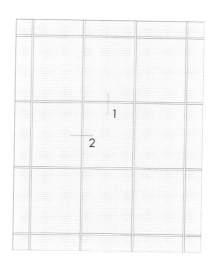

Außenansicht Oasis
Forest Holiday Village
Outside view Oasis
Forest Holiday Village

Bad Sulza, Germany

Planung
Design
Ollertz & Ollertz, Dipl.-Ing.
Architekten, Fulda

Mitwirkende Sachverständige
Consultants
Ing.-Büro Trabert & Partner,
Geisa/Rhön

Eine reizvolle Dachkuppelkon-
struktion bildet interessante
Glasflächen in der Badelandschaft mit Blickbezug zu den
Außenbecken. Sie mündet in
eine aufragende verglaste
Spitze. Die polygonalen Glasfassaden werden von einer
komplizierten Flachstahl-Unter-
konstruktion gehalten. Für
die Glasfassade wurde das
System FW 50.1 eingesetzt,
für die Lichtdächer SK 60.

An attractive domed roof
structure creates interesting
glass aspects in the surrounding
spa countryside, with a view
over the outside pools. It leads
into a rising glazed apex. The
glazed façades of the polygon
are supported by an intricate flat
steel substructure. The FW 50.1
system was used for the glass
façade and SK 60 for the
skylights.

Innenansichten
Toskana Therme
Inside views
Toskana Therme

Nijmegen, Netherlands

Planung
Design
AGS Architekten & Planners,
Heerlen

Eine Aluminium-Glas-Konstruktion überdacht die Schwimm- und Badelandschaft des Kurhauses. Das dafür gewählte Schüco System SK 60 kann auftretendes Kondenswasser aufnehmen und nach außen abführen. Als SK 60V wird das System in vertikalen Bereichen eingesetzt.

An aluminium glass construction covers the swimming and bathing pool of this convalescent centre. The Schüco System SK 60 selected for this project collects any condensation water and drains it to the outside. As SK 60V, the system is also used for vertical areas.

Außenansicht
Sanadome
Outside view
Sanadome

Sanadome

Jungfraujoch, Switzerland

Planung
Design
Anderegg Architekten,
Meiringen

Auf 3571 m war dieses die
höchste Baustelle Europas.
Nach dem Brand der alten
Station entstand das neue Berg-
und Touristenhaus mit einer ein-
zigartigen Aussichtskanzel.
Hochwärmegedämmte Alumi-
niumprofile und Sonnenschutz-
gläser schützen vor extremer
Witterung. Bewährt haben sich
die Schüco Systeme SK 60V.1
und Royal S 70.1.

At an altitude of 3571 m this
was the highest building site in
Europe. A fire destroyed the old
station, thus a new mountain
and tourist centre with an
unusual viewing platform was
erected. High thermally
insulated aluminium profiles
and solar control glass offer a
shield from the extreme weather
conditions. Schüco Systems
SK 60V.1 and Royal S 70.1 have
proven successful.

Detailansichten
Sphinx
Detail views
Sphinx

Graz, Austria

Planung
Design
Architekt Prof. DI Klaus Kada

Detailansichten
Stadthalle Graz
Detail views
Stadthalle Graz

Thessaloniki, Greece

Planung
Design
J/V GEK S.A. – Themeliodomi
S.A.

Ein von klassischen Ordnungs-
prinzipien geprägtes Gebäude.
Die großzügige von Rundsäulen
getragene Empfangs-Rotunde
lädt zum Besuch des Musik-
theaters ein. Sie besteht,
genauso wie das vorgesetzte,
abgehängte Glasvordach, aus
einer rahmenlosen Punktverglasung. Dieser offene, verglaste
Eingangsbereich steht in reizvol-
lem Kontrast zum restlichen
abgestuften steinernen Baukörper. Die eingesetzten Profil-
Systeme sind FW 50, SK 60 und
Royal S 65.

A building influenced by
classical principles. The
generous entrance rotunda
supported by round columns
invites visitors into the concert
hall. It consists of frameless
point-fixed glazing, as does the
suspended glass canopy at the
front. This open glazed entrance
area is delightful contrast to
the rest of the stepped stone
building. The profile systems
used here were FW 50, SK 60
and Royal S 65.

Außenansicht
Music Hall
Outside view
Music Hall

Stanserhorn, Switzerland

Planung
Design
Architekten Waser und
Achermann

Außenansichten
Rondorama
Outside views
Rondorama

Stuttgart, Germany

Planung
Design
RKW Rhode Kellermann
Wawrowsky, Architektur und
Städtebau, Düsseldorf

Detailansichten
UFA-Palast
Detail views
UFA Palace

Einkaufswelten werden in unseren Städten heute wesentlich von Einkaufs-Passagen, Shoppingcentern, Boutiquen und Stores bis hin zu Fachmärkten geprägt. In diesem innerstädtischen Gefüge werden an diese Bauaufgaben besondere Anforderungen gestellt. Menschen decken hier ihre Bedürfnisse nach Waren, die präsentiert und inszeniert werden – von funktional praktisch bis hin zu faszinierenden bunten Welten.

Shopping centres are today a hallmark in our towns and cities, from shopping arcades, malls, boutiques and stores through to specialist shops. These construction projects in inner-city developments pose particular demands. People satisfy their desire to buy goods which are showcased in attractive surroundings; from functional and practical presentations to eye-catching and colourful displays.

Einkaufswelten
Shopping centres

Berlin, Germany

Planung
Design
Klaus-M. Hoffmann, Berlin, für
ECE Projektmanagement GmbH,
Hamburg, in Zusammenarbeit
mit wmb Architekten, Berlin

Einkaufszentrum mit Büro-
flächen im Norden Berlins,
gekennzeichnet durch einen
dynamisch gestalteten Ein-
gangs-Turmbereich und eine
langgestreckte, gebogene
Fassade.

Shopping Centre with offices in
the north of Berlin, characterized
by the dynamic design of
the entrance tower and a long
curved façade.

Außenansichten
Gesundbrunnen Center
Outside views
Gesundbrunnen Center

Für den nach außen geneigten Turm wurde eine Structural Glazing-Sonderkonstruktion auf Basis SG 50N eingesetzt, die Fassade besteht aus dem Profil-System SK 60V.

For the forward sloping tower, a special construction in Structural Glazing based on SG 50B was chosen, the facade consists of the profil system SK 60V.

Innenansichten
Gesundbrunnen Center
Inside views
Gesundbrunnen Center

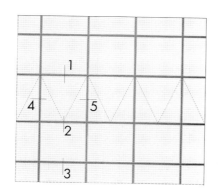

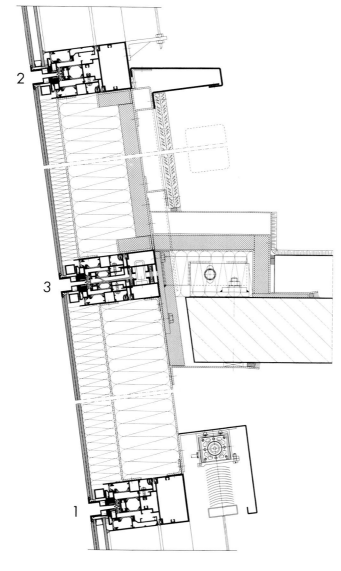

Innenansichten
Gesundbrunnen Center
Inside views
Gesundbrunnen Center

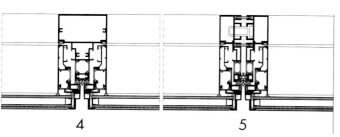

Gütersloh, Germany

Planung
Design
Gatermann + Schossig,
Architekten BDA, Bauplanungs-
gesellschaft mbH & Co. KG

Detailansichten
Karstadt
Detail views
Karstadt

Bleichenhof

Hamburg, Germany

Planung
Design
NPS – Nietz, Prasch, Sigl,
Architekten BDA, Hamburg

Projektleitung
Project management
Detlef Gäde-Schardin

Ein konsequent gestaltetes
Geschäftshaus mit typisch
hanseatischem Flair. Es bezieht
seine Wirkung aus der gelun-
genen Kombination von Aluminium, Glas und Klinker.

A consistently designed
commercial building with typical
hanseatic flair. The effect is
achieved by a successful
combination of aluminium, glass
and brickwork.

Außenansichten
Bleichenhof
Outside views
Bleichenhof

St. Pölten, Austria

Planung
Design
Architekt
Dipl.-Ing. Wolfgang Brunbauer,
Vienna

Aus dem schlanken System
FW 50 wurden alle Aluminium-
Bauteile für dieses Objekt gefer-
tigt; die Fassade der Halle, der
„Bug" des Hauptgebäudes, die
Verglasungselemente im EG und
die Fenster des Baus. Überall
einheitliche Profilansichten.

The slim sections of the FW 50
system were used for all
aluminium elements of this
project: the facade of the mall,
the "bow" of the main building,
the glazed units on the ground
floor and the windows of the
building. Throughout uniform
profile faces.

Außenansichten
Traisenpark
Outside views
Traisenpark

Debrecen, Hungary

Planung
Design
Hr. Csaba Tompos

Der elliptische Grundriss und der Kreissegment-First geben der Lichtdach-Konstruktion der großen Halle des Debrecen Plaza ihre dynamisch-futuristische Anmutung.
Alle tragenden Konstruktionsteile haben unterschiedliche Längen. Die Verwirklichung der Konstruktion stellte hohe Anforderungen an Produktion, Montage und Logistik. Die Schrägverglasung wurde mit dem Schüco System SK 60 ausgeführt.

With its oval outline and curved ridge, the skylight design of the large hall gives the Debrecen Plaza a dynamic and futuristic appearance.
All the supporting members within the structure are of different lengths. The realisation of the design was a challenge as far as production, assembly and logistics are concerned. The sloped glazing was created using the Schüco SK 60 system.

Debrecen Plaza
Debrecen Plaza

Tarquinia, Italy

Planung
Design
Dr. Arch. Leonardo Proli

Karstadt Warehouse

Magdeburg, Germany

Planung
Design
Dipl. Ing. Helmut Kriegbaum,
Berlin

Detailansicht
Centro Commerciale
Detail view
Centro Commerciale

Außenansichten
Karstadt
Outside views
Karstadt

Potsdam, Germany

Planung
Design
Planungsgemeinschaft
Stern-Center

nps und Partner
Nietz, Prasch, Sigl und Partner,
Architekten, Hamburg,
nhp Partnership
Architekten + Ingenieure
Bölinger, Hanke, Kreussler,
Hamburg

Innenansicht
Stern-Center
Inside view
Stern-Center

The Criterion

London, Great Britain

Planung
Design
RHWL Architects, London

Shopping Center Limani

Thessaloniki, Greece

Planung
Design
M. Papanikolaou,
S. Sakelaridou

Außenansichten
The Criterion
Outside views
The Criterion

Detailansichten Limani
Detail views Limani

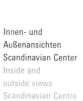

Århus, Denmark

Planung
Design
T. Skovgaard Sørensens
tegnestue A/S, Århus
Friis & Moltke A/S, Århus,
P. Andersen, Århus

Mitwirkende Sachverständige
Consultants
Arkitekt MAA
Kim Skovgaard Sørensen
Arkitekt MAA E. Dige Toft,
Arkitekt P. Andersen

Das Kongresszentrum erhielt
den Ariostea-Preis für die
Qualitität seiner Architektur. Die
eine Attraktion des Zentrums ist
die große Erschließungshalle mit
dem gläsernen Gewölbedach.
Die andere sind die Vorhang-
fassaden mit der reflektierenden
Verglasung. Das Dach, die
Giebelflächen und die Vorhangfassade sind aus dem System
FW 50.

The Congress Centre was
awarded the Ariostea Prize for
the quality of its architecture.
One of the attractions of the
centre is the circulation hall with
the glazed vaulted roof, another
is the curtain wall façades with
reflective glass. The roof, the
gable areas and the curtain wall
façade are system FW 50.

Innen- und
Außenansichten
Scandinavian Center
Inside and
outside views
Scandinavian Centre

Hanover, Germany

Planung
Design
ASW – Architekten Silcher,
Werner + Partner, Hamburg

Mitwirkende Sachverständige
Consultants
Dipl.-Ing. Michael Lange,
Hanover

Erneuerung der gesamten
Gebäudehülle. Dabei wurde der
Eckpunkt des Gebäudes zum
zentralen Blickpunkt. Auf voller
Höhe verglast mit besonders
weicher Rundung durch gebo-
gene Scheiben in der Schüco
System-Konstruktion SK 60V.
Fenster- und Nebeneingangs-
anlagen aus dem System
Royal S 65.

New cladding for the whole
building, the corner of the
building as central focus. Full
height glazing with a slight
curvature using curved panes of
Schüco System SK 60V.
Windows and side entrances of
System Royal S 65.

Detailansichten
Karstadt
Detail views Karstadt

Valence, France

Planung
Design
M. Pierre Traversier, Valence

Einkaufszentrum mit großzügiger Lichtdach-Konstruktion aus dem Schüco System SK 60. Das tonnenförmige Mittelteil des Daches wird von zwei Kuppelhälften abgeschlossen. Hier laufen jeweils 15 Profile auf einen Punkt. Klimatisierung durch vier Reihen elektronisch gesteuerter Lüftungsflügel.

Shopping centre designed with well-proportioned skylight construction using Schüco System SK 60. The barrel-shaped central part of the roof is closed off at each and by two cupola halves. Fifteen profiles meet at apex. Four rows of electronically controlled vents provide ventilation.

Detailansichten
Espace Victor Hugo
Detail views
Espace Victor Hugo

Dresden, Germany

Planung
Design
Architekturbüro
Dieckmann & Partner, Soest

Gebäudehülle aus zwei Schüco
Systemen in gleicher Elemente-
Abmessung und gleicher
Verglasung: SG 50N, das
Structural Glazing-System, als
Warmfassade sowie als Bänder
in den Attika- und Brüstungs-
Kaltbereichen. Royal S 65 für die
wärmegedämmten Fenster.

Two Schüco systems of equal
element dimensions and equal
glazing are used on the outer
skin of the building: SG 50N, the
structural glazing system as
warm facade as well as ribbon
elements in the parapet and
spandrel section. Royal S 65 for
the thermally insulated
windows.

Außenansichten
Modezentrum Dresden
Outside views Fashion
Centre Dresden

Planung
Design
de Architekten Cie, Amsterdam

Mitwirkende Sachverständige
Consultants
Prof. ir. P. B. de Bruijn

Außenansichten
Einkaufszentrum
Beursplein
Outside views
Shopping Centre
Beursplein

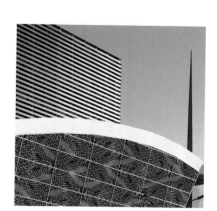

Ein neuentwickelter Wohn- und
Einkaufsbereich im Rotterdamer
Gebiet Beursplein erhielt eine
tiefergelegte Einkaufsstraße.
Große Teile dieses Zentrums
sind mit Lichtdachkonstruktio-
nen überdacht. Auch die
Fassaden, Fenster und Türen
wurden mit Schüco Systemen
realisiert.

A low-level shopping mall
was introduced into a newly
developed housing and shopping
sector in the area of Rotterdam
Beursplein.
A considerable part of the
centre is roofed with skylight
constructions; façades, windows
and doors also feature Schüco
systems.

Bauten für Lehre und Forschung
sind Stätten des Lehrens und
Lernens, der Bildung und
Forschung, sowie Kliniken, die
neben den ökonomischen Überlegungen optimierte logistische
Konzepte aufweisen, die mit
sozialer und kultureller Qualität
kombiniert werden müssen.

Centres for Education and
Research are institutions of
teaching and learning and of
education and research
including hospital clinics, which,
besides economical considerations, indicate optimised
logistical designs which need to
be combined with social and
cultural quality.

Bauten für Lehre und Forschung

Centres for Education and Research

Graz, Austria

Planung
Design
Architektengemeinschaft
o.Prof. Arch. DI
Günther Domenig +
Arch. DI Hermann Eisenköck,
Graz

Für die Stadt Graz ein markantes
Stück zeitgenössische Architek-
tur, für die Universität ein
EDV-Zentrum und die Erwei-
terung der Fakultätsräume sowie
der Bibliothek. Fassade und
Lichtdachkonstruktion aus den
Schüco Systemen SK 60V und
SK 60. Für die Fenster wurde
Royal S 70 eingesetzt.

For the City of Graz a striking
example of present day
architecture, for the University
a computer centre and the
extension of the faculty areas as
well as the library. Façade and
skylight construction using
Schüco Systems SK 60V and
SK 60. Royal S 70 was specified
for the windows.

Außenansichten
Resowi-Zentrum
Outside views
Resowi Centre

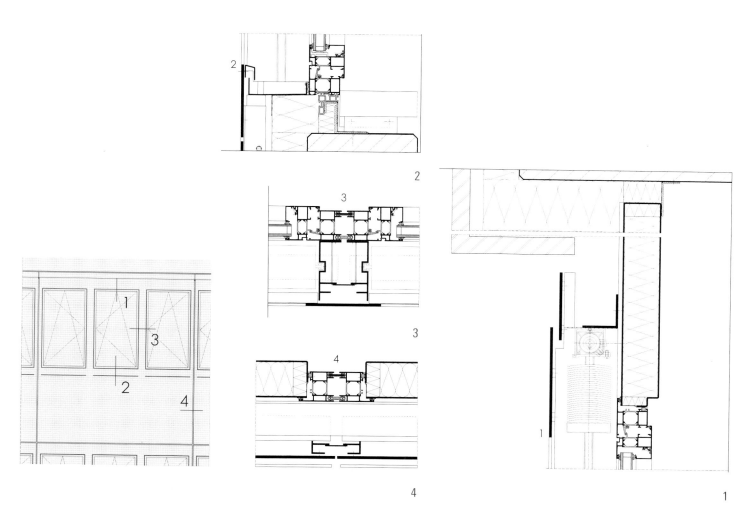

2

3

3

4

1

Levallois Perret, France

Planung
Design
Cabinet Roth, Paris

Außenansichten
Lycee Leonard de Vinci
Outside views
Lycee Leonard de Vinci

Hamburg, Germany

Planung
Design
Schaub + Partner, Architekten,
Hamburg

Mitwirkende Sachverständige
Consultants
Herr Martin Reiber,
Herr Dieter Hemming

Außenansichten
Hochschule
Outside views
of the college

Bath, Great Britain

Planung
Design
Alec French Partnership
Architects, Designers, Planners
Bristol

Das neue Konzept hieß: 24-Stunden-Bibliothek für flexibles Studieren. Der bestehende Bau aus den 60er-Jahren erhielt eine völlig transparente Erweiterung mit einem vorgelagerten Fußweg auf Höhe der 1. Etage. Dieser „Walkway" ist straßenseitig durch vorgespannte Gläser geschützt, die von 6 kreuzförmigen Stahl-Bäumen getragen werden. Die Fassade, geschosshoch verglast, ist aus dem Schüco System SK 60V.

The concept was: a 24-hour library for flexible studying. Added to the existing building of the 60's is a fully transparent extention with a pedestrian way set forward at first floor level. This walkway is protected on the roadside by prestressed glazing which is supported by 6 cross-formed steel tree-like supports. The storey-height glazed façade uses the Schüco Systems SK 60V.

Detailansicht
Universität Bath
Detail view
University of Bath

Dessau, Germany

Planung
Design
Kister Scheithauer Gross,
Architekten und Stadtplaner,
Dessau

Außenansichten
Hochschule Anhalt
Outside views
College Anhalt

International Neuroscience Institute (INI)

Hanover, Germany

Bauherr
Client
International Neuroscience
Institute GmbH, Hanover
c/o Prof. Dr. Dr. Majid Samii

Betreiber
Operator
Asklepios Kliniken GmbH,
Königstein-Falkenstein

Entwurfs- und
Ausführungsplanung
Design and construction
planning
SIAT Architektur + Technik,
Munich

Generalunternehmer
General contractor
ARGE Klinik INI Hanover,
Philipp Holzmann Direktion
Nord + Siemens
Gebäudetechnik Nord,
Hanover

Ausführung der Fassaden
Façade construction
Anders Metallbau GmbH, Fritzlar

Das im Juli 2000 eingeweihte
Institut soll ein „Center of
Excellence" auf dem Gebiet der
Hirnforschung und Neuro-
chirurgie werden. Sein Initiator
und ärztlicher Leiter ist Prof. Dr.
Dr. Majid Samii, Chefarzt der
Neurochirurgie an der Medizi-
nischen Hochschule Hannover
(MHH), der als einer der besten
Neurochirurgen auf der Welt gilt.
Das Institut wird eng mit der
MHH zusammenarbeiten.

The Institute, which was
officially opened at the end
of July 2000, is intended to
become a "Centre of Excellence"
for brain research and neurosurgery. Instigator and chief
medical officer is Professor
Majid Samii, Senior Consultant
for neurosurgery at the School
of Medicine in Hanover (MHH),
who is considered to be one of
the best neurosurgeons in the
world. The Institute will be
working very closely with the
MHH.

Aufgabenstellung, Entwurfskonzept und Funktionsanordnung

Das Institut soll als Spezialklinik und als Forschungszentrum für Neurowissenschaften u.a. die Entwicklung der „Neurobionik", d.h. der Verbindung biologischer und technischer Arbeitsmethoden zur Behebung von Defekten des zentralen Nervensystems und des Gehirns, vorantreiben.

Das in enger Zusammenarbeit mit Prof. Samii entstandene Konzept der Architekten für den Entwurf und die Funktionsanordnung sah von Anfang an eine Lösung vor, bei der die äußere Gestalt und die innere Struktur des Gebäudes Assoziationen zu Gestalt und Struktur des menschlichen Gehirns – bis hin zur „Furche" zwischen dessen rechter und linker Hälfte – weckt. Der Bau soll sich auf diese Weise signifikant von den üblichen Krankenhaus- und Forschungsbauten unterscheiden.

Im Sockelgeschoss sind im Wesentlichen die Räume für Forschung, Küchenanlage sowie für Ver- und Entsorgung untergebracht, im EG die Eingangshalle mit Empfang, das Casino und ein Vortragssaal, im 1. OG die radiologische Diagnostik, im 2.–4. OG die Pflegestationen mit zusammen 100 Betten, im 5. OG die OPs und die Intensivstation, im 6. OG die interdisziplinären ärztlichen Arbeitsräume und im 7. OG die ärztliche Leitung und die Konferenzräume.

Die gläserne Hülle des Gebäudes

besteht im Wesentlichen aus
- einer inneren Schale in thermisch getrennter Aluminium-Konstruktion als Klimahülle und
- einer imaginären äußeren Schale aus vorgehängten Streifen rahmenloser, punktgehaltener Gläser, die die horizontale Gliederung des Baues unterstreichen und mit ihrer Schrägstellung gewissermaßen die menschliche Schädelkontur nachzeichnen.

Lediglich die Glaswände des EG und 1.OG sowie der beiden „Furchen" in Structural-Glazing-Konstruktion sind 1-schalig.

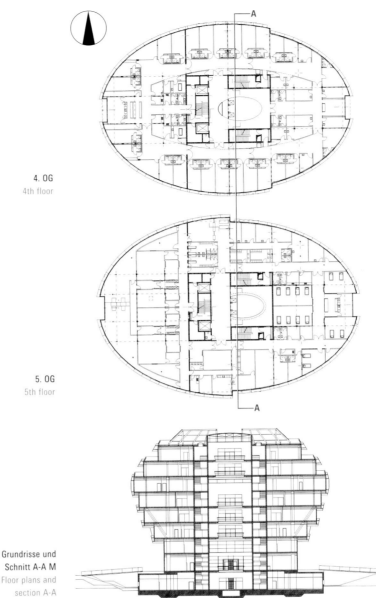

4. OG
4th floor

5. OG
5th floor

Grundrisse und Schnitt A-A M
Floor plans and section A-A

Areas of responsibility, design concept and organisation

The Institute is intended to be a specialist clinic and research centre for neuroscience, driving forward such areas as the development of "neurobionics", i.e. where biological and technical methodologies are combined to repair defects of the central nervous system and the brain.

Professor Samii and the architects worked closely together on the concept of design and organisation and the solution proposed right from the beginning was that the external appearance and internal structure of the building would suggest associations with the form and structure of the human brain – including the "furrow" between the left and right halves of the brain. The construction was therefore intended to be quite significantly different from the types of building typically used for hospitals and research institutes.

The basement houses, essentially, research labs, kitchens and services. The ground floor has an entrance hall with reception area, restaurant and lecture theatre. The first floor is devoted to radiological diagnostics. Wards with a total of 100 beds are on floors two to four. Operating theatres and the intensive care unit are on the fifth floor. Interdisciplinary doctors' consulting rooms are to be found on the sixth floor and clinical management and meeting rooms on the seventh floor.

Die unterschiedlichen Reflexionen

- der transparenten Fenstergläser und der rückseitig farbbeschichteten Glaspaneele der inneren Schale und
- der geneigten Glasstreifen der äußeren Schale mit ihrem Siebdruck-Muster

geben zusammen mit dem jeweils individuell eingestellten äußeren Sonnenschutz in Form von Rollscreens der Gebäudehülle einen gewollt patchworkartigen, lebendigen Charakter.

Die Konstruktion der inneren Schale

besteht aus geschosshohen, 2,50 m breiten Elementen in Pfosten-Riegel-Konstruktion des Schüco-Systems SK 60 V mit Dreh- und Kippflügeln im System Royal S75 B.1.

Alle Aluminium-Profile sind thermisch getrennt und entsprechen der Rahmenmaterialgruppe 1.0 nach DIN 4108.

Die horizontalen Elementstöße liegen jeweils in Ebene der

Montagepfosten (s. Horizontalschnitte). Die aus der Ellipsenform resultierenden unterschiedlichen Winkel im Anschluss an die Mittelpfosten werden von den EPDM-Glasfalzdichtungen aufgenommen.

Die Elemente wurden im herstellenden Metallbaubetrieb komplett vorgefertigt und am Bau mittels Kränen und Hubbühnen montiert. Sie sind im Bereich der Deckenkonstruktion mit Stahlblechen für den Transport ausgesteift und übernehmen zusammen mit der feuerbeständigen Füllung der Fugen zu den Deckenvorderkanten den Schutz gegen Feuerüberschlag von Geschoss zu Geschoss.

Auf den besonnten Seiten ist ein äußerer Sonnenschutz in Form von elektrisch betriebenen Rollscreens angeordnet. Die äußere Reinigung der Festverglasung erfolgt von den umlaufenden Terrassen bzw. Gitterrosten aus, wobei für letztere Anleinpunkte zur Absturzsicherung vorhanden sind.

Detailansicht
Detail view

Blick auf NW-Seite
View to NW-side

The glazed building envelope-primarily consists of:

- An internal shell which is a thermally broken aluminium structure designed as an insulated envelope
- A virtual external shell made of strips of frameless glass fixed at single points, which emphasise the horizontal lines of the building and which, because of their sloped position, resemble the shape of the human skull.

The only single-glazed sections are the curtain walling on the ground and first floors and the two "furrows" of structural glazing.

Different reflections given by:

- The transparent windows and glazed panels of the internal envelope which have coloured coatings on the back
- The sloping strips of glass in the external shell with a sieve-like pattern

together with the individually adjustable roller blinds on the building envelope to protect against the sun give it the desired patchwork, dynamic appearance.

The internal envelope structure
is made up of floor to ceiling 2.5 m wide mullion-transom units using profiles from Schüco's SK 60 V system with side hung and bottom hung windows from the Royal S75 B.1 system. All the aluminium profiles are thermally broken and fulfil the requirements of frame material group 1.0 in accordance with DIN 4108. The horizontal unit joints are each at the level of the split mullions (see horizontal section). The various different angles at the joints with the centre profiles which come from the oval shape are accommodated by EPDM glazing rebate gaskets. The units were completely

prefabricated by an aluminium fabricator and erected on site using cranes and hoisting platforms. They were reinforced with steel panels at floor RPW level for transport purposes, which, together with the fire resistant filling in the joints with the floor front edges, protect against flashover from floor to floor.

The side of the building facing the sun has electrically operated roller screens to provide external protection. The fixed glazing can be cleaned on the outside from the terraces and grilles surrounding the building. The latter have connection points for safety lanyards to prevent anyone working on them from falling off.

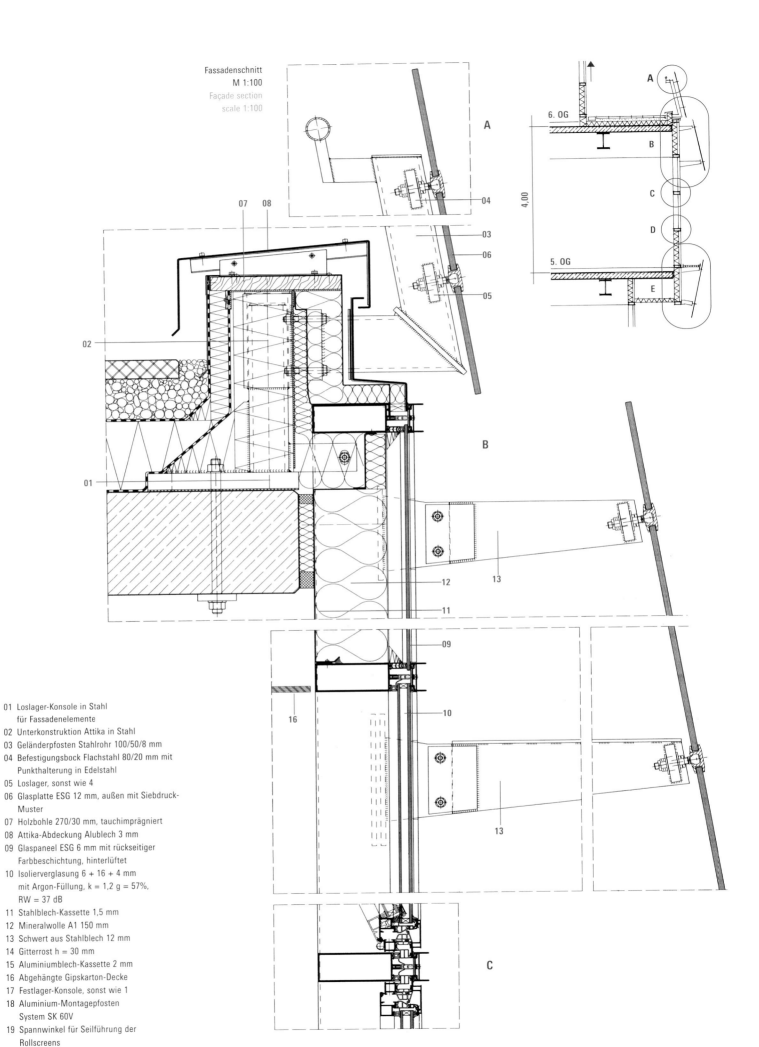

Fassadenschnitt
M 1:100
Façade section
scale 1:100

01 Loslager-Konsole in Stahl
   für Fassadenelemente
02 Unterkonstruktion Attika in Stahl
03 Geländerpfosten Stahlrohr 100/50/8 mm
04 Befestigungsbock Flachstahl 80/20 mm mit
   Punkthalterung in Edelstahl
05 Loslager, sonst wie 4
06 Glasplatte ESG 12 mm, außen mit Siebdruck-
   Muster
07 Holzbohle 270/30 mm, tauchimprägniert
08 Attika-Abdeckung Alublech 3 mm
09 Glaspaneel ESG 6 mm mit rückseitiger
   Farbbeschichtung, hinterlüftet
10 Isolierverglasung 6 + 16 + 4 mm
   mit Argon-Füllung, k = 1,2 g = 57%,
   RW = 37 dB
11 Stahlblech-Kassette 1,5 mm
12 Mineralwolle A1 150 mm
13 Schwert aus Stahlblech 12 mm
14 Gitterrost h = 30 mm
15 Aluminiumblech-Kassette 2 mm
16 Abgehängte Gipskarton-Decke
17 Festlager-Konsole, sonst wie 1
18 Aluminium-Montagepfosten
   System SK 60V
19 Spannwinkel für Seilführung der
   Rollscreens

Alle bewitterten bzw. verdeckten Bauteile in Stahl
sind verzinkt!

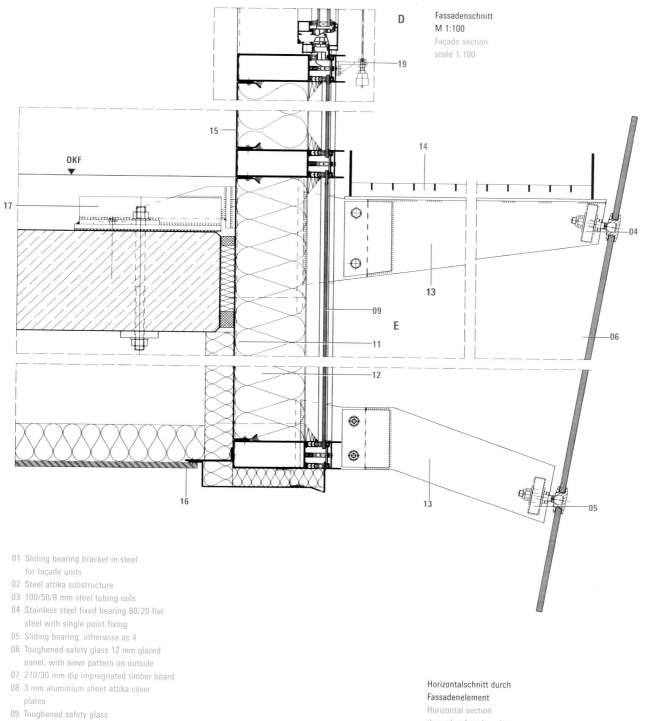

D

19

15

OKF

14

17

13

09

E

11

12

16

13

04

06

05

01 Sliding bearing bracket in steel
   for façade units
02 Steel attika substructure
03 100/50/8 mm steel tubing rails
04 Stainless steel fixed bearing 80/20 flat
   steel with single point fixing
05 Sliding bearing, otherwise as 4
06 Toughened safety glass 12 mm glazed
   panel, with sieve pattern on outside
07 270/30 mm dip impregnated timber board
08 3 mm aluminium sheet attika cover
   plates
09 Toughened safety glass
   6 mm rear ventilated glazed panel with
   colour coating on the back
10 Argon filled 6 + 16 + 4 double glazed unit ,
   k = 1.2 g = 57 %, RW = 37 dB
11 1.5 mm steel infill panel
12 150 mm A1 mineral wool
13 12 mm steel plate brackets
14 Grille h = 30 mm
15 2 mm aluminium sheet
16 Suspended plasterboard ceiling
17 Fixed bearing bracket, otherwise as 1
18 SK 60V aluminium split mullion
19 Angle for roller blind cable guide

All sections open to the weather and
concealed components made of steel
have been galvanised!

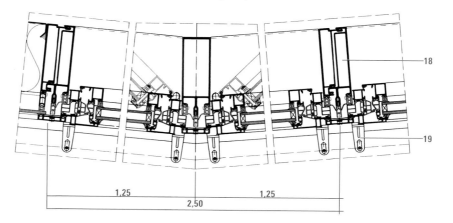

18

19

1,25

1,25

2,50

St. Gallen, Switzerland

Planung
Design
Dipl. Arch. BSA/SIA
Bruno Gerosa, Zurich

Kuppel und Glaswand
des Eingangs- und
Pausenfoyers
Dome and glass wall of
the entrance hall

Das Weiterbildungszentrum der Universität St. Gallen liegt auf einem anfangs flach, später steil nach Nordwesten abfallenden Gelände in fußläufiger Entfernung zum eigentlichen Universitätskomplex. Dank der topografischen Situation konnte der Baukörper mit seinem kuppelgekrönten, zweigeschossigen Eingangs- und Pausenfoyer so gestaltet werden, dass er bergseitig nur eingeschossig in Erscheinung tritt und so den Blick ins Tal wenig beeinträchtigt.

The centre of Continuing Education at the University of St Gallen is located on a site that slopes at first gently then more steeply towards the Northwest, and which is within walking distance of the main university campus. The topography of the site means that the building structure with its domed roof and two-storey entrance hall could be designed so that it appears to be a single-storey building when viewed from the mountain and therefore has a minimal impact on the view over the valley.

Die Gesamtansicht von
Osten in den Eingangs-
hof, darunter die
Ansicht von Südwesten
The overall view
towards the entrance
courtyard from the East,
underneath the view
from the South-west

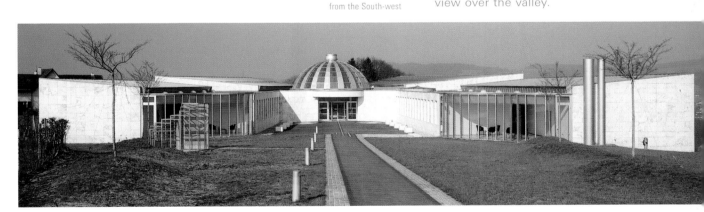

Manchester, Great Britain

Planung
Design
Mills, Beaumont, Leavey,
(R. Avery), Manchester

Mitwirkende Sachverständige
Consultants
Nelson Tectonics Ltd.

Die geschwungene Linienführung der Fassade wurde durch gebogene Aluminium-Formteile, Glasflächen und Aluminium-Profile erreicht.

The curved line of the façade was produced by curved aluminium panels, glass and aluminium profiles.

Außenansichten
Bibliothek Manchester
Universität
Outside views
Manchester
University Library

Zurich, Switzerland

Planung
Design
giuliani.hönger ag, Zurich

Mitwirkende Sachverständige
Consultants
Metall-Bau-Technik Reto Gloor,
Guntershausen

Außenansichten
Fachhochschule Sihlhof
Outside views
Technical College Sihlhof

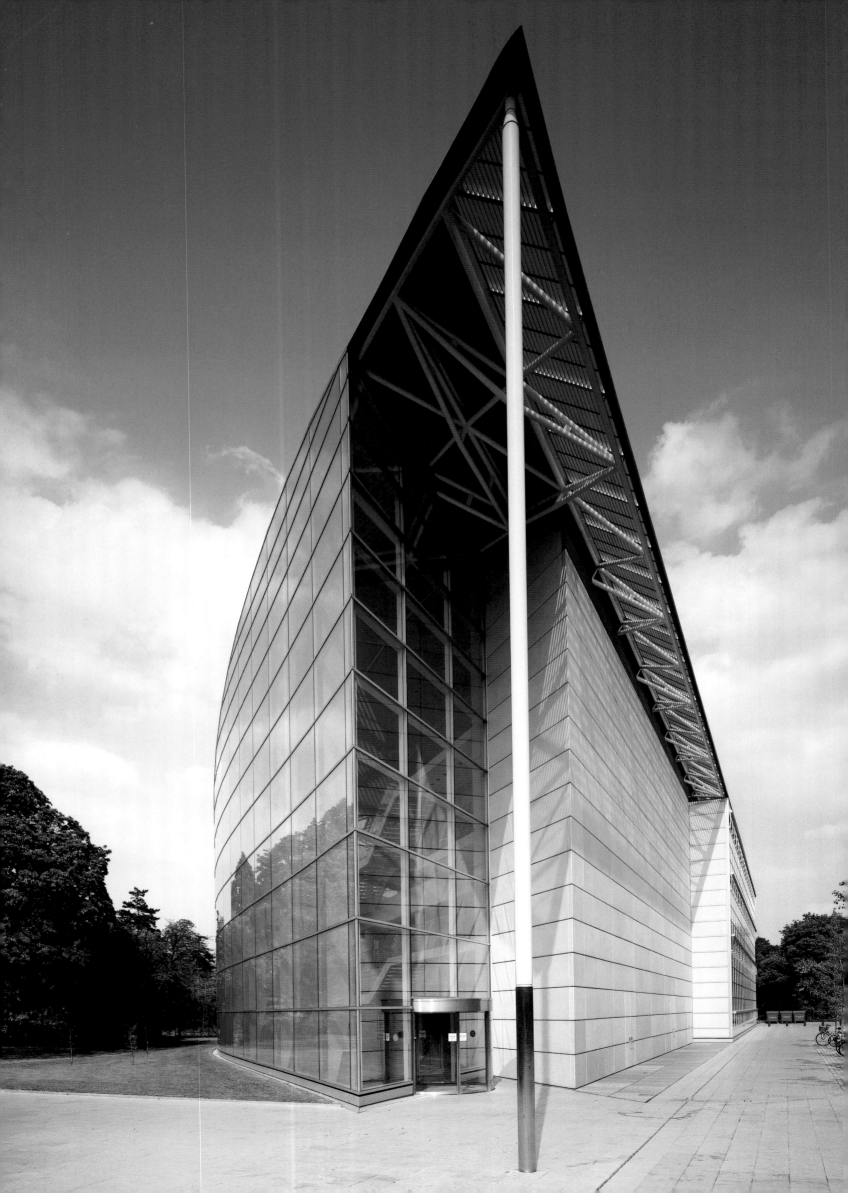

Cambridge, Great Britain

Planung
Design
Foster and Partners, London

Den Neubau auf dem Universitätsgelände bezeichnete das englische Architects' Journal als „technically sophisticated Design". Die gläsernen Teile der Gebäudehülle ruhen auf einer Sonderanfertigung des Systems SG 50, dem Structural-Glazing-System von Schüco: innen weiß beschichtet, nach außen dunkelbronze eloxiert.

The Architects' Journal rated the design of the new building on the University campus as "technically sophisticated". The glass members of the cladding are based on a special construction of system SG 50, the Schüco Structural Glazing System: internally coated white and externally anodized dark bronze.

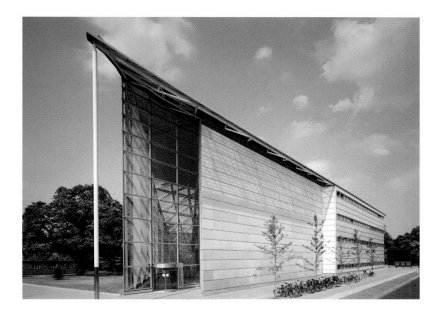

Außenansichten
Law Faculty Cambridge
Outside views
Law Faculty Cambridge

Cottbus, Germany

Planung
Design
kleyer.koblitz.architekten, Berlin

Mitwirkende Sachverständige
Consultants
KFE, Kucharzak Fassaden
Engineering, Berlin

Das klar konzipierte Bauwerk
dient dem Erforschen und Expe-
rimentieren mit Metallen. Entsprechend modern und sachlich
präsentiert es sich in der Spra-
che des Automobilbaus.
Die Stirnseiten und die schräg-
gestellte Westfassade der geschwungenen Halle sind verglast. Die anderen Seiten sind
durchgehend mit Aluminium
verkleidet.
Durchgesteckt ist ein roter Riegel, der weit sichtbar aus dem
Gebäude ragt und als Haus im
Haus das dreigeschossige Bauwerk durchläuft.
Er öffnet sich großzügig sowohl
zur Halle wie zum Außenraum
und beherbergt die Büros und
Besprechungsräume der
Wissenschaftler.

This centre specialising in metals
research and experimentation
has a clean design. Both modern
and industrial, the building uses
the language of automotive
manufacture.
The curved hall is clad throughout
with aluminium, whilst the end
walls and sloping west façade
are glazed.
A red bar juts conspicuously out
of the building and runs through
the structure on three floors, as
a building within a building.
Opening out onto both the hall
and the outside, it houses the
research offices and meeting
rooms.

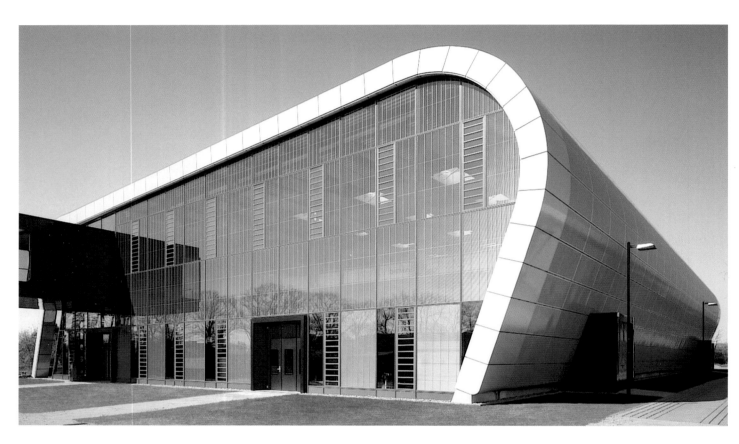

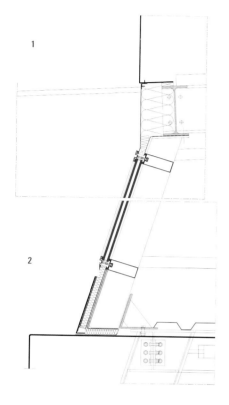

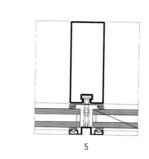

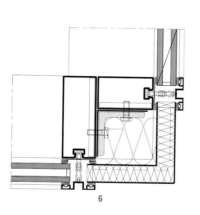

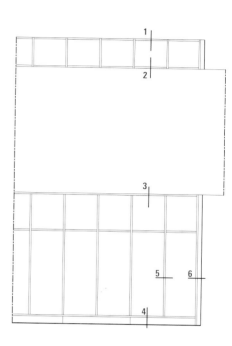

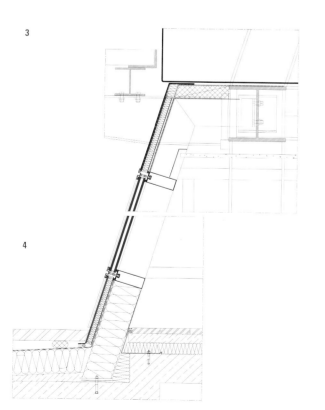

Samuel-von-Pufendorf-High-School

Flöha, Germany

Planung
Design
Allmann, Sattler, Wappner,
Architekten, Munich

Außen- und
Innenansichten
Outside and inside
views

Gesamtansicht
Pufendorf-Gymnasium
Aerial view
Pufendorf-High-School

Bitterfeld, Germany

Planung
Design
Scholl Architekten GmbH,
Bitterfeld

Detailansichten
Berufsschulzentrum
Detail views Vocational
College Centre

Lincoln, Great Britain

Planung
Design
RMJM-Architects, London

Auf 16 ha ehemaligem Eisen-
bahngelände entstand Phase 1
der Universitätsbauten für 1.500
Studierende. Das nach Norden,
zur Wasserfront gerichtete
Hauptgebäude besteht aus einer
Serie von 24 x 15 m großen
Modulen, vertikal gegliedert
durch Erschließungs- und
Haustechnik-Türme. Für
die großflächig verglaste
Fassade wurde das Schüco
System FW 50S gewählt.

Phase 1 of university buildings
for 1,500 students was built on
15 hectares of former British
Rail land. Towards the north,
facing the waterfront, the main
building consists of a series of
24 x 15 m sized modules,
vertical structuring emphasized
by staircases and service towers.
Schüco System FW 50S was
selected for large glazed façade.

Außenansichten
Universität Lincolnshire
Outside views
University Lincolnshire

Martin-Luther-King Comprehensive School

Marl-Lenkerbeck, Germany

Planung
Design
Kresing Architekten, Munster

Erfrischend positiver Neubau
einer Schule. Die Öffnungen in
der Fassade sind großformatig
und springen scheinbar zufällig
an ihre Position.
Das weit auskragende Dach
simuliert Schutz und orientiert
sich zur Natur hin.
Auch die Wahl der Materialien,
wie mit Bootslack beschichtetes
Holz an Verkleidungen und
Brüstungen, ist angenehm.

The design of this new school is
refreshingly positive. Openings
in the façade are large-format
and seem to fall into place as if
by chance. The overhanging roof
suggests protection and reveals
an inclination towards nature.
Another attractive feature is the
choice of materials, such as
the varnish-coated timber on
cladding and spandrel panels.

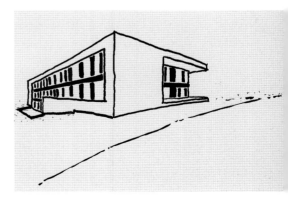

343

Außen- und
Innenansichten
Martin-Luther-King
Gesamtschule
Outside and inside
views Martin-Luther-
King school

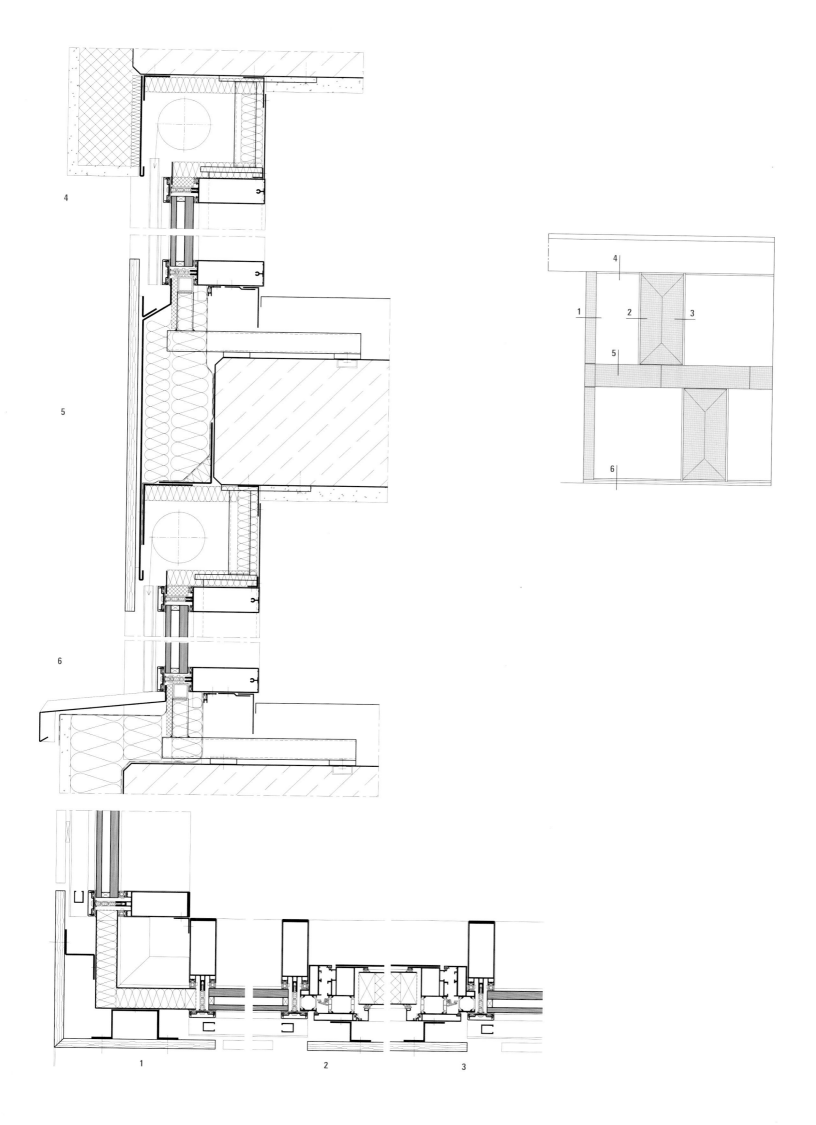

Cottbus, Germany

Planung
Design
Architektengemeinschaft
Bassenge, Puhan-Schulz,
Heinrich, Schreiber, Berlin

Außenansichten
Oberstufenzentrum
Outside views Further
Education Centre

Verkehrsbauten sind die Bauten
für Transport und Verkehr, wie
Flughäfen, Bahnhöfe, Parkhäu-
ser, Brücken, Verkehrsknoten-
punkte, Mautstationen und vie-
les mehr. Es sind Baustrukturen
besonderer Komplexität, die
hohe Ansprüche an Sicherheit,
Komfort sowie an Wirtschaftlichkeit und Nachhaltigkeit
stellen.

Transport nodes are buildings
for transport, such as airports,
railway stations, multi-storey car
parks, bridges, transport inter-
changes, toll stations and much
more. They are particularly
complex building structures that
require high levels of safety,
comfort, economic viability and
sustainability.

Verkehrsbauten
Transport nodes

Zacharias+Partner
WS Atkins & Partners Dirrix van Wylick
Derek Walker Associates Waser, Achermann Wörrlein & Partner
Engin Ünal and Ibrahim Öztürk Verhaegen Wartiainen Architects Lunde & Lövseth
Studio ADS Sp Studio E Architects Prof. Dr. Jeko Tilev Csaba Tompos Pierre Traversier
Arch. Z. Stanik, Arch. J. Lelatko Tadeusz Szumielewicz i Partnerzy, ARCA Architects & Consultans Percy Thomas
SIAT Architektur Siklósi és Társa Skovgaard Sørensens, Friis & Moltke, P. Andersen
RKW Rhode Kellermann Wawrowsky RMJM Schaub+Partner Schmidt-Schicketanz Prof. Schneider-Wessling Scholl Architekten
Hans-Hermann Seydel
Reinhardt+Sander Cabinet Roth Hartmut+Ingeborg Rüdiger Sam-Woo Architects Sauerbruch Hutton
Jo Rabaey Florian Riegler & Roger Riewe Renner Hainke Wirth Planungsring Ressel RHWL Architects M. Papanikolaou, S. Sakelaridou
Reinhard Müller Müller Reimann Leonardo Proli Puhl Antal Építész Irodája Dieter Punckt Pysall-Starenberg & Partner
John Portman & Associates Obermeyer Albis-Bauplan Ollertz & Ollertz Planteam West Renzo Piano
Raivo Puuseep Richard Meier & Partners van Mierop & Belaieff Müller-Hartburg ZT Cesar Pelli Novotny Mähner
Kosig+Kosig Kresing Architekten Arn. Meijs Mills, Beaumont, Leavey Murphy/Jahn J.S.K. Perkins & Will
Marki and Associates Kjelgaard & Pedersen Kwang Sung+Soren Mengler KG Meyer Adviesburo NBBJ-HUS-PKA Architects NPS NHP
Prof. Mäckler Kohn, Pedersen, Fox Kaci Archiplan Prof. Kada Kahlen+Partner Karres Hartmeyer Dreyer C. F. Møllers Morphosis Architects
Koch und Partner Michael Knoche Hyvämäki-Karhunen-Parkkinen IFB Planungsgruppe Helmut Kriegbaum Meyer en van Schooten
Kleyer, Koblitz Kister Scheithauer Gross Michel Jaspers Henning Larsens Henze+Vahjen Hochtief Prof. Kaup, Dr. Scholz, Jesse+Partner, Obermeyer Michaelsen und Michaelsen
KHR AS Arkitekter Michael Knoche Henn Architekten Prof. Holzbauer José Antonio Galea Fernández Gatermann+Schossig Prof. Kaup Ingenhoven Overdiek Julián Franco Lopez D. Manuel de Lorenzo
J/V GEK S.A. Themeliodomi S.A. Peter Henkel Prof. Fehringer Thomas Feiger Klaus-M. Hoffmann Daniel Libeskind
Häussler Gruppe Dieckmann & Partner Dissing+Weitling Prof. Domenig Gehry Partners Inros Planungsgesellschaft
Daller, Huber Prof. Bonatti Claude Bouney and Georges Guerin Alexander Freiherr v. Branca Dr. Finta Foster and Partners Hohaus+Partner Holder Mathias
BM+P BHLM Architekten Bieling & Bieling Dorin Stefan Gerber Architekten Giuliani Hönger HPP
Autorska Precownia Ecolo Architekten Wolfgang Brunbauer Bruno Gerosa gmp Grüttner Architekten
Baum and Kwiecinski, Stepa, Siudowski ASW ATEC Atelier 4A Atelier d'Art Urbain Biuro Projektowe BRT Architekten Alec French G+D Studiogroep GWB Planungsgesellschaft
Arte charpentier et associés Sattler, Wappner Blum/Spomizz de Architekten Cie Cabinet Guillemont Herbert Gergs
AGS Architekten AIC Bau-Planungs GmbH Allmann, Angerer & Feuser Bulanda-Mucha Architekci D.M.J.M. Grimm+Bauen
3xNielsen A Tasarim, Ali Osman Öztürk Aare Saks Anderegg Architekten Puhan-Schulz, Heinrich, Schreiber Uri Blumenthal
Daller, Huber Atelier Pak Atelier WW ATP Aviaplan Bassenge- Puhan-Schulz Grünuchi+ms Architekten
Architekt DEGW

Gardermoen, Norway

Bauherr
Client
Oslo Hovedflyplass AS, Oslo

Entwurfs- und Ausführungsplanung
Design and construction
planning
Aviaplan as, Oslo

Projektleitung
Project leader
Gudmund Stokke, Arch. MNAL

Fassadenplanung
Façade design
Christian Henriksen,
Arch. MNAL

Bauleitung
Site management
Oslo Hovedflyplass AS, Oslo

Tragwerksplanung
Structural engineers
Ove Aruo & Partners, London,
Great Britain
Reinertsengruppe Oslo

Generalunternehmer
General contractor
Selmer ASA, Oslo

Ausführung der Fassaden
Façade construction
Flex Fasader AB, Örebro,
Sweden
Bolseth Glass AS, Sandane

Oslos neuer Flughafen – 45 km
nordöstlich in der Nähe des
Ortes Gardermoen gelegen –
wurde nach nur 4-jähriger Bauzeit im Oktober 1998 in Betrieb
genommen. Er ersetzt den auf
einer Halbinsel im Oslofjord
gelegenen alten Flughafen
Fornebu, der nicht mehr erweite-
rungsfähig war und auch zu
nahe an der Osloer Wohnbebauung lag. Der neue Flughafen
ist – neben einer Schnellstraße –
durch eine Schnellbahn mit
der Stadt verbunden (Fahrzeit
19 Min.).
Der Auftrag für den Masterplan
und für das Passagierterminal
wurde direkt dem Architekten-
und Ingenieurteam Aviaplan as
erteilt, das 1989 schon einen
Projektwettbewerb für den an
anderer Stelle geplanten
Flughafen gewonnen hatte.

Oslo's new airport – 45 km
to the north east close to the
town of Gardermoen – became
operational in October 1998
after just four years of
construction. It replaces the old
Fornebu airport on a peninsular
in the Oslo Fjord which could
not be expanded further and
also was too close to urban
Oslo. The new airport is located
next to an expressway and
benefits from a high speed rail
link to the town (journey time
19 minutes).
The contract for the master plan
and for the passenger terminal
was awarded directly to
Aviaplan as, a team of architects
and engineers which had already
won the project for the airport in
a different location in 1989.

351

Das Entwurfskonzept des Terminals

Zwischen den in N-S-Richtung verlaufenden Start- und Landebahnen liegt das Terminal wie eine Spange. Es besteht aus einer großen zentralen Halle von 165 x 110 m und zwei seitlichen, je 330 m langen Armen mit 3-seitigen Andockmöglichkeiten für Flugzeuge, wobei der östliche Arm die interkontinentalen, der westliche die Inlandsflüge bedient.
Dieser insgesamt ca. 830 m lange Bau wird als „Pier A" bezeichnet und kann bei Bedarf durch Pier „B" und „C" erweitert werden. Die dafür erforderlichen Verbindungstunnel sind unter dem Vorfeld schon im Rohbau angelegt.

Die Führung der Passagiere im Terminal

Die Abflugebene mit Check-in-Schaltern, Pass- und Sicherheitskontrolle, Restaurants sowie Zugängen zu den Gates liegt im OG. Dagegen werden die ankommenden Passagiere in den Armen über der Abflugebene in die zentrale Halle und dort mittels Rolltreppen ins EG zu Passkontrolle und Gepäckausgabe geführt.
Die Schnellbahnstation liegt am Westgiebel der zentralen Halle auf UG-Ebene und ist durch Rolltreppen und Aufzüge mit dem EG und OG verbunden.
Das ganze Terminal zeichnet sich durch eine verblüffend einfache und sinnvolle Führung der Passagiere aus. Die großen Glaswände öffnen sich
- an der N-Seite auf das Flugvorfeld und die dahinter liegende Waldlandschaft,
- an der S-Seite auf die 2-geschossige Vorfahrt für Busse und PKW sowie auf ein Parkhaus für 4000 PKW und unterstützen damit die Orientierung.

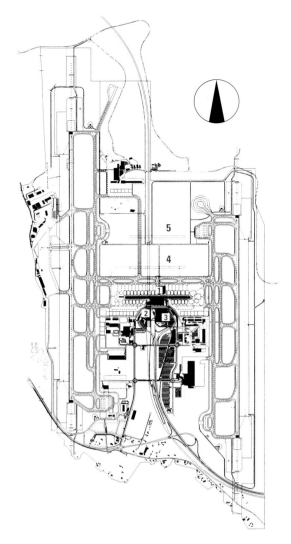

Lageplan
Location plan

1 Terminal Pier A
  Terminal pier A
2 Schnellbahnstation
  Express train station
3 Parkhaus
  Car park
4 Pier B
  Pier B
5 Pier C
  Pier C

The design of the terminal

The terminal building is located between the two north to south runways. It comprises a large central concourse measuring 165 by 110 m and two wings 330 m long, one at each side, with three-lateral docks for aircrafts. The east wing is for international, the west wing for domestic traffic.
This 830 m long structure is known as "pier A" and can be expanded if need be by means of piers "B" and "C". The initial structural work required below the apron for the tunnels linking the piers has already been completed.

Passenger flow within the terminal

The departure area with check-in desks, passport and security control, restaurants and gate access is located on the top floor. Arriving passengers are led through the wing blocks above the departure area into the central concourse and down escalators to the ground level where passport control and baggage reclaim are located. The station for the express train is located at the gable on the west side of the central concourse on the bottom floor and is linked to the ground and upper levels by escalators and lifts.

The best feature of the entire terminal is the amazingly simple and intelligent way in which passenger flow has been planned. The large glass walls open:
- Onto the apron and the forest behind on the north side.
- The two-level approach area for busses and cars and a car park with a capacity of 4000 cars on the south side, aiding orientation.

Passagierterminal von
Nordwesten
Passenger terminal
from the north west

Passagierterminal von
Südwesten
Passenger terminal
from the south west

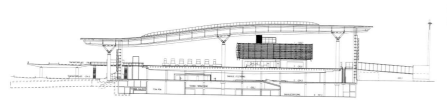

Schnitt A-A
Section A-A

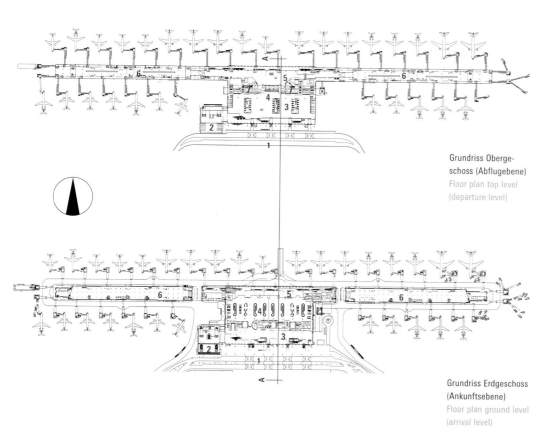

Grundriss Oberge-
schoss (Abflugebene)
Floor plan top level
(departure level)

Grundriss Erdgeschoss
(Ankunftsebene)
Floor plan ground level
(arrival level)

Legende Obergeschoss:
1 Vorfahrt Abflugebene
2 Luftraum Halle Schnellbahnstation
3 Check-in-Schalter
4 Pass- und Sicherheitskontrolle
5 Restaurant, Café usw.
6 Wartehalle und Gates
7 3-gesch. Bürotrakte
Legend top level:
1 Approach departure level
2 Clear area hall of the express train station
3 Check-in desks
4 Passport- and security control
5 Restaurant, café etc.
6 Waiting area and gates
7 Three-storey office section

Legende Erdgeschoss:
1 Vorfahrt Ankunftsebene
2 Halle Schnellbahnstation
3 Pass- und Zollkontrolle
4 Gepäckausgabe
5 Rolltreppen für ankommende Passagiere
6 Gepäcksortierung Abflug/Ankunft
Legend ground level:
1 Approach arrival level
2 Hall express train station
3 Passport- and customs-control
4 Baggage reclaim
5 Escalators for arriving passengers
6 Baggage sorting departures/arrivals

Die Gestaltung der zentralen Halle des Terminals

Der großartige Raumeindruck der Halle beruht auf ihrer Höhe, auf ihren großen Glaswänden und auf dem eleganten Schwung der weit gespannten hölzernen Binder-Paare mit den dazwischen abgehängten Lichtgittern. Sie lassen tagsüber diffuses Licht vom Dach durch, abends wirken sie als Reflektor für die starken Deckenstrahler. Zwei wie Möbel in die Halle eingestellte 3-geschossige, voll verglaste Bürotrakte für die Verwaltung des Flughafens und für die Fluglinien geben ihr den notwendigen Maßstab.

Die Konstruktion der großen Glaswände

Ihre Abmessungen betragen auf der N-Seite 165 x 26 m, auf der S-Seite 165 x 20 m! Beide Wände sind fest verglast und bestehen aus einer Pfosten-Riegel-Sonderkonstruktion auf Basis des Profilsystems FW 50. Die erheblichen horizontalen Lasten aus Winddruck und -sog sowie die vertikalen Lasten aus Eigengewicht (insbesondere der 3,0 x 1,5 m großen Isolierglasscheiben) werden jeweils in den Kreuzungspunkten der Riegel mit den Pfosten über 3-dimensional justierbare Anschluss-Elemente in die V-förmigen Arme und Stahlstützen eingeleitet, die in 1,2 m Abstand frei hinter den Glaswänden stehen. Diese Stützen spannen frei zwischen der Bodenplatte und der Dachschale der Halle und bestehen aus Stahlrohren von 300 bzw. 120 mm Ø, die mittels aufgeschweißter Bleche zu einem steifen Hohlprofil verbunden sind.

Die oberen Teile der Glaswände sind im Hinblick auf Verformungen der weit gespannten Dachkonstruktion durch Schneelasten von der Dachschale abgehängt. Ihre Alu-Konstruktion und die aussteifenden Stahlhängepfosten sind daher beweglich an die unteren Teile der Glaswände bzw. die jeweils obersten V-Arme der Stahlstützen angeschlossen.

Die thermischen Längenänderungen der Alu-Konstruktion werden horizontal in jedem Kreuzungspunkt der Riegel mit den Pfosten durch kompressible Dichtungsmanschetten aus Zell-Kautschuk, vertikal durch verschiebbare Pfostenstöße mit einer speziellen Abdichtungstechnik aufgenommen.

Die Eckausbildungen zwischen der N- bzw. S-Glaswand und den nur teilweise verglasten Giebelwänden können Bewegungen aus Windlasten in N-S-Richtung und in O-W-Richtung aufnehmen.

Vor den oberen Scheibenfeldern aller Glaswände sind in 60 cm Abstand Alu-Konstruktionen mit elektrisch betriebenen Rollscreens angeordnet, um direkten Lichteinfall bei flach stehender Sonne (im Sommer auch von der N-Seite!) zu verhindern.

Durch die geringe Ansichtsbreite der Alu-Profile und der Stahlstützen auf der Raumseite wirken die Glaswände im Verhältnis zu ihren Abmessungen außerordentlich leicht und elegant!

The design of the central concourse

The impression of space in the concourse comes from its height, the large glass walls and elegant flourish of pairs of wide span wooden trusses and the lighting gantries which are suspended between them. They allow light to diffuse through the roof during the day, and during the night they act as reflectors for the powerful ceiling-mounted lights.

Two three storey fully glazed office sections for airport administration and airline staff are placed in the immense concourse like pieces of furniture giving a sense of scale to the structure.

The construction of the large glass walls

The glass wall on the north side measures 165 x 20 m, and the wall on the south side measures 165 x 20 m. Both walls have fixed glazing and are custom built mullion/transom structures using the Schüco FW 50 profile system. The considerable horizontal loads from wind pressure and negative wind load and the vertical loads from dead weight (in particular the 3.0 x 1.5 m panes of double glazing) are transmitted via the intersection points between transoms and mullions into V-shaped arms and steel supports which are free standing 1.2 m behind the glass walls by means of three-dimensional adjustable connecting pieces. These supports are free standing between the floor slab and the roof shell of the hall and are made of steel tubes with a diameter of 300 or 120 mm, fixed to a rigid hollow profile by means of welded plates.

The top sections of the glass walls hang from the roof shell to cater for possible buckling of the wide span roof structure caused by snow load. For this reason, the aluminium structure and the rigid steel mullions have a flexible connection to the lower sections of the glass walls and each of the top V-arms of the steel supports.

Changes in the length of the aluminium structure due to fluctuating temperatures are transmitted horizontally into each of the transom/mullion junctions by means of compressible gasket sleeves made of cellular rubber and vertically through flexible mullion joints using unique gasket technology.

The corners between the north and south glass walls and the gable walls which are only partially glazed are designed to allow for movements from wind loads in a north-south direction and in an east-west direction.

There are aluminium structures with electrically operated blinds every 60 cm from the top panes in all the glass walls to prevent the direct entry of light when the sun is low in the sky (including the north side in the summer).

The slim face width of the aluminium profiles and the steel supports on the inside, the glass walls appear to be much lighter and more elegant than would be expected from their actual dimensions.

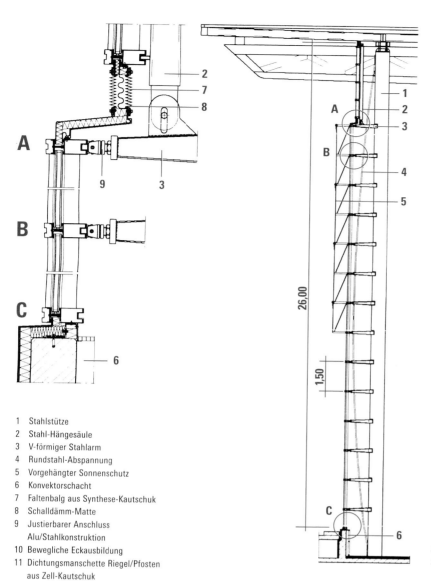

A

B

C

9   3

B

C

6

26,00

1,50

A

B

C

1 Stahlstütze
2 Stahl-Hängesäule
3 V-förmiger Stahlarm
4 Rundstahl-Abspannung
5 Vorgehängter Sonnenschutz
6 Konvektorschacht
7 Faltenbalg aus Synthese-Kautschuk
8 Schalldämm-Matte
9 Justierbarer Anschluss
   Alu/Stahlkonstruktion
10 Bewegliche Eckausbildung
11 Dichtungsmanschette Riegel/Pfosten
   aus Zell-Kautschuk

1 Steel supports
2 Steel mullion
3 V-shaped steel arms
4 Steel rod bracing
5 Solar shading
6 Convector heating shaft
7 Synthetic-rubber
   concertina wall
8 Sound insulation mat
9 Adjustable connector aluminium/steel
   construction
10 Corners which absorb movement
11 Cellular-rubber transom/mullion
   gasket sleeve

E

D   F

3,00   3,00   3,00

6

Schnitt A-A
Section A-A

Grundriss Glaswand
NO-Ecke
Outline of glass wall
NE corner wall

E

1

3

7   11

D

10

9

11

F

Blick in die Abflughalle
nach Nordosten
View into the departure
hall to NE

Blick auf Glaswand N
(links Draht-Skulptur)
View on the
glass wall N (lefthand
rod-sculpture)

Blick durch die
Glaswand N auf
Flugvorfeld und Wald
View through the
glass wall N on apron
and forest

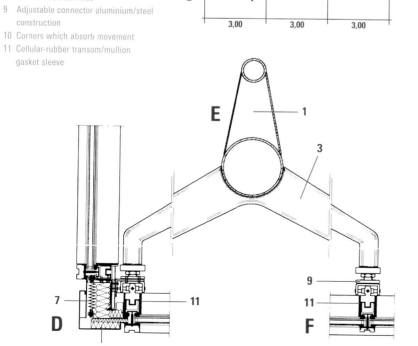

355

Fryderyk Chopin
International Airport

Warsaw, Poland

Planung
Design
HOCHTIEF

Außenansicht
Flughafen Warschau
Outside view
Warsaw Airport

Graz, Austria

Planung
Design
Architekten Florian Riegler &
Roger Riewe, Graz

Mitwirkende Sachverständige
Consultants
Bauph. Dr. Thomberger

Der langgestreckte Flachbau
hat eine flächenbündige
Structural-Glazing-Fassade, die
jedoch durch vorgesetzte
Aluminium-Elemente aufgebrochen und dynamisiert wurde.
Schmal-lange Fassadenfelder
und ebensolche Senkklapp-
Fensterflügel verstärken die horizontale Dynamik.

The long low building is
designed with a flush structural
glazing façade interrupted by
mounted aluminium elements
which give the façade a
dynamic effect. Long low façade
elements and top hung windows
of the same system emphasise
the horizontal fenestration.

Detailansichten
Flughafen Graz
Detail views
Graz Airport

Stockholm, Sweden

Planung
Design
van Mierop & Belaieff
Arkitektkontor

Mitwirkende Sachverständige
Consultants
Rob van Mierop, Dennis Belaieff,
Leif Nilsson

Außenansicht
Sky City
Outside view
Sky City

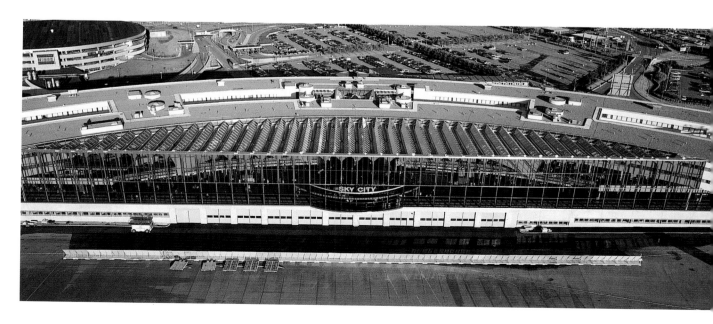

Latnisko Gdansk

Gdansk-Rebiechowa, Poland

Planung
Design
Pracownia Arch. Baum und
Kwiecinski
Andrzej Stepa, Lech Siudowski

Außenansichten
Latnisko Gdansk
Outside views
Latnisko Gdansk

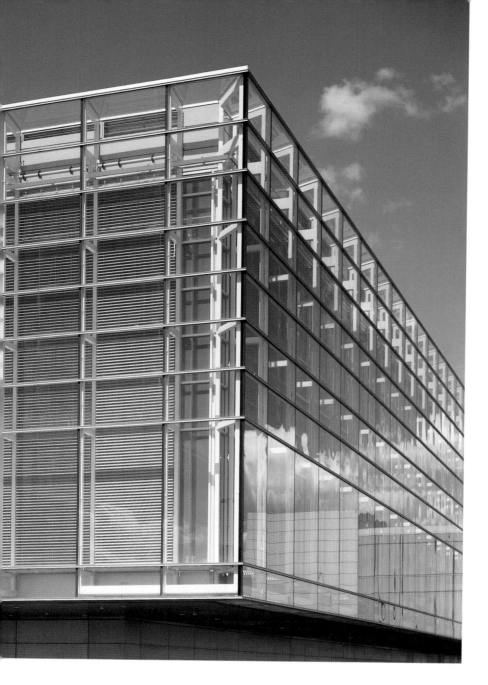

**Außenansichten
Arlanda Flughafen**
Outside views
Arlanda Airport

Inchon, South Korea

Planung
Design
KACI Architecture, ARCHIPLAN
INC. Architects & Planners

Mitwirkende Sachverständige
Consultants
Yusin Engineering, Dawoo
Engineering

Außenansichten Inchon
International Airport
Outside views Inchon
International Airport

Vienna-Schwechat, Austria

Planung
Design
Architekt Prof. Dipl.-Ing.
Franz Fehringer, Vienna

Der optische Effekt einer gebrochenen Fassadenfläche hat eine ganz solide Basis: das Schüco Fassadensystem SK 60V. Hier in einer Sonderkonstruktion in Kombination mit Structural Glazing-Elementen.

The optical effect of an apparently broken façade surface has a very sound base: the Schüco façade System SK 60V. A special construction combined with structurally glazed elements was used for this project.

Außenansichten
Flughafen Wien
Outside views
Vienna Airport

367

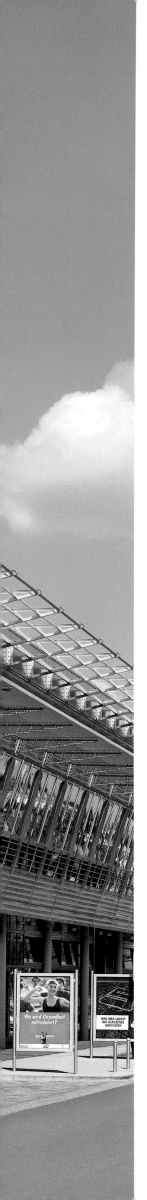

Greven, Germany

Planung und Bauleitung
Design and site management
J.S.K. Perkins & Will,
Dipl.-Ing. Architekten,
Frankfurt/Düsseldorf

Fassadenplanung
Eternal skin
Ingenieurbüro Memmert &
Partner, Neuss

Außenansicht Flughafen
Münster/Osnabrück
Outside view
Münster/Osnabrück
Airport

Hamburg, Germany

Planung
Design
renner hainke wirth architekten,
Hamburg

Tragwerksplanung
Structural engineers
Wetzel & von Seht,
Ing.-Büro für Bauwesen

Tragkonstruktion
Structural planning
Buthmann Stahlbau, Glinde

Fassadenplanung
Eternal skin
PBI Planungsbüro für
Ingenieurleistungen, Wertingen

Fassadenausführung
Façade construction
Georg Kammenhuber
GmbH & Co., Hamburg

Stahlprofile
Steel profiles
Jansen AG Oberriet

Außenansichten
Flughafen Fuhlsbüttel
Outside views
Fuhlsbüttel Airport

Mit Fliegen und Gleiten,
Leichtigkeit und Dynamik asso-
ziiert man schon von weitem das
neue Empfangsgebäude der
Lufthansa Technik. In weniger
als einem Jahr Planungs- und
Bauzeit setzte das Hamburger
Büro Renner Hainke Wirth den
Traum vom Fliegen in eine ein-
zigartige Architektur aus Stahl
und Glas um. Die filigranen
Stahlprofile unterstützen dieses
gestalterische Konzept.

From afar, the new reception
building at Lufthansa Technik
demonstrates a clear association
with flying, gliding, lightness
and dynamism. In less than a
year for design and construction,
the Hamburg-based company
Renner Hainke Wirth created the
dream of flying in a unique piece
of architecture in steel and
glass. The fine lines of the steel
profiles support the concept of
this creation.

Schüco –
das Unternehmen
Schüco –
the Company

Mission
Mission statement

Geschichte
History

Geschäftsbereiche
Activities

Beratung
Consultancy

Globale Präsenz
Global presence

Wir geben Visionen eine Gestalt.
Shaping ideas.

Mission
Mission statement

Die Gebäude auf den vorangegangenen Seiten sind mehr als eine Auswahl faszinierender Ideen und konsequenter Umsetzungen. Sie sind ein eindrucksvoller Beleg dafür, dass man Außergewöhnliches erreichen kann, wenn man an seine Ideen glaubt – und wenn man die richtigen Partner findet.

Schüco ist Europas Nummer 1 und weltweit tätig in der Realisierung von Gebäudehüllen. Das Unternehmen steht für intelligente Systeme, das breiteste Spektrum an Technologien und Werkstoffen, starke Markt- und Kundenorientierung sowie für weitreichenden Service. Dabei sehen wir unsere Aufgaben nicht nur darin, anspruchsvolle Vorgaben perfekt und zuverlässig umzusetzen. Unser Ziel ist es auch, neue Möglichkeiten aufzuzeigen, neue Ideen des Machbaren zu inspirieren oder einfach Träume zu wecken.

Innovationskraft ist nur die eine Seite unseres Schaffens. Auf der anderen Seite steht für uns das, was man heute gerne mit Nachhaltigkeit bezeichnet. Wir nennen es lieber Zeitlosigkeit. Mit Zeitlosigkeit ist nicht nur der gestalterische Aspekt gemeint. Neben klarem, ansprechendem Design geht es beim Bauen vor allem darum, Jahre voraus zu denken. Die dauerhafte Kompatibilität unserer Produkte, Langlebigkeit und Beständigkeit tragen ebenso dazu bei, nachhaltige Werte zu schaffen. Gründe, warum wir schon seit langem weltweit die höchsten Qualitätsmaßstäbe setzen in Technik, Design, Produktion und Testing.

Um aus Ihren Ideen bleibende Werte zu schaffen, sind wir immer auf der Suche nach der besseren Lösung.

The buildings on the pages of this book are more than just a selection of fascinating ideas and their ultimate implementation. They are an impressive testament to the fact that extraordinary things can be achieved if you believe in your ideas and if you find the right partners.

Schüco is Europe's No. 1 and is involved globally in the creation of building envelopes. The company stands for intelligent systems; the widest spectrum of technologies and materials; strong market and customer focus and comprehensive service. Our job, as we see it, is not merely to transform demanding requirements perfectly and reliably into reality. Our aim is also to demonstrate new possibilities, to inspire new, workable ideas, or simply to awaken dreams.

The power of innovation is only one side of our creativity. On the other hand, we stand for what is nowadays referred to as sustainability. We prefer to call it timelessness. And timelessness doesn't just refer to design. Apart from attractive designs, building is, above all, about thinking years ahead. The durable compatibility of our products, their lasting quality and high standards contribute just as much to creating sustainable value. These are the reasons why we have always set the highest quality standards worldwide in engineering, design, production and testing.

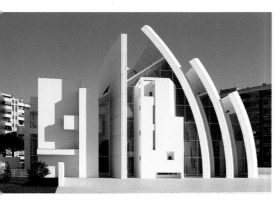

Dives in Misericordia, Rome, Italy

McLaren Technology Centre, Woking, Great Britain

Ein globales Unternehmen
kann man nur mit Profis bauen.
A global company can only be
built with professionals.

Die Erfolgsgeschichte von
Schüco startet 1951 mit dem
Bau von Schaufenstern und
Fassadenelementen aus Alu-
minium. Durch ganzheitliches
Denken, Perfektion und Inno-
vationskraft entwickelt sich
schnell ein Systembaukasten.
Nachdem Schüco 1963 zur Otto-
Fuchs-Gruppe (Meinerzhagen)
kam, begann der Aufstieg zum
weltweit tätigen Unternehmen.

In den 70er-Jahren expandiert
Schüco zunächst ins europäi-
sche Ausland und wird dann das
erste weltweit tätige Unternehmen seiner Branche. Heute sind
4.100 Mitarbeiter und 12.000
Partnerbetriebe in über 60 Ländern aktiv: als leidenschaftliche
Konstrukteure, als kundenorien-
tierte Macher, als qualitätsbe-
sessene Ausführer. Und immer
als zuverlässige Partner arbeitet
ein hochmotiviertes Team mit
der Kraft und Schnelligkeit des
Familienunternehmens.

Moderne Managementmethoden
in der Mitarbeiterführung, per-
manente Wertanalysen (Rationalisierung), die Suche nach
zukunftsweisenden Lösungen
(Innovation), sowie die Ver-
breitung erfolgreich eingesetzter
Systeme (Multiplikation) sind der
Garant für Schüco, seit 50 Jahren
erfolgreich zu wachsen.

In order to create lasting value
from your ideas, we are always
searching for better solutions.

The Schüco success story
started in 1951 with aluminium
shop fronts and façade units.
Through integrated thinking,
powers of innovation and the
pursuit of perfection a system
of building components was
soon developed. When Schüco
became part of the Otto-Fuchs
Group (Meinerzhagen), its rise to
world company status began.

In the 70s Schüco expanded
into the rest of Europe and then
became the first in the industry
to operate worldwide. Today
it has 4,100 employees and
12,000 partner companies in
over 60 countries; passionate
designers and customer-
focused, quality-conscious
people of action. And always, a
highly motivated team with the
strength and speed of a family
firm works as a reliable partner.

Modern management methods
in employee leadership, constant
value analyses (rationalisation),
the search for solutions of
the future (innovation), and
the expansion of sucessfully
implemented systems
(multiplication) have guaranteed
Schüco's successful growth
for 50 years.

Geschichte
History

Der Weg zum Erfolg
The path to success

Rationalisierung
Rationalisation

Innovation
Innovation

Multiplikation
Multiplication

Unser Fundament
heißt ganzheitliches Denken.
Our cornerstone is integrated
thinking.

Aluminium-Systeme
Praxisgerechte Profile für Fassaden, Lichtdächer, Fenster, Türen, Sonnenschutz, Wintergärten, Balkone, Geländer, Schutz- und Sicherheitskonstruktionen

Aluminium systems
Comprehensive range of profiles for façades, skylights, windows, doors, conservatories, balconies, balustrades, protection and security constructions

Stahl-Systeme
Zusammen mit dem Partner Jansen AG bietet Schüco Stahlrohr- und Stahlprofilsysteme für Fassaden-, Tor- und Türtechnik

Steel systems
In partnership with Jansen AG, Schüco offers solutions for façade and door technology from high quality steel tubes and steel profile systems

Kunststoff-Systeme
Breitgefächertes Produktprogramm und große Gestaltungsvielfalt aus hochwertiger Kunststoff-Systemtechnik

PVC-U systems
A broad spectrum of products and a wide variety of design options from high quality PVC-U system engineering

Bauelemente
Fertigelemente für individuelle Bauideen aus den Werkstoffen Kunststoff und Aluminium für alle Anforderungen des Neubaus oder der Renovation

Standard units
Standard range units made for individual building ideas from PVC-U and aluminium available for all your new build or renovation needs

Solar-Systeme
Als führender Anbieter von Photovoltaik- und Solarthermie-Elementen garantiert Schüco ein einheitliches Montagesystem und somit besonders ressourcenschonende Technik

Solar products
As the leading supplier of photovoltaic and solar heating units, Schüco guarantees uniform system of assembly and thereby also particularly efficient technology

Schüco Design
Als Spezialist für Aluminium-Systemtechnologie bietet Schüco für den Maschinenbau, die Industrie- und Werbetechnik und die Möbelindustrie umfassende Produktlösungen

Schüco Design
As a specialist in aluminium system technology, Schüco provides comprehensive product solutions for engineering, industrial technology, advertising and the furniture industry

Effizientes Energiemanagement, Steuerung des Innenraumklimas sowie Schutz vor Außeneinflüssen wie Lärm, Hitze, Kälte oder Sonneneinstrahlung gehören heute zu den Anforderungen an ein modernes Gebäude. Dabei übernimmt die Gebäudehülle auch die Rolle einer Funktionsschicht zwischen Umwelt und Gebäudeinnerem.

Die Entwicklung und Realisierung von Systemen für diese Gebäudehülle ist die technologische Kompetenz von Schüco. Sie umfasst Fassaden, Glasdächer, Fenster, Türen sowie Gebäude- und Solartechnologie. Hier beherrscht Schüco die ganze Werkstoffpalette. Aus diesem gebündelten Know-how entsteht ein Systembaukasten, der bis heute in seiner Breite einzigartig ist. Und der zu einer Minimierung der Qualitätsprobleme an den Schnittstellen einzelner Komponenten führt.

Efficient energy management, interior climate control, protection against external influences such as noise, heat, cold or the sun's rays are some of the fundamental requirements of a modern building. In this, the building envelope takes on the role of a functional layer between the external environment and the building interior.

The development and implementation of systems for this building envelope is what Schüco technological expertise is all about. It includes façades, glass roofs, windows, doors, as well as building management and solar technology. Here, Schüco commands the whole range of materials. From this collective know-how, a system of building components was developed which is still unique in its scope. And one which leads to minimising of quality problems at the interface between different components.

Das Schüco Technologie-Zentrum in Bielefeld ist eine der leistungsfähigsten Prüfzentren für Fenster-, Fassaden- und Solartechnik weltweit. Es steht für die hohe Qualität, Langlebigkeit und Sicherheit aller Schüco Produkte. Hier wird schon im Vorfeld der offiziellen Institutsprüfungen sichergestellt, dass alle Neuentwicklungen die aktuell gültigen Normen erfüllen und übertreffen. Auf dem Schüco Fassadenprüfstand können zweigeschossige Fassaden-Elemente unter extremen Belastungen bis hin zur Orkan- oder Erdbeben-Simulation getestet werden. Die geprüfte Schüco Systemsicherheit durch das Technologie-Zentrum hilft allen Architekten und Planern, aus individuellen Entwurfs- und Konstruktionsideen abgesicherte und genehmigungsfähige Lösungen zu realisieren.

Technologische Kompetenz ist die eine Seite, Planung und Durchführung sind die andere. Bei Schüco kommt der umfassenden Beratung aller Baubeteiligten in technischen und ästhetischen Fragen eine hohe Bedeutung zu. So gibt es spezielle Software-Lösungen für Konstrukteure, Architekten, für Kaufleute und Verarbeiter. Mit dem Know-how und der Zuverlässigkeit deutscher Ingenieurskunst garantiert Schüco weltweit die reibungslose Umsetzung anspruchsvoller Projekte.

The Schüco Technology Centre in Bielefeld is one of the most efficient test centres for window, door, façade and solar technology worldwide. It represents the high quality, durability and reliability of all Schüco products. Before being assessed by official test institutes, all of our new developments are tested here for their compliance with current industry standards. On the façade test rig, we can test two-storey façade units under extreme loads and even simulate a hurricane or an earthquake. Schüco's system reliability, tested at the Technology Centre, helps architects and designers to create secure, approved project solutions from their individual design ideas.

Technological expertise is one side, design and implementation the other. At Schüco, a high level of emphasis is placed on comprehensive consultancy with everyone involved in the building project, covering all technical and aesthetic questions. There are special software solutions for designers, architects, for sales staff and fabricators. With the know-how and reliability of German engineering, Schüco guarantees the smooth implementation of sophisticated projects in the field of commercial architecture worldwide.

Sicherheit ist bei uns ein eigenes Haus.
Security has a place of its own at Schüco.

Der wichtigste Baustein ist nach wie vor der Mensch.
The key component is still people.

In über 60 Ländern sind
4.100 Mitarbeiter und über
12.000 Partnerbetriebe für
Schüco aktiv.

With 4,100 employees and more
than 12,000 partner companies,
Schüco operates in over 60
countries.

۩ Schüco International KG
Karolinenstraße 1–15
33609 Bielefeld
Germany

Telefon +49 521 783-0
Telefax +49 521 783-451
www.schueco.de

USA www.schuco-usa.com

Argentina www.schueco.com.ar
Brazil www.schueco.com.br

Die Corporate Partnership mit
dem West McLaren Mercedes
Formel 1 Team ist Symbol und
Verpflichtung für die führende
Position in Qualität und Zuver-
lässigkeit der Hightech-System-
konstruktionen von Schüco
International.

The corporate partnership with
the West McLaren Mercedes
Formula 1 team is a commitment
that symbolises the leading
position of Schüco International
in terms of quality and
reliability of its high tech system
constructions.

Algeria www.schueco.com
Chad www.schueco.td
Egypt www.schueco.com
Morocco www.schueco.ma
Mauritania www.schueco.com
Nigeria www.schueco.ng
Sudan www.schueco.com

Austria www.alukoenigstahl.com
Bosnia-Herzegovina www.schueco.com
Belgium www.schueco.be
Bulgaria www.alukoenigstahl.bg
Croatia www.alukoenigstahl.hr
Czech Republic www.schueco.cz
Denmark www.schueco.dk
Estonia www.schueco.ee
Finland www.schucofin.com
France www.schuco.fr
Germany www.schueco.de
Greece www.schueco.gr
Hungary www.alukoenigstahl.hu
Ireland www.schueco.co.uk
Iceland www.schueco.is
Italy www.schueco.it
Latvia www.schueco.lv
Lithuania www.schueco.lt
Luxembourg www.schueco.lu
Macedonia www.schueco.com
Netherlands www.schueco.nl
Norway www.schueco.no
Poland www.schueco.pl
Portugal www.schueco.com
Romania www.alukoenigstahl.ro
Russia www.schueco.ru
Serbia a. Montenegro www.schueco.com
Slovenia www.alukoenigstahl.si
Slovakia www.schueco.sk
Spain www.schueco.com
Sweden www.schueco.se
Switzerland www.jansen.ch
Turkey www.schueco.com.tr
United Kingdom www.schueco.co.uk

Bahrain www.schueco.com
China www.schueco.com.cn
Iran www.schueco.com
Israel www.schueco.co.il
Japan www.schueco.jp
Jordan www.schueco.com
Kazakhstan www.schueco.kz
Kyrgyzstan www.schueco.kg
Kuwait www.schueco.com
Lebanon www.schueco.com
Mongolia www.schueco.com
Oman www.schueco.com
Qatar www.schueco.com
Saudi Arabia www.schueco.com.sa
South Korea www.schueco.com
Tajikistan www.schueco.com
Turkmenistan www.schueco.tm
Ukraine www.schueco.ua
United Arab Emirates www.schueco.com
Uzbekistan www.schueco.com
Yemen www.schueco.com

Impressum

Translation from German into English: Translation Team UK, Schüco International KG

A CIP catalogue record for this book is available from the Library of Congress, Washington D.C., USA.

Bibliographic information published by Die Deutsche Bibliothek

Die Deutsche Bibliothek lists this publication in the Deutsche Nationalbibliografie; detailed bibliographic data is available in the internet at http://dnb.ddb.de.

© 2004 Schüco International KG, Bielefeld
Birkhäuser – Publishers for Architecture, P.O. Box 133, CH-4010 Basel, Switzerland.
Member of Springer Science+Business Media

Printed on acid-free paper produced from chlorine-free pulp.

Project management:
Jochen Wilms
Layout and typography:
Manfred Kronenberg, Beelen
Litho:
scanlitho.teams, Bielefeld
Printing:
Kunst- und Werbedruck,
Bad Oeynhausen

Printed in Germany

ISBN 3-7643-7061-0

9 8 7 6 5 4 3 2 1

http://www.birkhauser.ch